INDIANAPOLIS

The Story of a City

INDIANAPOLIS
The Story of a City

BY

EDWARD A. LEARY

The Bobbs-Merrill Company, Inc.

INDIANAPOLIS / NEW YORK

Aerial view of Indianapolis, 1970,
courtesy of William Oates. All other photos courtesy of
the Indianapolis Star/Indianapolis News.

The Bobbs-Merrill Company, Inc.
A Subsidiary of Howard W. Sams & Co., Inc., Publishers
Indianapolis / Kansas City / New York

To My Wife, Linda

Contents

1. Capital in the Wilderness   3
2. Triumphs and Tragedy   10
3. Progress, Murder, Melodrama   21
4. Watershed Years   30
5. Arrivals and Departures   42
6. War, Politics and a Prediction   53
7. School Bells and Railroad Bells   61
8. All 'Board for Prosperity   68
9. Poetry, Panic, Banks   79
10. Farewell to Union   87
11. Wartime Capital   97
12. Oliver P. Morton, War Governor   104
13. Death of a President   113
14. "Change Was Over All"   116
15. Greenbacks and Bread   129
16. Oh, Those Golden Years   135
17. A President and a Monument   148
18. The Golden Age of Literature   157
19. Wheels for a Nation   167

20. A Sound of Engines   175
21. New Century, New Voices   180
22. Of War and Peace   188
23. The Man Who Was the Law   200
24. Crisis and Upheaval   207
25. World War II—and After   215
26. New City: Indianapolis 1970   224
     Appendix I.   Mayors 1847-1968   233
     Appendix II. Population,
                   City of Indianapolis   235
     Appendix III. Territorial and
                   State Governors   236
     Bibliography   238
     Index   243

Acknowledgments

Many people and organizations provided valuable assistance in the preparation of this work. I am especially indebted to the staffs of the Indianapolis Public Library; the Indiana Division of the Indiana State Library; Eugene S. Pulliam, assistant publisher of Indianapolis Newspapers, Inc., publishers of the *Indianapolis Star* and *Indianapolis News;* and Larry Arany, librarian, and his library staff of Indianapolis Newspapers, Inc. Mr. Arany also indexed the book.

Many people loaned books and materials, including James E. Farmer, James M. Rogers, Mrs. Karl Zimmer, James R. Sweeney, William Darnaby and Dr. and Mrs. James Norton. Interest and encouragement were provided by Mrs. Jeannette Covert Nolan, who was kind enough to read some parts of the manuscript; James T. Morris, Mr. and Mrs. Roberton Williams, Mrs. Edward A. Tyler, Elmer Wohlfeld, Mrs. Howard Gustafson, and George Diener, chairman of the Indianapolis Sesquicentennial Commission. Mrs. Elsa Rollins typed the manuscript.

Edward A. Leary

INDIANAPOLIS

The Story of a City

Nothing great is lightly won. . . .

—SARAH T. BOLTON,
Indianapolis

Chapter I

CAPITAL IN THE WILDERNESS

It WAS A LAND OF DENSE and primeval forests and sunlit glades, of scattered plains and swamps, where the game was plentiful, the fishing was good and the corn grew tall. For moons without number it had been the home of the Indian, and his fathers lay buried in its soil. But now this land at the junction of the creek and the river the Indians called Wapehani and the "Long Hairs" called the White River was something more than level land, trees and marshes and a place to hunt and fish. It was real estate: real property to be marked off, bargained for, built upon, sold and resold. As real estate it offered opportunity, profit, assets and a point of departure for dreams without limit.

The change from land to real estate had taken place at a tiny village called St. Mary's, in Ohio. There in 1818 the chiefs of the Delaware, Miami, Wea and Potawatomi tribes, meeting with three United States commissioners, had signed a treaty which transferred to the white man the middle third of the new State of Indiana, including the land at the junction of the creek and the river. The treaty, known as the "New Purchase," represented a great bargain and a distinct triumph for the new nation and the fledgling state. For several thousands of dollars a year and the promise of new hunting grounds west of the Mississippi the Indians had relinquished a vast diamond-shaped tract of some 8,000,000 acres, or the equivalent of 20 counties. It was the largest land purchase to be negotiated with the Indians, but, most important of all, the treaty provided that the red men would move off the land within three years.

One of the commissioners, the handsome, dark-haired, fastidiously turned out Jonathan Jennings, could take special pride in the treaty. The youngest of the three 12-dollar-a-day U. S. government commissioners, he was thirty-four years of age and serving his first three-year term as governor of the new State of Indiana. He had long advocated the removal of the Indians and the opening of their lands and he had been growing impatient with the fact that his people, estimated at 75,000 when Indiana attained statehood in 1816, were confined to a cluster of 15 counties in the lower third of the state, hemmed in by the Ohio River on the south and by the "Ten O'Clock Line" and the boundaries of other Indian treaties on the north. For a population that was growing by the minute, this was intolerable, and land-hungry settlers, speculators, empire builders and those who merely wanted more elbow room had been looking over the boundary lines to the virgin lands beyond. Now Governor Jennings could announce that within the space of three short years men could start the work of building a big and important state and converting the forests and hunting grounds to farms and villages and waving fields of corn. It also meant that Governor Jennings' plan for establishing a new capital in the very center of the state, envisioned as somewhere on the White River, could be realized.

When Indiana became a territory in 1800, its capital was Vincennes, a logical choice because it was in the Northwest Territory's very center of population. With the organization of Illinois as a territory, residents of eastern and southeastern Indiana protested that the seat of government was too far away. Accordingly, the territorial legislature selected Corydon as its new capital and moved there in 1813.

The new capital was a tiny village of a few hundred inhabitants in the center of Harrison County back from the Ohio River and surrounded by high hills. The hills offered remarkable vistas, but in a day of horses and wagons and incredibly bad roads, the new capital was difficult to reach in the best of seasons and in winter was often inaccessible. The capitol building was the two-story Harrison County courthouse, a limestone structure 40 feet square, which was leased by the state.

Although it appeared there was general acceptance for Governor Jennings' plan for a capital in central Indiana, scattered but not unexpected opposition developed. The village of Corydon, unwilling to give up the prestige and the extra revenues of a state capital, was against any and all removal plans. Other residents of southern Indiana, acting on the belief that Corydon was out of the running, but desirous of keeping the seat of government in their part of the state, offered Salem and Madison as alternatives. Madison, a thriving pork-packing center, was particularly anxious to obtain the new capital. To help its cause, Madison offered a thousand dollars, cash on the barrelhead, to have the capital moved to their city. Vincennes came forward to press a claim. It was the state's oldest city, with a history that extended back to the days of French occupation and therefore, so the argument went, it was the logical and proper place for the new capital.

None of these claims, however, could hold a candle to the persuasive argument of Governor Jennings and his supporters. It was only a question of time, they said, before central and northern Indiana would be settled and now was the time to plan ahead and to locate the capital in the very center of the state, where it could be easily and conveniently reached by everyone. Capitals of other states had sprung up by accident or sentiment, but Indiana had an opportunity to plan and build a seat of government that could be tailored to its present and future needs. There was no need to compromise on an existing town or village, no need to adapt existing land and buildings. Indiana could build its new capital and create the proper facilities for carrying on the functions of government at little or no cost, for under the terms of the Enabling Act all proceeds from the sale of land within the four-square-mile donation could be used for building the capitol and other public structures.

It was a powerful argument and its combination of vision and logic appealed to dreamers and empire builders, as well as hard-headed businessmen and land speculators. It was also the winning argument, and Governor Jennings, now serving his second three-year term, was authorized to name a commission of ten men from as many counties to select a site for the new capital in the "New Purchase" lands.

The governor lost no time appointing his commission: George Hunt of Wayne County; John Conner of Fayette; Stephen Ludlow of Dearborn; John Gilliland of Switzerland; John Bartholomew of Clark; John Tipton of Harrison; Jesse Durham of Jackson; Frederick Rapp of Posey, and Thomas Emison of Knox. William Prince of Gibson County was also appointed but did not serve.

It was agreed the commissioners would start out in the early spring and meet at the farm of John Conner's brother, William, near the west fork of the White River about four miles south of the present city of Noblesville. From this point the men would ride out and take a look at the Jacob Whetzel settlement at Waverly and the so-called Fall Creek Settlements near the junction of the creek and the White River.

The Conner farm and the two prospective sites were the first settlements in central Indiana. Each had a different background, but the stories of their settlement were symbolic of what enterprising men could accomplish in the wilderness.

The William Conner prairie farm, the first white settlement in central Indiana, consisted of about 150 acres of White River bottomland and fertile prairie. A frontier landmark, the farm was a profitable Indian trading post as well as a prosperous and virtually self-sufficient farming and home-manufacturing operation. It grew most of its own food, including an annual yield of several thousand bushels of corn; and besides the abundant game in the nearby woods and fish from the White River, the farm kept sheep, hogs, and cattle. Its outbuildings included a barn, storage buildings, a springhouse, a milk house, a distillery for making corn whiskey and a loom house which turned out blankets and clothing.

William Conner's farm and trading post and John Conner's settlement, Connersville, nearly 60 miles to the northeast, represented what could happen on the frontier if you were able to get along with the Indians and were part of the Indian establishment. The Conner brothers had lived among the Indians most of their lives, spoke their language and dialects, and were the equal of many braves when it came to hunting, fishing and trapping. Both were married to the daughters of important Indian chiefs. Their story, with some variations, was the story of many pioneer Americans who became involved with the Indians at an early age, usually as captives, and exploited their knowledge of Indian ways to obtain land and trading concessions which later formed the basis of family empires and fortunes.

Born in pioneer Ohio, William and John Conner were the only sons of Richard and Margaret Boyer Conner, Moravian missionaries dedicated to converting the Indians to Christianity. Shortly after William's birth at the Moravian settlement of Schoenbrunn in 1777, the family moved to Michigan to live with a group of Christian Indians. It was there the brothers' future was determined. Taken captive by a Shawnee raiding party, the Conner family were marched to the British garrison at Detroit, where the British released them but forced them to live with a group of Christian Indians near the fort.

The Conner brothers were strapping young men wise in the ways of the Indians when they left the village in 1796 and returned to Ohio, where they put their Indian lore to good use as fur traders. About 1800, when both were in their twenties, they moved to Indiana. William tried his luck at the mouth of Fall Creek on the White River, then a main crossing route for the Indian trappers, and John started out along the Whitewater River, establishing a trading post first at Cedar Grove, Brookville, and later, in 1808, building Fort Conner (Connersville) in Fayette County.

From the beginning both men prospered. The Indians liked to do business with men who understood their ways and were honest and aboveboard in their dealings. William, traveling up and down the White River visiting the many Delaware villages, became a close friend and confidant of Chief Anderson at the village of Wapeminskink, the site of the present city of Anderson. On one of his visits he married the chief's pretty young copper-skinned daughter, Meskinges, and in 1802 brought his bride to the prairie near the White River which he had selected as a site for a permanent trading post and farm. He built a large, double log cabin, divided it into living quarters and a trading post, and set about making plans for a settlement.

Captain Jacob Whetzel's farm near Waverly in northeastern Morgan County was still new in 1820, located at the terminus of a trace which the captain, his son, Cyrus, and three axemen had finished cutting only the year before. The trace was the only trail suitable for traveling and the first east-west route in central Indiana. Some 60 miles in length and wide enough for a pair of oxen, the trace started at Laurel on the Whitewater River in Franklin County, crossed what would later be Rush, Shelby and Johnson Counties and terminated at the bluffs of the White River in Morgan County.

Whetzel had been an Indian fighter, scout, frontiersman, a member of General Harrison's militia and a veteran of the Battle of Tippecanoe and the War of 1812. A native of Virginia, the son of Dutch parents, he came to Indiana in 1811 from Kentucky and settled near the present site of Laurel, on the west fork of the Whitewater River. After the War of 1812, Whetzel selected a tract of land near Worthington, in present-day Green County, and discovered that the trip from Worthington to Laurel through primeval forests required several weeks.

The grizzled fifty-three-year-old Indian fighter decided the only solution lay in cutting a trace through the south-central part of the state and, despite the fact that he knew nothing about surveying or engineering, roughed out a plan for a trail from Laurel to White River. But the land still belonged to the Delaware Indians and it was necessary to obtain the permission of Chief Anderson. Whetzel's timing, however, was right. It was 1818, the year of St. Mary's and the "New Purchase," and Chief Anderson readily gave his permission, probably on the grounds that he had nothing either to gain or to lose.

Whetzel, his son and the axemen finished the trail the next year. It was a remarkable feat, and when it was completed the old Indian fighter decided to give up the land at Worthington and resettle at Waverly. The land was cleared, several acres of corn planted, and Jacob and Cyrus returned over the trace to bring the family and their belongings to the new site.

In 1820, the year the new capital would be selected, the farm was prospering and Jacob and his son were making plans for further expansion.

The Fall Creek Settlements consisted originally of two families of pre-emptors, or "squatters," the George Pogues and the John McCormicks. Both had come down from Connersville and staked out claims and were taking their chances that eventually their blazed boundaries would be translated into legal titles. Which of the two families came first in the spring of 1820 has never been accurately established, but it is certain they were the original settlers.

Pogue was a large, powerful man, as befitted his trade as blacksmith. A native of North Carolina, he had homesteaded in the "Gore" near the Ohio line, moved to Connersville and become the first smithy in "New Purchase." Pogue, who sometimes affected the flowing cape and wide-brimmed hat of the Pennsylvania Dutch, was fifty years old when he arrived with his wife and five children on the banks of the White River. He followed the river to the mouth of Fall Creek, where he staked out a piece of high ground with a small stream on it, selected a site for a double log cabin and started clearing the land. Pogue's land was located about where present-day Michigan Street crosses Pogue's Run, the name later given to the stream.

In a time when men judged the fertility of the soil by the number of trees on it, the sober blacksmith from Connersville was pleased with his selection. The clearing away of the dense forest was a discouraging job even for a man with George Pogue's powerful shoulders and strong back, but he managed by working from sunup to sundown to clear an acre every three weeks. Sometimes, as Pogue told it later, he could "tromp" over his clearing on the fallen trunks of trees and "never touch a foot to the ground."

John McCormick and his family, accompanied by his brothers, James and Samuel, had traveled part of the way on the Whetzel Trace and then hacked their own way to Fall Creek with the help of axemen and teamsters who also made up the party. The McCormick brothers built cabins on the east bank of the White River, below the mouth of the creek, John's cabin north of present-day Washington Street. James McCormick made his home on the river near the Riverside Dam and later ran a ferry boat.

Other squatters, mostly farmers from the Whitewater settlements, came later that spring and summer. Among them were John Cowan, John Maxwell, Henry and Samuel Davis, Isaac Wilson, Robert Harding, Robert Brownhill, Jeremiah Corbaley and Van Blaricum. From Frankfort, Kentucky, came the Nowlands, Matthias, his wife and mother and several children. They were the first of many who would come up from Kentucky.

The new arrivals filled the air with the thud of axes, the crashing of falling trees, and the pungent smell of wood smoke as they burned away the branches and the thick underbrush of the forests. Although no man could know it in the spring of 1820, a city was being born.

The wet and rainy spring of 1820 forced the commissioners to delay their visit. It was not until May 17 that Governor Jennings, accompanied by John Tipton, one of the commissioners, and a black boy, Bill, started their ride of some 120 miles from Corydon to William Conner's farm. En route they picked up Durham and Bartholomew, and the party arrived at Conner's farm about one o'clock on May 22. Two other commissioners arrived later in the day.

The men relaxed after their long ride and enjoyed William Conner's warm hospitality that included good food, corn whiskey, and knowledge-able comments about the area. On May 24 the commissioner rode to the mouth of Fall Creek, which the Indians called Sak-pe-hel-luk, and spent the next three days studying possible sites.

After exploring the area and meeting again, the commissioners agreed each of the three sites offered many possibilities. Further discussion, how-ever, some of it heated, eliminated the Conner and Whetzel sites, and on May 27 the commissioners agreed on the Fall Creek site and voted to "locate the Township 15 degrees north of R. 3 E which township was not divided into sections." A survey was ordered to "locate" the four sections to be accepted as a Congressional donation, and on June 7, 1820, the com-missioners met at John McCormick's cabin and, on the motion of John Tipton, officially defined the Fall Creek site as the new capital.

The commissioners viewed their work with pride and in their report to the legislature called attention to the capital's location, its level and fertile soil and its proximity to the advancing National Road. Special stress was laid upon the fact that the land was located on a navigable river, an im-portant factor in a day when there were no roads and water offered the single surest and best means of transportation and communication. The report emphasized the high, dry banks of the White River, "twenty-five to thirty feet above the stream which insure certain passage in times of high water."

There were few who would quarrel with the decision of the commis-sioners. Their selection of the Fall Creek site generally reflected careful thought and good judgment. There was only one flaw in their choice, but this would not be discovered until later. The White River was not navi-gable, except for some small craft, and the river would play little or no part in the new capital's future.

Chapter 2

TRIUMPHS AND TRAGEDY

T HE GENERAL ASSEMBLY OF 1821, meeting in Corydon, accepted the recommendations of the commissioners for the site of Indiana's new capital, named Christopher Harrison, James W. Jones and Samuel P. Booker to map and plat the town, and appointed John Carr as agent for the state with powers to advertise and hold a sale of lots. These actions left only one problem: to select a name for the new capital.

The choosing of a name touched off a sharp and heated debate. Marston G. Clark of Washington County, a strong advocate of Indian place names, proposed "Tecumseh," and when it was shouted down, suggested still others. The name "Suwarrow," or "Tuwarrow," was offered and shot down to the accompaniment of jeers and laughter. Legislators with classical backgrounds suggested names compounded from the Latin or Greek, but took their seats when their efforts met stony silence or loud snickers.

In his room at the Old Capital Hotel that evening Judge Jeremiah Sullivan of Madison had an inspiration. Why not combine the word Indiana with the Greek suffix "*polis*," meaning "city," thus forming the word "Indianapolis," or City of Indiana? He wrote the word down on paper, said it aloud several times and decided it looked right and sounded right. Flushed with his creative effort, he tried it on Samuel Merrill of Switzerland County and Governor Jennings. Neither, it is reported, shared Judge Sullivan's enthusiasm for the name, but they agreed and promised their support. The next day Judge Sullivan proposed the name "Indianapolis." There were some jeers, but by now everybody was tired of the whole business and it was generally agreed the name did make sense, and it was adopted.

Public announcement of the capital's new name brought more brickbats. Some people said the new name was downright "ridiculous" and that no one would ever learn to pronounce it. Particularly caustic was the editor of the *Indiana Sentinel,* who wrote:

One of the most ludicrous acts of the sojourners at Corydon was their naming of the new seat of government. Such a name, kind readers, you would never find by searching from Dan to Beersheba; not in all the libraries, museums, and patent offices in the world. It is like nothing in heaven, nor on earth, nor in the waters under the earth. It is not a name for man, woman or child; for empire, city, mountain or morass; for bird, beast, fish nor creeping thing; and nothing mortal or immortal could have thought of it, except the wise men of the East who were congregated at Corydon. It is composed of the following letters: I-N-D-I-A-N-A-P-O-L-I-S. Pronounce it as you please, gentle readers—you can do it as you wish—there is no danger of violating any system or rule, either in accent, cadence or emphasis—suit your own convenience and be thankful you are enabled to do it by this rare effect of the scholastic genius of the age.

There was more of the same in other pieces that followed. The articles found a ready audience, especially among readers in southern Indiana. The removal of the capital from the lower part of the state still rankled and readers were glad to seize upon the strange new name and hold it up to ridicule. Unhappily, the jeers would continue as the new capital struggled for recognition.

Christopher Harrison of Salem, one of three commissioners appointed to "lay off" the town and the only one to appear, rode into the new capital in the wilderness in April 1821. Harrison, a native of Maryland, was a moderately wealthy man, regarded by his neighbors as a recluse, dilettante, and eccentric. He had been elected the state's first lieutenant governor in 1816, an ideal post for a recluse, as the duties were few except to preside over the senate for a few weeks each year.

In 1818 he had proclaimed himself governor on the grounds that Jennings had disqualified himself by serving as commissioner for the U.S. government during the "New Purchase" negotiations. The violation was clear, as the state constitution forbade dual officeholding. An investigating committee, however, failed to recognize Harrison's claim and he resigned in a huff.

To help plan the new capital, Harrison had selected and hired Elias Fordham and Alexander Ralston as surveyors and appointed Benjamin Blythe as clerk. Fordham, an Englishman, had been a pupil of George Stephenson, who would unveil the world's first practical steam-driven locomotive. Ralston, a gentle white-haired bachelor then in his fifties, had come to America from his native Scotland as an assistant to Major Pierre Charles L'Enfant, the imaginative Frenchman engaged by President Washington to plan the nation's capital. Ralston had gone on from the Washington post to the Southwest, where he had been employed as a surveyor for Aaron Burr at a time when the former Vice-President was involved in a complex and questionable web of activities which eventually led to Burr's arrest on a charge of treason. Ralston apparently was merely a paid employee of Burr and not privy to the former Vice-President's secrets, but it cast a shadow on his reputation.

Ralston is generally credited with creating the plan for the town, with the encouragement and approval of Harrison. There is no doubt that in laying out the city, Ralston was influenced by L'Enfant's design for Washington, D. C. Some engineers and historians, perhaps influenced by local pride, have characterized the plan as "strikingly original" and unlike any to be found in the world. More objective engineering opinions suggest Ralston's plan as a genuine improvement and simplification of the Washington design or a happy combination of Thomas Jefferson's Federal City of regular squares and the famous Versailles "Spider Web."

Ralston started out by visualizing the new capital as one mile square because, as he later said, he didn't believe the city would ever be any larger than that. At first, his square mile was set directly in the center of the four-mile square of the federal donation, but he shifted it slightly to the north and east to avoid the low, marshy ground along Pogue's Run. Almost in the center of Ralston's square mile was a high, grassy knoll of nearly four acres which he staked off into a circle 333 feet in diameter with a street 80 feet wide running around it. This knoll would be the starting place for the city and it would be crowned by the residence of the governor.

With the knoll as his base, Ralston proceeded to lay out his streets. First, Meridian Street, running north and south from the Circle (as it came to be called), and then four avenues, radiating out in four directions like an enlarged X. These he named Massachusetts, Indiana, Virginia and Kentucky Avenues.

The first street south of the Circle, Washington Street, he saw as the town's principal business thoroughfare and he made it 120 feet wide. Pennsylvania was the first street to the east, Illinois the first to the west and Ohio the first street to the north. The remainder of the city was laid off in a uniform arrangement of squares. In all, there were nine streets running east and west and nine streets running north and south. The entire square was bounded by streets which were appropriately called East, West, North and South Streets.

Besides making provision for a governor's mansion on the knoll in the

Circle, Ralston set aside an entire block for a statehouse and another for a courthouse. A large tract between Meridian and Pennsylvania was reserved for a university. The area outside the mile square, a large portion of it low and swampy, was referred to as the "outlots" and it was a generally shared opinion they would never be put to use.

It was a neat arrangement and it looked very pretty on paper, but it was far removed from reality. Lot lines and streets ran through some dense forests, and virtually all of the lots were heavily timbered. Ralston himself appears to have been struck with the contrast between his plan and the wilderness about him, for it is reported that on one occasion he shook his head and commented: "It will be a beautiful city—if it is ever built."

Even as Ralston and Fordham drove their stakes and marked off lots in the woods, new settlers were arriving on foot, in wagons or on horseback. Among them were Thomas Byrnes, James B. Hall, Conrad Brusell, Mitchell Ingals, George Smith and Milo R. Davis. Daniel Shaffer opened the first store and Alexander Russell and Robert Wilmot, partners, opened the second one. Two lawyers, Obed Foote and Calvin Fletcher, hung up their separate shingles.

Dr. S. G. Mitchell, the town's first doctor, arrived with his black manservant, Ephraim Ensaw, a freedman who worked for wages. Ensaw would be the first black man to become a permanent resident. Earlier John Maxwell had brought Aaron Wallace to Indianapolis, but Wallace hadn't liked the place and moved away. Other Negroes would come later, including David Mallory, who would become the town's first barber. In common with other free states, Indiana in 1821 didn't encourage black men to settle and they were not allowed to vote, join the militia, serve on juries or enjoy the other benefits of first-class citizenship.

Mordecai Harding was born that spring, the first child to be born in the new capital, and Jerry Johnson married Jane Reagan in the village's first wedding ceremony. Because Connersville was the county seat, Johnson had walked 120 miles, round trip, to obtain the marriage certificate. Governor Jennings appointed the village's first justice of the peace, James McIllvaine, who held court at the door of his cabin on the southwest corner of Ohio and Meridian Streets. Jeremiah Corbaley became the first constable and bailiff. McIllvaine's jurisdiction covered only petty cases, and the administration of justice in the little town was pretty much "administration by bluff." (The town's early history is filled with stories of prisoners permitted to escape or crimes that went unpunished in order to save townspeople the trouble and expense of transporting the culprits to trial or to jail at Connersville.)

Two inns (taverns) dispensed whiskey, meals and lodgings and provided sheds for horses. Hawkins' tavern, the Eagle, was on the north side of Washington Street between Meridian and Pennsylvania, and

Carter's tavern, the Rosebush, a double log cabin, was situated east of Illinois and north of Washington Street. Travelers not only shared the same roof, but often the same bed. Around their huge fires in the barrooms local citizens and travelers exchanged news and views, and talked and planned for the future.

The first men of the cloth also came the first spring. The Reverend John McClung of the "New Light" denomination became the first resident preacher and held meetings on the knoll in the Circle. In late spring the first circuit rider, the Reverend Rezin Hammond, a preacher of great repute, rode into town. In his honor Ralston laid some logs in a pewlike arrangement on the street surrounding the Circle and nailed together a rough platform. The Reverend William Cravens, a circuit rider for the Missouri Conference of Methodists, also came that spring, riding in with his family, a Bible and a hymnbook under his arm. In August the Reverend Ludwell G. Gaines, a missionary from Ohio, held an open-air meeting.

Most of these early preachers had little or no religious training, but they made up for this lack with an enthusiastic espousal of the Lord's work and an ability to exhort their congregations. In a day where there was little entertainment and most people lived Thoreau's lives of quiet desperation, these services were something more than religion—they were a diversion, a show, an important outlet for pent-up emotions. The strong sermons and the dedicated work of these lay and secular ministers had a great impact on the little village. They provided a moral brake for a place without law and gave untold comfort to a people whose life-span was short and who walked daily in the shadow of death.

Church services on the Circle also had their social and practical side. They offered an opportunity to meet friends, neighbors and newcomers, to complete a business deal, to arrange a cooperative work project, to exchange news, recipes and cures, and for many a mother, a chance to do some matchmaking.

Early in the spring a community or common garden was established on some 100 acres on the northwest corner of the donation, where an invasion of caterpillars had laid waste to the trees and foliage. For families who had to plan their food a year ahead and whose farms were still being hacked out of the wilderness, the garden was a godsend. Everybody got together and cleared the land and divided it up so that each family had its own "turn rows" in which to plant their corn, pumpkins and beans. It was known for years as "The Big Field."

Meat was generally plentiful in the form of wild game: rabbits, ducks, geese, partridge, passenger pigeons, wild turkeys and deer. Some families had brought cows and hogs with them. The hogs usually were left to roam at will, but cows and horses were confined by split-rail fences or kept tethered, attesting to their value.

That same spring a renegade Indian, Wyandotte John, showed up at George Pogue's farm and stayed overnight. Pogue was still smarting over the theft of some horses from his farm, and when Wyandotte John offered the information that he had seen some shod horses at an Indian camp near Buck's Creek, Pogue pricked up his ears. Wyandotte John couldn't promise they were Pogue's horses, but they wore iron shoes and obviously were horses belonging to white men.

The next morning Pogue took down his rifle and headed into the wilderness in the direction of Buck's Creek. It was the last anybody saw or heard of him, and as the weeks went by the supposition grew that he had been killed by the Indians, an assumption that kept the little settlement excited for weeks. Pogue thus earned the dubious distinction of being the last white man to die at the hands of Indians in central Indiana.

There were already fewer Indians in the vicinity of the little village. They had started moving out under the terms of the "New Purchase" treaty. Among the first to depart was Chief Anderson, in September 1820. The chief took with him, in accordance with tribal law, his daughter Meskinges, the wife of William Conner, and the six half-Indian Conner children. With Meskinges went 60 horses, her share of the Conner trading venture. Remnants of the Delawares remained and there were Miami, Seneca and Shawnee hunting parties to be found in the woods. Residents were often startled to run across an Indian at their spring or find one cutting across the lower part of their farm.

Robert Wilmot, the storekeeper, had his own personal Indian trouble. It began with the sale of some goods on credit to a Deleware brave named Jim Lewis, who pledged some silver headbands as security. When Lewis, who had a reputation as a "bad Indian," appeared to pay his debt and redeem his headbands, he discovered Wilmot had sold them to another Indian. The angry Lewis vowed to "get" Wilmot and went about town brandishing a knife and promising to scalp the storekeeper the first chance he got. Wilmot, after living in abject fear for a few weeks, fled the town one dark spring night. Reports filtered back that he had returned to his old Kentucky home.

The first summer in the new capital was hot, close and humid. A malodorous stench arose from the lowlands, the swamps, from musty foliage and decaying plants. The White River got lower and lower. Fall Creek became a series of stagnant pools. From mist-hung Fletcher's swamp to the northeast and Pogue's Run on the southeast and from the floor of the forests came clouds of buzzing mosquitoes.

The epidemic started in the cabins near the river and spread like wildfire. Cattle, horses and hogs sickened and died. Then the chills and fever, the hot and cold sweats and the feeling of great weakness touched everyone including the children. The settlers, the sons and daughters of pioneers of other times and places, knew the "ager" had come among them. Their parents had called it the "summer sick" and classified its fevers: the Dumb, the Shaking and the Chill, with their "intermittent and remittent attacks."

Misery and death came to the rude cabins, clutching their victims in malarial fingers of fire and ice. Daniel Shaffer, the storekeeper, who only a week before had helped to select a site for the village cemetery, was the first to be interred in what would later be called the "Old Graveyard." Mrs. Maxwell was the first woman to die. Between July and October everyone in the settlement, at one time or another, was confined to bed, and at one high point, in mid-July, according to the account of one old settler: "Every person in the donation was down in his bed, except Enoch Banks, Thomas Chinn and Nancy Hendricks. These three nursed and cared for the rest of us as best they could." As the nights grew cooler and autumn crept close, the struggling little village learned that death had claimed 72 men, women and children—one out of every eight persons—during the long, hot summer of sickness.

The cooler nights brought relief to the sick and the grief-stricken village. Doctors no longer worked around the clock. Dr. Mitchell and a Dr. Livingston Dunlap, who had come out from New York to relieve Mitchell, were both struck down early in the epidemic, but recovered sufficiently to care for other patients. Dr. Isaac Coe proved to be the real life saver. He had brought with him some cinchona bark, which was then proving effective against malaria in experiments in the East, and prescribed pills made of the bark and generous sips of wine or whiskey. Although people joshed about the size of his pills, they apparently saved many a life. As for the epidemic itself, the doctors blamed the vapors from the swamps and lowlands and recommended they be drained to prevent further outbreaks. Medical science had yet to determine that the mosquito was one of man's deadliest enemies.

As the little village slowly recovered there were those who decided they had had enough. They cursed the place, packed up their belongings and returned to their former homes on the Whitewater. Some families, in the hope of escaping future outbreaks of the "summer sick," moved to higher and drier ground and built new cabins. The believers and the more optimistic talked knowingly about the need for a place to be "seasoned" before it became healthy and promised things would be different next year and the year after. But there was doubt beneath the brave talk. Who could prove that the others weren't right—the others who declared Indianapolis was a God-forsaken place and that it would never be the state's capital because men would eventually come to their senses and move the capital back to southern Indiana where it really belonged?

While the epidemic raged, the *Indiana Sentinel* at Vincennes carried an announcement that lots in the "Town of Indianapolis" would be offered for sale at public auction on the second Monday of October. The advertisement, which appeared August 11, 1821, described the village as "located on a high, dry plain which extends for several miles perfectly free of floods, marshes and ponds . . . beautiful and fertile . . . and probably the best land in the state." The advertisement promised "good, wholesome water at a depth of twenty feet" and declared: "It is confidently expected that the Great National Turnpike Road from Washington to Missouri will pass through Indianapolis."

Indianapolis readers of the *Sentinel* could point to at least one inaccuracy in the advertisement—there *were* marshes and ponds—but this could be overlooked in view of the promise that the National Road would pass through the city. The road, already under construction and designed to link the Eastern seaboard with the Western states, was originally planned to cross Indiana about 15 miles below Indianapolis. More recently the States of Indiana, Illinois and Ohio had petitioned Washington that the turnpike route be changed in order to link their state capitals. Obviously, Indiana "confidently expected" approval of the petition, an expectation that turned out to be right, because in 1825 Congress changed the route to pass through the Indiana capital.

For weeks before the sale the residents of the town prepared for the expected visitors. Bread was baked, doughnuts fried, extra meat cured or dried. Temporary sheds and fences were erected for horses, the rooms in cabins and taverns were cleaned and aired, extra corn whiskey and rum were brought in, and spaces were cleared for the expected wagons.

Visitors and prospective purchasers began to arrive early. Christopher Harrison, who had fled at the outbreak of the epidemic, returned. John Carr, the state agent, arrived, selected Matthias Nowland's recently opened tavern near Washington Street west of Missouri Street as sale headquarters and engaged a room for the auction officials. The town's taverns were soon filled to overflowing and many settlers opened their homes. Other visitors camped in the clearings or lived in their wagons. At night their many campfires blazed under the trees.

To those who came from older and established settlements, the new capital appeared primitive and unprepossessing. Most of the area was a vast wilderness infested with bears, wolves and wildcats and isolated from the rest of the state. Indians still outnumbered the white men. Except for Whetzel's and Berry's Traces, there were no roads, the nearest town was 60 miles away through the woods, and the closest point to the Ohio River, pioneer lifeline and main artery of commerce, was 85 miles. The few trails and wagon ways were not usable for several months of the year, particularly in spring, because of mud and swollen unbridged streams. As a consequence, everything that came into the village commanded the highest prices. Residences were crude cabins. There was as yet no sawmill and the nearest grist mill was at Whitewater, 60 miles away. To cap it all, the visitors were dismayed to find the surrounding land low and swampy and to learn the town had only just recovered from an epidemic.

The sale of lots opened on October 9, with overcast skies and high, chill winds. Tommy Carter, the auctioneer, banged his hammer and announced: "I am about to lavish upon every man, woman and child present a fortune—whether you wish it or not." James Ray served as clerk.

The first lot to be sold, located on the south side of Washington Street between Missouri and West Streets, went to Jesse McKay for $152.75. Two lots at the northwest corner of Delaware and Washington Streets, west of the block set aside for the new courthouse, brought the most money: $500 for one and $560 for the other. Lots to the north and east in the mile square also brought high bids, marking a distinct trend away from the river. The sale continued over several days and resulted in the sale of 314 lots for $35,596.25. Actual cash receipts were $7,000, the balance in promissory notes running over a period of four years.

The auction receipts were woefully short of anticipation. The state's disappointment would have been greater had it known that 161 of the lots would never be paid for and that ten years later the state would still own three-fourths of the lots in the mile square and nearly all of the outlots. In fact, it would not be until 1842 that the state would finally dispose of all the land in the donation for a total of less than $150,000.

The first winter in the new capital proved to be a hard one with much snow, but everyone managed somehow. Joseph C. Reed, one of the new arrivals, started a school in his one-room cabin at the intersection of Kentucky and Illinois Streets. Like many early Western schools, it was a "blab" school, where the children learned their lessons by reciting them aloud and in unison. The blackboard was a slab of wood hung on the wall, the benches were half-logs set on wood-slab legs and the windows were of paper covered with bear grease. Apparently the settlers put greater store by those who could write and figure, as the fee for writing and arithmetic was $2.50 per quarter; for reading and spelling, 50 cents less. As there was little gold and silver in town, tuition was generally paid in coonskins, the basic medium of exchange in pioneer Indianapolis.

The John Wyants, owners of the largest cabin in town, gave the first dancing party, with fiddlin', cider, whiskey and good food. Mr. Wyant collected 25 cents from each guest to help pay for the liquid refreshments. The party opened with Matthias Nowland and Mrs. Wyant leading the dancers, when Mr. Wyant appeared, stopped the music, tapped Nowland on the shoulder and advised all and sundry that at this party every man was to dance with his own wife. Nowland retired in confusion and the dance went on. The party furnished talk and gossip for many weeks. There were also shooting matches when the weather was good, with muzzle-loading long-barreled Kentucky rifles, and shooting was "off hand." Nathaniel Cox, known affectionately as "Uncle Nat" and a brother of George Smith's wife, and Robert Duncan captured most of the prizes.

On the last day of the year 1821, the General Assembly, which still met annually in December at Corydon, organized Marion County. Indianapolis was designated as the county seat and $8,000 appropriated to build a courthouse 50 feet square and two stories high. The county's new name was not without a wry touch. Following a common practice of naming Indiana counties for war heroes, the new county had been named after Francis Marion, an American Revolutionary War general. Marion had earned the nickname "Swamp Fox" for his guerrilla-like raids on British communications and supply depots and his ability to disappear with his men in the nearby swamps.

Attached to the new county for judicial purposes was the area now comprising the counties of Johnson, Hamilton, Hancock, Madison and Boone. William W. Wick was appointed judge, Hervey Bates was made county sheriff, and plans went forward for an election of other county officers in the spring.

The same legislature also took cognizance of the fact that the new capital was hard to reach and appropriated $100,000 to open up and construct roads to Indianapolis. Two main roads were planned to connect the capital with southern Indiana, one from the Ohio River near Lawrenceburg, the other from Madison. In addition, roads were planned to link Indianapolis with the older settlements, including Noblesville and Crawfordsville.

The town's first newspaper, the weekly *Indianapolis Gazette*, appeared on January 28, 1822, with George Smith and his nineteen-year-old stepson, Nathaniel Bolton, as publishers. The paper, printed on a two-pull Rampage hand press, consisted of four pages each about half the size of a standard newspaper.

Smith, a native of Kentucky, had learned the printing trade as an employee of the Lexington (Kentucky) *Observer* and the Cincinnati (Ohio) *Liberty Hall and Gazette*. While working on the Ohio newspaper, he had met and married the widow of James Bolton, and in 1820 he came to Indiana with his new wife and stepson, Nathaniel, settling first in southern Indiana. Sensing opportunity in the new capital, Smith came to Indianapolis for the 1821 sale and purchased two lots at the corner of Maryland and West Streets at the intersection of Missouri Street. Two weeks before Christmas in the same year, after following a blazed trail through the wilderness, Smith and his family arrived in Indianapolis and moved into a buckeye cabin.

Besides their household goods and clothing, the Smiths brought with them the basic equipment for printing a newspaper, including type, cases, stands, paper and the small hand press. Smith and Bolton set up the equipment in one corner of the cabin, laboriously fashioned additional wood type by hand, compounded ink from a solution of tar and, in lieu of inking rollers, made hand applicators of deerskin rolled into balls and stuffed with wool.

The lead article of the first issue was devoted to reprinting the bill passed by the General Assembly appropriating funds for the laying out of roads into the capital. It announced: "Deer skins, dressed or undressed, will be received as payment for the *Gazette*. Butter, honey and poultry will be received for any debt due the printers."

The *Gazette* remained the only newspaper in town until May 7 of the following year, when *The Western Censor and Immigrant's Guide* started publication. The new paper was published by Harvey Gregg, an attorney, and Douglass McGuire, and offices were in a cabin near the site of the present Washington Hotel.

Nathaniel Bolton eventually became the manager, editor and publisher of the *Gazette*, which was published in later years at Georgia and Tennessee Streets. In a few years it became the *Indianapolis Democrat* and, in 1841, the *Indianapolis Sentinel*. The *Censor* was destined to become the *Indianapolis Journal* in 1825.

The week following the *Gazette's* debut the town inaugurated its first postal service. For two years Connersville had served as the nearest post office, and mail was dispatched to Indianapolis whenever someone passed through on his way to the new capital. On arrival the letters were passed about until they reached their owners. This situation added to the community's growing sense of isolation. As a result, a citizens' meeting was held at Hawkins' tavern and a private mail route was established, with Aaron Drake hired to ride regularly to Connersville, pick up the mail and deliver it to Hawkins' tavern, where it could be called for.

The town's private mail system had been in operation only a few weeks when President Monroe ordered the extension of U.S. postal service to Indianapolis and appointed Samuel Henderson as postmaster. Henderson opened his office in a log cabin near Missouri Street during the first week in March, later transferring the post office to his tavern, Washington Hall, which he built on Washington Street. Mail was brought in by horseback until some six years later, when the first stage lines came into the town.

Chapter 3

PROGRESS, MURDER, MELODRAMA

IN THE SPRING OF 1822 the *Gazette* estimated the town's population at 500, some 400 persons living in the mile square and another 100 in the outlying areas. The newspaper could also count two water-powered sawmills, one grist mill, a brick yard and a ferry across the White River. Forty new residences had been built, among them the first two-story frame house and the first brick house, John Johnson's, on Market Street. Spring also brought the first of a series of floods which would plague the little town for many years, the receding waters leaving stagnant water that provided breeding places for malaria-carrying mosquitoes.

That year the town voted for the first officers of "the newly formed Marion County." As there was no formal nominating machinery, a citizen had merely to put his name down on the lists and announce his candidacy, usually by standing a round of drinks at a local tavern.

The campaign demonstrated greater geographical than political division within the community. Those who had come up from the Whitewater settlements lined up behind James M. Ray and became the "Whitewater" faction; those from the Blue Grass State formed the "Kentucky" group, with Morris Morris as their candidate and leader. On election day voters cast their ballots at two polling places in Indianapolis and others in Anderson, Noblesville, Pendleton and Strawtown. Of the 336 ballots counted, about 100 were cast in Indianapolis.

The "Whitewater" faction emerged victorious. James M. Ray was elected clerk; Joseph C. Reed, the schoolmaster, recorder; James McIllvaine and Eliakim Harding, associate judges; John McCormick, William McCartney and John T. Osborne, county commissioners. Upon his election, Reed closed his school, but it was taken over a few months later by Mr. and Mrs. R. B. Lawrence.

The newly elected county commissioners held their first meeting, a full and busy session, on April 15, 1822, at a house on the corner of Ohio and Meridian. Daniel Yandes was appointed treasurer, a county seal was adopted, and bids were published for a new courthouse and jail. The new commissioners also divided the county into townships: Anderson, Center, Decatur, Delaware, Fall Creek, Franklin, Lawrence, Perry, Pike, Washington, White River and Wayne. Fees were established for toll on the only ferry across the White River: one wagon, four horses or oxen, 62½ cents; for one man or woman, plus one horse, 12½ cents. The commissioners also fixed prices for the taverns: meals, 25 cents each; lodging 12½ cents; whiskey, 12½ cents a half pint; imported rum, brandy or wine, 25 cents a half pint; peach and apple brandies, 18½ cents a half pint.

Turning from this pioneer version of price fixing, the commissioners tackled the problem of taxes and established personal property rates at 37½ cents for every horse and mule; 25 cents for an ox; $1.00 for a two-wheeled pleasure vehicle; 20 cents for a silver watch and 50 cents for a gold watch. (Records show there were but two watches in Indianapolis in the first taxable year.)

At the behest of the settlers, the commissioners ordered trees cut down in order to open the streets. On Washington Street, the town's main and fastest-growing thoroughfare, the trees were cut down, but the low stumps posed a serious threat to horses and wagons and it was no mean feat to drive around them. In rainy weather when the mud was deep, wagons would sink so deep in the mire that the axletree would hit a stump and strand the wagon for hours.

During their May 29 session the commissioners adjourned to the banks of the White River for an important event: the landing of two large keelboats. The *Eagle*, "15 tons burthen," from Kenhawa brought salt, tobacco, whiskey and dried fruit, and the *Boxer* from Zanesville, "33 tons, Captain Wilson," brought Hugh Walpole and his family, a piano, household furnishings and several tons of merchandise for the store that Walpole was opening opposite the courthouse. The boats were the first to land in the town and lent support to Ralston's theory that the White River was navigable "at least four months of the year."

A general camp meeting sponsored by the Methodist Church was held in the spring at the James Given farm on the outskirts of the village. A large temporary camp was set up and the Reverend James Scott held audiences spellbound night after night with his fervent preaching. People got religion "in droves." A highlight of each evening was the "testifying" in the eerie light of flaming torches.

Religious services, however, were no longer confined to visiting preachers and camp meetings. The Baptists and the Presbyterians formally organized in 1822, the Baptists with the Reverend Benjamin Barnes as their minister, and the Presbyterians sharing the Reverend C. Proctor with fellow Presbyterians in Bloomington. The Presbyterians were also the first to build a church, a simple frame structure costing $1,200, on the northwest corner of Market and Pennsylvania Streets.

The Methodists, who had earlier been represented by circuit-riding preachers, organized the same year under the Reverend William Cravens. The next year the Methodists purchased a hewed log house on Maryland Street near Meridian, which became their first church.

Indianapolis was one of the first cities in the nation to have a Sunday school. It was organized by Dr. Isaac Coe, and, starting April 5, 1823, sessions were held in Caleb Scudder's cabinet shop on the south side of the Statehouse square. James M. Ray was superintendent and James Blake the teacher. The following year the school, then called the "Union Sunday School," met in the new Presbyterian church and, as befitted its new name, was attended by boys and girls of all denominations.

That summer the town formally celebrated its first Fourth of July. There was an opening sermon by the Reverend John McClung and speeches and readings by Judge Wick, Obed Foote and John Hawkins. The Reverend John Brenton pronounced the benediction. Following the solemn and patriotic part of the program, 14 toasts were drunk, and everybody joined in feasting on a barbecued buck deer that Robert Carter had killed near the lower end of Washington Street. In the evening a big bonfire lit up the sky and there was a gay ball at Jacob Crumbaugh's house at the corner of Market and Madison Streets.

A militia regiment, the Fortieth, was organized to comply with Indiana's law that required, under penalty of fine, that all able-bodied men eighteen to forty-five years of age attend musters, "Negroes, mulattoes and Indians excepted." Conscientious objectors were excused on condition they pay an annual assessment equal "to the lowest fines assessed on those privates ... who may neglect or refuse to perform military duty." Following the custom of the times, the men elected their own officers: James Paxton, colonel; Samuel Morrow, lieutenant colonel; and Alexander Russell, major. Except for the officers, the little company had no uniforms and weapons were few. Those who didn't own a sword or musket marched with a hoe handle or a cornstalk over their shoulder. The company, however, bravely held musters and regularly requisitioned equipment from Corydon.

The first session of the circuit court was held on September 26, 1822, and, in the absence of a courthouse, Judge Wick convened court in the cabin of Jonathan Carr, the largest and most pretentious house in town. Calvin Fletcher was named prosecutor. After admitting ten lawyers to practice, the court approved the naturalization of one Richard Cooke "lately from the kingdom of Ireland" (sic) and impaneled a grand jury that returned 22 indictments. Most of those indicted were charged with selling whiskey without a license, but there were cases of assault and battery and failing to pay justly incurred debts. Under Indiana law, a man could be jailed for failing to pay his debts but could be freed by "delivering up his estate for the benefit of his creditor or creditors." As there was no jail, the court established certain streets as boundaries and ordered that prisoners be confined to the area until such time as the judgment of the court was satisfied.

The summer passed without an epidemic, although there were some cases of the "summer sick." As the summer waned and the days grew shorter, the town was visited by a new plague: gray squirrels. They came from nowhere by the tens of thousands, swimming the White River and descending upon the village like a plague of locusts. They were everywhere: in the trees, grass, fields and gardens; in the cabins, under beds, in lofts and chimney corners. They devoured everything in sight, including the corn in the fields or stored for the winter. Everybody joined in fighting the invaders. Women and chlidren beat the bushes with flails and brooms, rang bells and beat on pans. Men plowed deep furrows and ditches to protect their crops. But still they came, scrambling up and down the side of the ditches, detouring the women and children and their noise.

Then one morning the town woke to find the squirrels gone, and everyone went about the business of cleaning up and listening to the recollections of other men and women who told stories of other times and places where the invaders had also struck and just as quickly disappeared.

More settlers came in 1823, to push the town's population to about 700, but others who might have come shied away. There was still talk around the state that Indianapolis was a place of pestilence, death, poor crops, swamps and few conveniences and would eventually be abandoned. The talk and gossip stiffened local pride, but merchants, doctors, lawyers, land owners, speculators and traders continued to feel uneasy. They had invested time and money in Indianapolis on the premise it was going to be the state capital. Then, three years later, there was little solid evidence that the capital would really be moved.

There were at least three good reasons why the capital hadn't been moved to Indianapolis. The little village as yet had no suitable place for the legislature to meet and there was doubt the local taverns offered sufficient accommodations for the legislators. Besides, section 2 of Article XI of the State Constitution provided that Corydon was to be the state capital until 1825 "and until removed by law."

However, the new Marion County Courthouse was under construction that summer and the successful bidders, John E. Baker and James Paxton, promised it would be ready the following year. Plans were also afoot for at least one new tavern and Carter's Rosebush was being enlarged again. As for the law, Marion County's newly elected representatives, Senator James Gregory and Representative James Paxton, were already at work drafting a bill for introduction in the next session of the legislature. Under its terms, the capital would be moved to Indianapolis before the 1825 session of the General Assembly.

There was other evidence of the town's permanency. More houses were being built of brick and frame, cabins were being improved and the paths and trails were becoming rough roads. The town's second newspaper, *The Western Censor and Immigrant's Guide*, started publication. A newly formed Indiana Central Medical Society was functioning under its president, Samuel Mitchell. Through the efforts of Dr. Coe, Calvin Fletcher and James Blake, the original crude school of James Reed was abandoned and, under the supervision of Mr. and Mrs. Rice B. Lawrence, moved to the new Presbyterian church. Besides the three R's, English grammar and geography were offered for two dollars per quarter. It was no longer a "blab" school and Mrs. Lawrence offered lessons in needlepoint for a slight extra charge.

The stores offered a wider variety of merchandise, but prices remained distressingly high because of the cost of transporting goods by wagon and pack horse over trails or muddy roads. There was little hard money about and customers bartered at a disadvantage. It required, for example, about two bushels of oats to buy a pound of nails; a bushel of wheat or two bushels of corn to buy a yard of calico or a pound of coffee. A yard of silk could command as high as 80 bushels of corn, and good broadcloth 100 bushels of corn a yard. On the other hand, prices on farm products were low, with dressed pork averaging a dollar per 100; wheat, 37½ cents a bushel; corn, 10 to 15 cents; eggs, 3 to 5 cents a dozen; turkeys, 15 to 25 cents each; young cattle, $2.50 each; milk cows, $5 to $10.

With the high water that spring the White River seemed about to fulfill its promises. Several loaded canoes were sent downstream and Van Blaricum took down a flatboat. When he returned, he brought the first oranges and coconuts to the little village. The high water subsided, however, leaving the question of the river's navigability open to debate.

The town's first theatrical production was announced for New Year's Eve in the dining room of Carter's tavern. A Mr. and Mrs. Smith, "late of the New York theater," would present a number of specialties, two short plays with music and a farce. Billy Bagwell, a local cigar maker, was engaged to play the accompaniment on a fiddle.

Carter, an elder in the Baptist Church, had some misgivings when he was originally approached by the Smiths, but he was a tolerant man and though he held no truck with drinking, cardplaying, dancing or shows, he was not a man to force his views on others. Neither was he a man to pass up the chance to make a dollar or take some trade away from his rivals. He booked the Smiths with the understanding theirs was a refined and genteel performance.

Despite a high admission charge, 37½ cents, the room at Carter's was packed when the curtain went up on the improvised stage lighted by flickering coal oil lamps. Mrs. Smith appeared, dressed in a sweeping skirt of velvet and satin, and opened the show with "The Star-Spangled Banner." As the last notes of the national anthem died away, Billy Bagwell switched to a fast jig-time tune on his fiddle, and Mrs. Smith, now blindfolded, went into her specialty: doing a sailor's hornpipe in and around several dozens of eggs with the promise not to break any of them during her spirited dance.

From the rear of the hall, Carter had been enjoying his few brief moments as an impresario, but as the fiddle moved into the lively and toe-tapping music of the hornpipe, a scowl crossed his face. A moment later he strode down the aisle, climbed up on the stage and stopped the show. "There will be none of this jig-time music played in my tavern," he announced. "If there is to be music, it must be confined to hymns or psalms."

The curtain went down, the Smiths held a hurried conference with their accompanist, and the curtain went up on the first musical skit. But the contrast between the doleful hymns and the farce on stage brought laughter and jeers. Finally the Smiths called for the curtain to be rung down and Indianapolis' first show was over.

Fear of an Indian uprising came in March 1824 and for months the little capital lived in a state of nerves. It started when a party of nine Indians—two braves, three squaws and four small children—pitched their camp in February at Lick Creek, northeast of Indianapolis, to hunt and trap.

In early March a settler named John Harper, with a reputation for deep-seated prejudice against Indians, spied the camp and decided to raid it and seize the Indians' piles of valuable furs. He enlisted the help of

James Hudson, Andrew Sawyer, John T. Bridge, Sawyer's brother-in-law, and Bridge's eighteen-year-old son, John, Jr. On the morning of March 22 the five men walked into the Indian camp, made gestures of friendship and asked for help in finding some lost horses. The braves, a Shawnee called Ludlow and a Miami named Mingo, agreed to help.

The two braves had no sooner entered the woods than Harper and Hudson, according to plan, shot them in the back, and Sawyer and the two Bridges opened fire on the helpless women. To make the nine killings look like the work of other Indians, the men mutilated the bodies and left them unburied. The killers then plundered the camp, divided their loot, packed everything on horses they had earlier hidden in the woods and rode away.

A trapper came across the carnage the next day and carried the news to Pendleton. Despite the killers' attempts to make the murders appear to be the work of Indians, the experienced eyes of frontiersmen and Indians quickly determined the nine people had died at the hands of white men. Settlers felt a shiver run down their spines. This was just the kind of thing that could bring on equally bloody and retaliatory attacks on the settlements.

Thoughtful men suggested that, if the murderers could be captured and made an example of, the Indians might be held in check. Posses were organized and grim-faced men fanned out over the countryside. Within a week four of the five killers were rounded up and locked up in the log jail at Pendleton. Harper, the ringleader, escaped into Ohio and was never caught.

Meanwhile, the nearest Indian agent, John Johnson at Piqua, Ohio, had been notified, and he joined William Conner in visiting the bands of Delawares and Senecas in the area and meeting with their chiefs. They asked the Indians to take no action until the white man's government had a chance to act. The chiefs agreed to wait and see.

But despite the promise of the chiefs, the settlers remained uneasy. Who could guarantee that some young brave would not ignore his chief and set out, perhaps with other angry braves, to wreak vengeance on the white man? Men in Indianapolis kept their weapons close at hand and wives and children were warned against straying far from their cabins. Laws forbidding the sale of whiskey to the Indians were rigidly enforced.

The circuit court convened in April and the four alleged killers were indicted for murder and their trials set for fall. In July Hudson escaped, but was speedily recaptured. The four separate trials attracted a great deal of attention. No white man had ever before been indicted and brought to trial for the killing of an Indian, and pioneers argued on both sides of the proposition. There was, in fact, a good deal of sympathy for the prisoners, especially by those who would ask, "Why all the fuss over killin' a few damned Indians?"

The trial included some of the best legal talent in Indiana. Judge Wick of Indianapolis was presiding judge, assisted by Andrew Winsell (or Winchell), the village blacksmith, and Samuel Holliday, a farmer. It was explained that the two laymen were appointed so that the legal proceedings might be "tempered with common sense." U.S. Senator James Noble of Brookville, Indiana's first senior U.S. senator, represented the Department of Indian Affairs and assisted Prosecutor Calvin Fletcher in the presentation of the state's case. The four defendants were represented by outstanding attorneys from Indiana and Ohio. The jurymen added a touch—they wore moccasins and carried hunting knives in court.

The prosecution's case was based on the need for respect for law and that all must be equal before the law; the defense shifted as much of the blame as possible to the missing Harper and dwelt upon prior outrages suffered at the hands of the Indians. The jury found the defendants guilty and Judge Wick sentenced all four to death by hanging. The cases were promptly appealed to the Indiana Supreme Court, but Judge Isaac Blackford, in a historic decision, upheld the convictions and the death penalty. James Hudson, who had made a full confession in the hope of leniency, was the first to be hanged publicly. He died on the gallows before a large crowd on January 12, 1825, and thus acquired the doubtful honor of being the first white man in America to be executed for killing an Indian. Sawyer and the two Bridges managed to stave off their executions for a few months, but eventually the date of their execution was set for June 3, 1825.

Huge crowds turned out on the appointed day, including bands of Indians who had been invited as special guests to view this example of white man's justice. The gallows were set up on the north bank of Fall Creek in what is now the City Park at Pendleton. Sawyer and the elder Bridge were hanged first and their bodies cut down and laid out in nearby pine coffins. Young Bridge was led up the scaffold steps, the rope adjusted and the black cap fitted over his head.

At this point a hard-riding horseman pushed his sweating, foam-flecked mount through the crowd of people to the foot of the scaffold. He dismounted, clambered up the steps of the gallows until he reached the platform and faced the condemned teen-ager. Dramatically holding up his hand for silence, the horseman announced in stentorian tones:

There are only two powers on earth who can save this boy from death. One is God Almighty and the other is Governor James Brown Ray of the State of Indiana. . . . I am Governor Ray and I hereby pardon this boy. . . . I order him released at once.

There are two versions of what happened next. One has it that when the black cap of the hangman was removed, the boy stood stock still staring straight ahead because "all reason had fled" and he remained helplessly insane the rest of his life. The other and happier version is that the young man lived to become a useful member of his community.

Chapter 4

WATERSHED YEARS

THE BILL INTRODUCED in the 1824 legislature to move officially the state's capital to Indianapolis drew opposition from many of the legislators representing the southern counties, but the bill passed both houses, was signed by Governor Hendricks, and Senator Gregory and Representative Paxton returned home to find themselves cast in the role of conquering heroes.

Preparations to move the capital began in the fall to meet the law's requirement that the capital "be removed from Corydon before the second Monday in January." Samuel Merrill, the state treasurer, who had been appointed by the legislature to superintend the move, auctioned off state-owned furniture and fixtures that could not be "advantageously" taken to Indianapolis; packed the state's silver, records and documents in heavy wooden boxes; and contracted with a Mr. Seibert for four horse-drawn covered wagons to make the overland trip of some 160 miles.

The party of 14 that set out in November consisted of Merrill, his wife and four daughters, Priscilla, Jane, Julia and nine-month-old Catharine; John Douglass, the state printer, and his family; and Seibert and his teamsters, who would double as axemen. One of the wagons carried the state's treasury and records and another was loaded with the state printing press, type, cases and equipment. The remaining wagons were filled with the furniture and household goods of the two state officials.

Seibert optimistically figured the journey from Corydon to Indianapolis would take about eight days. The trip, however, consumed nearly two weeks: the best day's travel was 11 miles and on one particularly bad day the little caravan managed only two and a half miles. Besides swollen rivers, rotting corduroy roads and seas of mud, there were blocked trails, and in some places axemen had to cut their way through dense virgin timber to provide passage for the wagons. At night the women and children slept in the wagons or were lodged in nearby cabins. The men generally slept on the ground. The conscientious Merrill, two loaded pistols within easy reach, slept near the wagon containing the state's treasury and records.

Samuel Merrill's oldest daughter, Priscilla, left this description of the journey:

The road was laid with rails or logs for miles, then covered with water that seemed bottomless. When the horses and the wagons would go down my sister and I would scream with fright. The water on the roads was too deep to drive through and trees had to be felled to make a road through these places. One of the wagons stuck and had to be pried out. I walked all the way, except when we came near Columbus, as it was raining. Mr. Seybert, the teamster, put bells on the teams whenever he came near a town. We begged him not to do this when we drove into Indianapolis but he would not listen to us. So we entered the capital in covered wagons drawn by fine, large, strong horses strung with bells. The sound brought the good people out to stare at us. I was glad I was in a covered wagon at the time.

Miss Merrill was right about the good people coming out to stare. Nearly everyone in the village converged on the little caravan as it pulled up in front of Blake and Henderson's store. The capital had finally arrived.

In January Samuel Merrill submitted his bill to the legislature, which not only reimbursed him but voted him a $100 bonus in appreciation for a job well done.

The 1825 legislature rode into the new capital on horseback, proposed legislation reposing in their saddlebags. The legislators represented cash for the taverns and the merchants. Senators and representatives were paid two silver dollars a day during sessions of the General Assembly and two dollars for each 25 miles "they shall severally travel on the most usual route." The General Assembly convened on January 10 in the new Marion County Courthouse, a two-story brick structure facing Washington Street, with an adjoining log jail whose walls were a foot thick.

The legislators made some effort to improve the town. Fifty dollars was appropriated to clean out Pogue's Run, a source of pestilence, and the outlying portions of the town were ordered sold or leased in four-acre tracts for farming. Midway through the session Carter's Rosebush was destroyed in a spectacular midnight fire which led to the formation of the town's first fire-fighting group, a bucket and ladder company.

The first stagecoach lines came to Indianapolis in 1825 and 1826 and connected the capital with other parts of the state as well as providing for downstate connections to adjoining states. Survey teams for the National

Road arrived the following year. The highway, known variously as "The Old Pike" and "The Cumberland Road," would enter Indiana at Richmond in 1829, advance through the woods to Indianapolis, continue on to Terre Haute and cross the Illinois line to Vandalia. Equally important was the proposed Michigan Road. An 1826 treaty with the Potawatomi Indians provided for the removal of the last of the Indians from Indiana, and plans had been launched for the Michigan Road, a 100-foot-wide highway to extend from the Ohio River to Lake Michigan. The road started at Madison and proceeded to Versailles, Greensburg, Indianapolis, South Bend and Michigan City. Work on the highway began in the spring of 1828. Today a marker at the junction of Southeastern Avenue and Washington Streets denotes where the north-south Michigan Road crossed the east-west National Road.

The first stagecoach line into the capital, The Madison and Indianapolis Stage, connected the town with the Ohio River, but it took from 7:00 A.M. on Thursday until Sunday at 4:00 P.M. for the trip. Fare was 6¼ cents a mile for "grown persons," and passengers were "privileged to carry small packages not exceeding fifteen pounds." The coaches of the Madison line were built in the East and carried nine passengers, with an additional seat on top beside the driver. Exteriors were elaborately and gaily decorated and interiors were generally upholstered in crimson red. To absorb shocks and "render passengers comfortable," each coach rested on heavy leather straps called "thorough-braces" which attached to stiff iron standards at each end. Coaches were drawn by four- to six-horse teams, the harnesses studded with shiny brass and bells jingling on an iron frame mounted above the collar. Besides the bells, each driver carried a horn which was blown loudly as the coach approached a town.

Besides the coaches, stage lines operated mail and freight stages that also carried passengers, but in a great deal less style and comfort. These were big, lumbering wagons covered with heavy canvas and drawn by six-horse "line teams." Most mail stages carried feed troughs for the horses that could be readily detached from the rear of the wagon and set up on the tongue at feeding time. Horses for coaches and stages were exchanged at relay stations established at regular intervals along the way. Additional horses and a postillion rider were often stationed at the foot of steep hills to provide extra horse power if the stage had difficulty in negotiating the grade.

A journey by stage was an adventure in uncertainty. Roads were unbelievably bad and there were few bridges. In the spring and in heavy rains, mud and swollen streams could play havoc with passengers and schedules. Coaches frequently bogged down in the mud and everybody had to get out and lend a hand in prying out the heavy vehicle with poles and fence rails. Where there were no bridges, streams had to be forded and coaches often toppled over in midstream, disgorging passengers and baggage into the water. Axles and springs were often smashed on hidden stumps or boulders and passengers were faced with the choice of continuing the journey on foot or sitting in the middle of the wilderness while the driver set out for help. Sometimes the team was unhitched and passengers rode into town on one of the big horses.

The population count for 1826 showed 762 residents, and four years later the U.S. Census reported the population standing at an official 1,085. A little arithmetic disclosed that an average of 108 persons or perhaps 27 families a year had moved into the capital during its first decade. The reason behind the snail-like growth was well told in little Catharine Merrill's diary. Confiding to its pages the fact that her mother had predicted that some day Indianapolis would have a population of 5,000, she wrote:

Pa says, too, that Indianapolis may be that large, but I heard some men tell him this morning that he was mistaken. They said it was situated in a vast mud-hole which could never be dried up so as to be depended upon.

Indianapolis still had much to live down and much to live up to.

Since the little town's beginning, the knoll on the Circle had been a pasture for horses, cows, sheep, goats and hogs, but in the spring of 1827 a rail fence was put up to keep them out and workmen started construction of a two-story brick house. It was the long-planned governor's house authorized by the legislature in January.

The house was 50 feet square with a modified mansard roof, a widow's walk which afforded a view of the little town, a spacious attic and a semi-basement. Doors on all four sides opened into wide halls which divided the lower floor into four large, high-ceilinged rooms. The same plan was repeated on the second floor. The house was both elaborate and impractical, and before it was finished Governor Ray made it clear he didn't like the place, nor did he intend to live in it, and the legislature appropriated no further funds. Mrs. Ray, it was reported, was displeased with the house because it had no kitchen or pantry and was horrified at the thought of publicly hanging out the family wash in the center of town for all to see and comment upon. As a result, the house was left unfinished.

Several public offices and a bank were later installed in the partially completed building, but their occupants complained of chills and drafts and soon departed. For a time the house was occupied by John Strange, a preacher, one or two other homeless men, and the widowed and ailing Judge Isaac Blackford, who not only lived there but carried on his work of editing the Indiana law reports. Following the deaths of the judge and the preacher, the house fell into further disrepair and became a haven for tramps, bats, rats and stray animals. It even acquired a reputation for being "haunted" before it was sold at auction in 1857 and torn down. The knoll was converted to a park, but continued to be used for a cow pasture until well after the Civil War.

As for Indiana's governors, they were on their own until 1839, when the legislature ordered the state officers to purchase a proper building for a governor's mansion.

The National Road, forerunner of east-west Route 40, crossed Washington Street in the 1830s and marked Indianapolis' beginning as a major transportation center. An 80-foot highway of broken stone with a gravel bed in the center, the road widened at Indianapolis to follow the 120-foot contours of Washington Street, returned to its original width at the end of West Washington and headed west for Terre Haute and Vandalia. A covered toll bridge, built of wood and resting on stone piers, afforded passage over the White River. A contemporary writer described the road as looking "more like the leading avenue of a great city than a road through a rural district" and told of counting "twenty four-horse coaches in line at a time on the road." Big, broad-wheeled Conestoga wagons laden with merchandise and drawn by six large horses were "visible all day long at every point." Besides the coaches and the freight wagons, there were also people afoot, on horseback and in wagons making their way to new homes in the West.

Indianapolis, with a number of other roads now radiating out from the town, became an important link in the state's and nation's highway systems. Stores and taverns enjoyed new prosperity. Store tea replaced sassafras and spice bush. Merchants, with a more liberal supply of goods, began to specialize. Communications improved. Mail took only 60 hours to reach Indianapolis from Washington by stagecoach. John L. Young and a contractor for building bridges on the National Road, William Werneg, built the town's first brewery on the south side of Maryland Street in 1834. The J. & P. Vorhees Company established a coach-making and repair shop on the southwest corner of Maryland and Pennsylvania. A tobacco factory was built and a linseed oil mill, a paper mill, a flour mill, a woolen mill and a soap factory. John Wood opened a steam foundry. Samuel Walton's spinning wheel factory invited customers to "Come in and Buy and Go and Spin / Dress Your Household Neat Within." Fresh fruits and vegetables in season were on sale daily at a new market house, "Wednesdays and Saturdays two hours after daylight."

George Smith left the *Gazette* in 1830 to launch the *Indiana Farmer* with the motto "Born of No Master, of No Party Are We." This was obviously a potshot at the *Gazette*, which had become a pro-Jackson paper and changed its name to the *Indiana Democrat and Spirit of the Constitution*, later shortened to simply *Democrat*. Newspaper advertising was sold by the "square" and advertisements printed on the front page.

Rewards of one or two cents were offered for runaway indentured apprentices, usually described as blue-eyed boys of twelve or fourteen years of age. The post office advertised uncalled-for mail.

The first Irish came to town as $8- to $12-a-month laborers on the National Road. A Temperance Society was organized, met regularly, issued tracts, wrote letters to the newspapers condemning the evils of rum, castigated judges for the light sentences doled out for drunkenness and raised funds to build a hall. Carter's tavern became the Indianapolis Hotel, David Buchanan purchased the Traveler's Hall, Elizabeth Noland opened a tavern and boardinghouse, and Nathaniel Bolton's wife, Sarah, gaining fame as a poet and a hostess, opened a tavern in their home on Mount Jackson near the National Road. Mrs. Bolton was helping her husband pay off debts he had incurred by the careless signing of notes for equally careless friends. The ubiquitous Samuel Merrill opened a book and stationery store in 1838 in the new brick Temperance Hall and laid the groundwork for the city's largest and most respected publishing house, The Bobbs-Merrill Company. The first insurance company was organized two years earlier, with Douglass McGuire as president and Jacob Scudder, the cabinetmaker, as secretary. Like the publishing business, insurance would also play a major role in Indianapolis' future.

While the National Road was nearing Indianapolis in 1831, the White River got new attention. A small boy fishing on the river on April 11 looked up from his bobber to find a steamboat on the river headed for Indianapolis. He dropped his fishing pole and headed for town to spread the momentous news.

The boy's shouts brought half the town to the banks of the river to gaze in disbelief at a small steamboat, resplendent in its white paint and gold trim, maneuvering inshore for a landing. The boat was the *Robert Hanna*, named for its owner, General Hanna, one of the contractors engaged to build a stretch of the National Road. Hanna had listened to stories downstate that the White River was navigable and he figured it would be cheaper to haul men, material and supplies by water than overland by horse and wagon over bad roads. Accordingly, he purchased a small steamboat on the Wabash, loaded it with timber and supplies, and tied on a barge loaded with stone to be used for the piers and abutments of the National Road Bridge. The journey had tested the mettle of the steamboat and its pilot. The river proved to be winding, filled with treacherous shoals, sandbars and overhanging trees. But the sturdy little steamer had made it despite all the obstacles, and as Hanna watched the gathering crowds on shore, he viewed his gamble with satisfaction.

Hanna's welcome to Indianapolis was exuberant and boisterous as befitted a man who appeared as the harbinger of a glorious future. Captain

Blythe's hastily summoned artillery company lined up and set off a thundering salute on their antique cannon. Governor Noble made a little speech in which he declared the landing was the "realization of our sanguine expectations."

General Hanna, basking in the warm glow of his reception, delayed departure of his steamboat in order to take groups of townspeople on a series of short excursions up and down the river. All went well until the last trip of the day, when the boat failed to steam out of range of some overhanging boughs that lined the banks. The boughs knocked down the boat's chimneys, smashed the pilothouse and wrecked a wheel housing. There was a brief moment of panic among the passengers and several leaped overboard and swam ashore. No one was seriously injured, but the steamboat was badly crippled.

Emergency repairs were made overnight, and the next day the little steamboat left the dock for its return journey to the Wabash. It had not proceeded far down the river when it ran aground on Hog Island. Men and horses rushed to the boat's assistance, but despite heroic efforts to free it, it remained fast, and there it sat all summer long in the middle of the White River—an inglorious symbol of a town's dashed hopes. It left in the fall with the high waters and a derisive whistle toot, and as Max Hyman, a chronicler of Indianapolis history, later wrote: "She was never seen in these latitudes again."

Nor were any other steamboats. Governor Noble, who persisted in the belief that the river was navigable, posted a $200 reward for the first steamboat to dock at the town. His offer tempted two steamboat captains. One managed to reach Spencer in Owen County before running aground; the second got a little farther up the river but decided the risk was too great and turned back. Wiser men shook their heads. It was no use arguing that the White River was navigable. Even keelboats and flatboats were abandoning efforts to navigate the river. Mr. Ralston and the others had been wrong and Indianapolis wasn't ever going to be an important steamboat landing.

The bustling 1830s saw the construction of the state's first public building in the little capital. Since Indiana's beginnings, even back in territorial days, the state had housed its government in leased buildings, first in Vincennes, then in Corydon and in the 1820s in the Marion County Courthouse. On February 10, 1831, the legislature authorized the construction of the first statehouse. Its site was the block between Washington and Market Streets and bounded by what are now Senate and Capitol Avenues.

The legislators estimated the cost of the structure at $56,000, to be amortized by the sale of the considerable number of lots which the state still owned in the original four-mile square. This second sale of public lands, however, proved as disappointing as the first. In the final days of the sale, the state land agents were reduced to offering choice downtown lots for as little as ten dollars each—probably the biggest real estate value in the city's history. Virtually all of the outlots continued on the unsold list and were rented for cow pastures, except for a few that were sold or leased for farms.

The statehouse design competition and a $150 prize was won by Ithiel Town and Arthur J. Davis, well-known New York architects. The talented Town submitted a design in the then popular Greek-revival style— a two-story Doric temple with ten classical pillars on the north and south and crowned with a Roman dome and cupola. Town and Davis were awarded a contract for $58,000 and the building was started September 26, 1832. Governor Noble, Morris Morris and Samuel Merrill acted as building commissioners for the state.

Eighty feet wide by 180 feet, the building was constructed of brick stuccoed to resemble stone. Specifications called for the use of oak, ash, poplar and walnut for interiors, "all to be found in abundance within a four or five mile radius of the site." It was a well-planned building, efficiently heated and ventilated. Six chimneys equipped with chimney pots poked their way up through the classic roof to carry off the smoke and fumes from the fireplaces at each end of the legislative halls and the Supreme Court rooms and the enormous stoves set up on each floor. The Senate, on the second floor, was a spacious room 36 by 70 feet, and the House, on the lower floor, 48 by 70 feet. Although the ten pillars and the cupola were given several coats of white paint, the zinc dome was left ungilded as an economy measure, and instead of glistening with gold in the sunlight, it merely sat and glinted.

When the building was finished, in December of 1835—in time for the first legislative session—there were those who hailed the new statehouse as the "finest and most beautiful building in all the West." This may have been a slight exaggeration, but to the proud residents of Indianapolis, every word was true.

A new attempt to find a suitable home for Indiana's governors was made in 1839. The state purchased the largest and handsomest house in town—the home of Dr. John H. Sanders, a large, rambling three-story house on the west corner of Illinois and Market Streets. But, like the house on the Circle, it proved to be an unhappy choice. Governor Wallace moved in and his family found it damp and unhealthy. Other governors who lived in it complained of frequent illnesses in their family caused by the house. Governor Whitcomb blamed it for his wife's death and Governor Wright lost two wives during his occupancy. Governor Morton, after a short stay in the house, refused to live in it, and it was sold in 1865.

The building of the National Road brought problems as well as prosperity. Many undesirable characters had floated into town, including gamblers, a few shady ladies and a number of hard-drinking toughs who worked on the road and spent their evenings brawling and fighting. Some of these young delinquents banded together in a "Chain Gang" led by a quick-tempered giant of a man named Dave Burkhart (or Buckhart) who was generally called "Old Dave Burkhart." Burkhart's gang took particular pleasure in terrorizing a small settlement of Negroes on the outskirts of the village. The bullying and night raids went on for a few weeks until the Negroes decided to fight back. Under the leadership of one of the town's most respected blacks, John Overall, they quietly acquired a number of shotguns and one night, as Burkhart's gang approached, drove them off with volleys of buckshot.

The Negroes' victory marked the beginning of Burkhart's downfall. A few nights later, filled with corn whiskey and accompanied by a few of his gang, Burkhart visited a Methodist camp meeting which was being held under the direction of the Reverend James Havens. Burkhart interrupted the services by shouting obscenities and singing off-color songs and, when ordered to leave the grounds, challenged Havens to throw him out. Havens left the pulpit, strode down the aisle, grabbed the surprised Burkhart by the shirt, gave him a thrashing and saw to it that the gang leader was hauled off to the town jail. The next day Burkhart was run out of town.

The Burkhart case and the alarming increase in vice and crime resulted in a public meeting of concerned citizens on September 7, 1832, and the organization of the first town government under the state's general incorporation act. Five trustees were elected: Samuel Merrill, Henry P. Coburn, John C. Brown, John Wilkins and Samuel Henderson, the former postmaster, who was elected president of the board. Salaries were fixed at a dollar for each regular monthly meeting the trustees attended.

The new town government adopted a general ordinance that served as a charter. It established five wards, defined the duties of the trustees, and banned kite flying, the galloping of a horse or the shooting of a gun within the city limits. The ordinance also forbade anyone to keep stallions on Washington Street, in the interests of safety on the National Road; established a $1 fine for allowing a stovepipe within two inches of the woodwork, $2 for leaving the cellar door open on the road or sidewalk (a real hazard for late-returning gentlemen in their cups), and $3 for leaving a team unhitched.

Four years later, 1836, the town petitioned the legislature for legal approval of its acts and requested a special charter which, "in the cause of good government," would increase the town's police powers. A reincorporation act passed February 17, 1838, provided for six wards and government by a board of councilmen, and gave the town the right to prohibit gambling, regulate amusements, abolish nuisances, repair streets and control markets. It gave the town jurisdiction over the four-square-mile donation, but limited its taxing powers (set at a maximum of one-half of one percent) to the mile square. It also gave the town the right to levy taxes on property owners for street improvements and construction of badly needed sidewalks.

A "law and order" board of councilmen was elected in September 1838, with James Morrison as president. Under the new charter, Morrison also had the jurisdiction and powers of a justice of the peace, and the marshal, William Campbell, those of a constable. In 1839 a change in the laws provided that councilmen would serve two-year terms instead of one and increased salaries to $24 a year.

Receipts of the town government were under $3,000 until the 1840s. In 1835, total receipts were $1,610 and expenditures $124.

Perhaps the only important purchase of the new town government was a Merrick hand-drawn "end brake" pumper with rack ladders and 25 leather fire buckets. The action was taken after prodding by the legislature who were desirous of obtaining improved fire protection for the new statehouse building. The shiny red and gold pumper with its glistening brass was hauled over the National Road from Philadelphia and housed in a new two-story brick building on the Circle. Manned by 28 men, the pump could throw a one-inch stream of water some 100 feet. In 1835 the old bucket and ladder company was absorbed by the newly organized Marion Fire, Hose and Protective Association. Caleb Scudder was named fire chief. The second floor of the firehouse, besides providing a social club for the volunteer firemen, served as a meeting room for the board of councilmen.

Indianapolis was a Northern town, but it was Southern in its style and the inflection of its voice. The sturdy, uneducated yeomen who came to the town from Kentucky, Tennessee, the Carolinas, Maryland and Virginia gave the language color and new, imaginative twists. If a child longed for something, he "honed" for it. Something on a bias was "siwhickety" or "cattawampus." A "sod soaker" was a heavy rain. There was both respect and disrespect in calling a rigid churchman a "Forty-

Gallon Baptist" or saying of a minister, "He could pray his congregation
to hell and back." And there was secular realism in a common comment
that dispensed with formalities at the start of a meal—"Grace was said
when the hog was shot."

It was a time of many superstitions. If a boy killed a toad, his father's
cow would give bloody milk; if a dog howled in the night, it meant death
in the house; if a cat rubbed his face frequently, the weather was going to
be dry; if one killed a snake and left it lying belly upward, there would
be rain before night.

It was also an age of nicknames and men had "handles" for almost everything, including states and regions. New Englanders were Yankees,
residents of Illinois were Suckers, Ohioans were Buckeyes. In the 1830s
Indianans became Hoosiers.

No one is sure to this day how the word originated, but there are a
great many theories. One of the most popular is that visitors to the state,
upon hailing a pioneer cabin or knocking on its door, were greeted with
a "Who's yere?" and Indiana became the "Who's yere?" or Hoosier
State. Another theory in wide circulation is that brawling Indiana river-
men were so often successful in trouncing or "hushing" their opponents
that they became known as "hushers" and eventually "Hoosiers." There
is also the story of a contractor named Hoosier employed on the Louisville and Portland canal who preferred to hire laborers from Indiana.
They became known as "Hoosier's men" and, in time, all Indianans were
called Hoosiers. Less colorful and more acceptable is the theory of Jacob
Piatt Dunn, highly respected Indiana historian and long-time secretary of
the Indiana Historical Society. Dunn tracked the word back to the word
"hoozer," from a dialect in use in England's Cumberland district. He
theorized that descendants of English immigrants who settled and named
the Cumberland Mountains brought the name with them when they
settled in the hills of southern Indiana.

Although the origin of the name "Hoosier" is obscure, how it came
into wide circulation is a story that begins in Indianapolis with a common
custom of the newspapers of the day—the publishing of a "Carrier's
Address" on the first day of each new year. The "Address" was usually a
long poem of special merit with artistic embellishments. These were given
free to newsboys, who sold them and pocketed the proceeds as their New
Year's gift from customers and publishers.

On New Year's Day, 1833, the *Journal* served up a long ten-stanza
poem, "The Hoosier's Nest" by John Finley of Richmond, Indiana. Finley's poem, which glorified Indiana and the West, told the story of a
sturdy pioneer who came to Indiana, built a cabin, hacked a farm out of
the wilderness and found happiness and contentment in his growing

family and fortunes. Along the way the rambling rhymes paid tribute to honest toil and all of the homely virtues.

One stanza is worth repeating for its description of a pioneer cabin of the 1830s:

> *One side was filled with divers garments,*
> *The other spread with skins of varmints;*
> *Dried pumpkins overhead were strung,*
> *Where venison hams in plenty hung;*
> *Two rifles placed above the door,*
> *Three dogs lay stretched upon the floor,*
> *In short, the domicile was rife*
> *With specimens of Hoosier life.*

"The Hoosier's Nest" wasn't particularly good poetry and far from Finley's best work, but it was an immediate success. The *Journal* was besieged for additional copies. Newspapers across the country reprinted all ten stanzas and found them immensely popular with readers. The stanzas also reached Europe, where they appeared in English newspapers as an example of backwoods American poetry. It became the first poem by a Westerner to achieve international fame. Finley's use of the word "Hoosier" was not the first time the word had appeared in print, but the tremendous popularity of the ten stanzas and their wide currency started the word well on its way into the American vocabulary.

"Hoosier" became a friendly or a fighting word depending upon the speaker's context, his attitude and the inflection of his voice. If used in friendly banter, no one need take offense, but if used derisively, it meant that a man was an illiterate and uncouth rustic, a hayseed, a rube, a "yahoo." Although the word is used and abused by contemporary editorial writers, headline writers, politicians and members of the country-lane, covered-bridge school of writing, the title evokes a certain belligerence among many people to this day. Several manufacturers and chambers of commerce omit the word entirely from their printed material, especially that designed for recruiting new employees from out of state.

Chapter 5

ARRIVALS AND
DEPARTURES

Hard Money Remained Scarce and even in the late 1830s most trade was conducted by barter. The few coins in circulation included a large copper penny, several Spanish coins ranging in value from 6¼ cents to 12½ cents, the latter called a "bit," and an occasional French franc. It was 1838 before Indianapolis saw its first American dimes and half-dimes. These were exhibited in Foster's Jewelry Store and placed in the cornerstone of the Christ Church, the town's first Episcopal church.

Bills on the State Bank of Kentucky were acceptable in trade but the early banks of Indiana, including the State Bank of Indiana, had failed or fallen into disrepute as the result of embezzlement or other crimes. Their bills, if they turned up, were worthless. On January 28, 1834, the Indiana General Assembly set out to remedy this intolerable situation by chartering the Second State Bank of Indiana, with a capital stock of $1,600,000 and an authorized life of 25 years. Under the act, the state owned half the bank stock, retained supervisory powers and the right to name key officers. The bank was prohibited from speculating in real estate, which had proved the downfall of some earlier banks.

The main office of the Second State Bank, whose powers were limited to supervision of its ten branches, was located in the "governor's house" on the Circle until 1840, when it was moved to a new building at the corner of Kentucky and Illinois Streets. Samuel Merrill, completing his term as state treasurer, was appointed president, and the first directors were Calvin Fletcher, Seaton W. Morris, Robert Morrison and Thomas

R. Scott. James M. Ray was appointed cashier. Hervey Bates, the town's first sheriff, was named president of the Indianapolis branch, and Betheul F. Morris, cashier. Calvin Fletcher later succeeded Bates to the presidency.

The ten branches of the bank, including the one in Indianapolis, did commercial banking and issued paper money. Samuel Merrill's conservative administration and the requirements of law provided a close working relationship of the branches which ensured their solvency. In the bank's first year of operation it reported a paid-in capital of over $800,000. In 1836 its capital was increased to $2,500,000.

The Second State Bank of Indiana provided money, credit and balance to the growing community of Indianapolis and gave impetus to business and industry. The bank's paper money (notes) were as "good as gold," and although it was forced to suspend specie payments—that is, redeem paper with coin—in the panic of 1837, it weathered the storm and continued sound and healthy until 1859, when it wound up its affairs and gave the State of Indiana a profit of $3,700,000.

Two private banks were also launched. John Wood, the steam foundryman, started one in 1838, but it failed three years later. Stoughton A. Fletcher, a brother of Calvin, joined with William D. Wygart and opened a bank at 30-34 Washington Street which later became the Fletcher and Churchman Bank, Fletcher's Bank, and eventually the oldest continuous bank in the state.

The 1832 legislature approved a petition of the town of Indianapolis for a county seminary. Alexander Ralston's original plat had set aside a block bounded by Meridian, New York, Vermont and Pennsylvania Streets for a state university, but this had only proved to be another of the town's unrealized hopes and the lot remained vacant, filled with trees and brush. With the legislature's permission, the ground was leased and a county seminary, a two-story stucco building surrounded by a graveled yard and a high fence, was opened two years later. It admitted boys only and charged tuition.

On the day the seminary opened, Miss Hooker's Female School opened its doors and was immediately followed by other female schools. Among them were Gilman Martson's Franklin Institute, Mary J. and Harriett Axtell's Indianapolis Female Institute, the Gregg school and schools of Clara Ellick and Laura Kise. Besides the basic subjects, the schools offered "the accomplishments"—drawing, painting and needlework.

New churches went up to symbolize the arrival of German and Irish immigrants. The First English Lutheran church was built on Ohio near Meridian in 1837, and three years later Zion's Church was organized by members of the first Lutheran church who had withdrawn to start a

German-speaking congregation. The Reverend Theodore J. E. Kuntz served as their first pastor until he transferred to the newly organized St. Paul's German Lutheran Church in 1844. The first Catholic church, with both German and Irish as parishioners, was built in 1840 by the Reverend Vincent Bacquelin of the Holy Cross Church, Shelbyville.

The small but growing Negro section formally organized their first Methodist church about 1840 and held services in a small frame house on Georgia Street. A leading force in the church was Augustus Turner. The Reverend W. R. Revels was one of their best-known pastors. A regular visitor was Bishop Paul Quinn of Baltimore, of the Colored Methodist Church, whose arrival was generally the signal for a series of revival meetings.

Among the new arrivals in Indianapolis was the Reverend Henry Ward Beecher, a native of Litchfield, Connecticut, graduate of Amherst College and Lane Seminary, brother of the famous Harriet Beecher Stowe, author of *Uncle Tom's Cabin*, and son of the Reverend Lyman Beecher, a noted Calvinist preacher. The Reverend Henry Ward Beecher and his bride, the former Eunice Ballard, came to Indianapolis from Lawrenceburg, Indiana, in answer to a call from a committee of 15 members of the original Presbyterian Church who had withdrawn (in a division over "new" and "old" schools of thought) and formed the Second Presbyterian Church. Beecher arrived in Indianapolis July 31, 1839, and two years later, October 4, 1840, a two-story frame Second Presbyterian Church building was completed on the corner of the Circle and West Market Street.

The handsome, square-set Beecher was eloquent, brilliant, and dynamic and he entered the religious and secular life of the community with what can only be described as gusto. His popular series of "Lectures to Young Men," dealing with sex and morality, were marked by the conversion of several of the town's "fast" young men and brought him national fame. Collected and brought out in book form, the lectures became a best seller and made Beecher a national figure. A relentless foe of slavery and whiskey, Beecher's thundering denunciations of both created loyal friends and implacable enemies. His first sermon on the evils of slavery so aroused the ire of several members of his congregation that they got up and walked out on his fiery words, some never to return. An acrimonious debate with a whiskey distiller resulted in a challenge from the distiller to meet the temperance crusader "anywhere at any time." Beecher met the challenge by replying in a letter to the editor of the *Journal* that he would bring "a woman and a Quaker for his seconds."

Harriet Beecher Stowe was a frequent visitor to her brother's vine-covered home in Indianapolis, and years later, when *Uncle Tom's Cabin* was published, many guessed that her *Uncle Tom* was patterned after a much-beloved elderly Indianapolis Negro, Uncle Tom Magruder, an ex-slave who lived with his family in a cabin built for him by Governor Noble's family. The names of three of the Magruder children, Moses, Louisa and Topsy, were also used in Mrs. Stowe's story. When the book went on sale in Indianapolis, there were some unkind enough to suggest the Magruder family may have well been the only Negroes Mrs. Stowe had ever known.

The Reverend Henry Ward Beecher left Indianapolis in October 1847 for New York City, to gain new fame and to rank with P. T. Barnum and Horace Greeley as the town's leading celebrities. But memories of the Reverend Beecher and Mrs. Beecher were to linger on. Mrs. Beecher, who had been unhappy during her years in the town and occasionally snubbed, wrote a novel, *From Dawn to Daylight*, in which she poured out her dissatisfaction with Indianapolis and Indiana. The book enjoyed a wide sale but was banned in Indianapolis and was the subject of controversy in the city library for 30 years.

A cholera epidemic swept the state in 1832 and 1833. Brought to America on ships from Europe, it arrived in Cincinnati from the East Coast. In Indianapolis some said the disease claimed 62 lives in a single month. Doctors who relied on bleeding their patients, or dosing them with calomel or herbs, stood helplessly by. The story is told of one doctor who advised the family of a cholera victim: "Give him this medicine every hour until he dies." It was probably sound advice, as there was little anyone could do to stop an epidemic. Sanitation was virtually unknown; there was no sewage system, no organized or common removal of trash or garbage. Families were large and as many as ten or 15 people might live in a small, unventilated cabin or house; in the taverns as many as 16 men might sleep in a single room. Screens were unknown and many cabins had no windowpanes, an open invitation to disease-carrying flies and mosquitoes. Many people went barefoot and men regarded the outdoor privy as effeminate. Small streams and creeks were often polluted with wastes from foundries, mills, and pork-packing plants and drainage from the streets. In winter there were no fruits or vegetables, and families subsisted on corn, pork and game. Bathing was infrequent and some took baths only three or four times a year. It was a cooperative society with every man a carrier.

The epidemic had one good result. A board of health was organized consisting of five doctors and five citizens. The town appropriated $1,000 and appointed a sanitary commissioner for each ward. A section of the "governor's house" on the Circle was converted to a hospital, with Dr. John E. McClure as superintendent. The germ theory of disease was yet to gain credence, so the board of health and the sanitary commissioners confined their efforts to filling in lowlands and swamps, as their vapors and odors were generally believed to be a source of pestilence.

During the winter of 1838 the town had its first theatrical season. John Lindsay came to town and set up a theater in Ollaman's wagon shop and presented a program of tragedies and melodramas. He also engaged an orchestra consisting of a fiddle, a clarinet and a brass horn that provided background music and accompaniment for the comic songs and turns between the acts. The churches regularly denounced the theater and dancing as immoral, but Lindsay's shows were well patronized and returned for several seasons.

Dancing and the theater, however, were not the only targets of the puritanical churches. Indianapolis ministers, including Beecher, were turning their righteous wrath on whiskey drinking, setting in motion the great temperance crusades of the 1830s and 1840s. Few could deny that whiskey was a problem. It was cheap and was consumed as generally as another age would drink coffee. In 1827, for example, 213 barrels of corn whiskey and other alcoholic beverages were imported and another 71 barrels of "Bayou Blue" were turned out by an Indianapolis distillery on the White River, ten gallons of liquid lightning for every man, woman and child in the donation—enough to quench many a monumental thirst.

It was considered a personal offense if a man refused a drink offered by another and hardly anyone refused a drink in public or in private. Women took a "little" with water. Regarded as "good for worms," it was given to children with a little tansy added. Mixed with wild cherry bark or a combination of dogwood bark and prickly ash, it was reputed to alleviate chills and fever.

Close on the heels of the formation of a state board of agriculture, a county agricultural society was formed, in 1835, with Nathan B. Palmer as president and Douglass MacGuire as secretary. Its first exhibit in the courthouse yard distributed $184 in premiums and Calvin Fletcher announced that the 1,300 farms in Marion County had produced 1,300,000 bushels of corn. James Blake, proprietor of the town's first wholesale dry goods house, who grew hemp and was experimenting with silkworms, served as president of the state board.

The county built its first poorhouse for the aged and the indigent in Wayne township during the 1830s, marking the beginning of an institution that would remain until the 1940s and Social Security. A benevolent society was organized in 1835 to collect clothes, household goods and groceries for the town poor. Lacking a home for the insane, mental cases were sent to the county poorhouse.

Express mail was inaugurated during Van Buren's administration and riders galloped daily up Washington Street on the National Road, blowing little tin horns, to the delight of every small boy in town. Indianapolis churches denounced the transporting and delivery of mail on Sunday. Aaron Wallace, the first Negro to arrive in and leave Indianapolis, returned to spend his declining years. The town's barbers were Negroes and included John Britton, who was married to Chaney Lively. Teenage boys prowled the woods hunting wolves in order to collect a 12½-cent state bounty.

Families made spruce beer at home and no one could ever eat enough of the town's favorite treat—gingerbread. The town started the initial leveling and graveling of sidewalks, but there was resistance from property owners who were unhappy over being assessed for the improvements. A new and larger market house was erected on the west side of Tennessee Street where Ohio crossed. The county was governed at different times by a board of county commissioners or a board made up of justices of the peace, depending upon the political climate of the legislature, but finally, in 1837, the commissioner system was made permanent.

Few men wore beards; they were regarded as "dandyish" and would be so regarded for another ten years. A man's masculinity was subject to challenge if he wore a mustache, an "imperial" or a goatee. Clothes, for the most part, were still made at home. But at least two tailor shops in town could turn out suits cut of imported cloth in the fashionable Eastern style. Women wore gingham, calico, wool or cotton dresses that hugged the neck and dropped below the ankle.

The town's first murder took place on May 8, 1832. Michael Van Blaricum, a ferryman on the White River, was arrested for purposely upsetting his boat in midstream and, in full view of several persons on the riverbank, drowning one William McPherson. McPherson, who was a bit of a dude, had incurred the dislike of the ferryman, but Van Blaricum claimed he had only meant to duck his passenger and "spoil his clothes." The ferryman was sentenced to three years in the penitentiary but was pardoned after serving 18 months.

There were also stories and gossip to be savored. Fletcher, the town prosecutor, had been waging a relentless crusade to stop the extended fighting and brawling in town, and then one day in his office he forgot himself and traded punches with Squire Obed Foote. Fletcher went to court the next morning, disclosed his breach of the law, pleaded guilty and paid a fine.

There was also the "Buffalo Boy" story. The lad, a black boy in his teens, had appeared in town in an outlandish hat with a crimson band, leading a grizzled old buffalo which he sometimes rode, to the delight of the town children. Arrested for some minor offense and clapped into the

log jail, he set it on fire during the night and in the excitement escaped
by riding off on his buffalo.

To the early settlers of Indianapolis and Indiana, land represented
power and independence, but the magic key that assured prosperity was
transportation. Insulated and landlocked, no town or city in Indiana was
perhaps more aware of this hard fact than Indianapolis. With no hope of
becoming a river port, the town had welcomed the National Road, the
Michigan Road and the other crude roads and pikes that then radiated
from the capital. These brought a trickle of new settlers, laborers with
money to spend and some new business and industry, proof that the
town's central and highly strategic location could be translated into
progress and prosperity with improved transportation.

But roads were not the answer. They were incredibly bad most of the
year and horse and wagon transport was slow, costly and uncertain. According to the movers and shakers, what Indianapolis needed to set its
feet on the way to real prosperity were canals and railroads. These were
already proving of tremendous benefit to other cities and towns across
America; without these modern means of transportation, Indianapolis
would remain just another backwoods town.

Central to all the talk was the success of the Erie Canal that had spurred
Indiana and Ohio to build what would prove to be the world's longest
canal, the Wabash and Erie, starting at Toledo on Lake Erie and termi-
nating at Evansville on the Ohio River. Financed in part by federal funds
in the form of land grants and a percentage of the proceeds from the sale
of public lands, the canal would be 450 miles long, 380 miles in Indiana.

For most men in Indianapolis whose earlier lives and fortunes had been
linked with water transportation, canals were something they understood. A canal was safe, sure, economical. "Pencil engineers" spent long
hours sketching possible routes for a connecting waterway to the Wabash and Erie and trying to prove that income from tolls would quickly
pay its original cost. A further stimulant to the drawings on the backs of
worn envelopes was that a bushel of corn worth 12 to 20 cents in Indianapolis brought 50 to 60 cents on the Ohio River or the East Coast.

Not everyone favored canals. There were "railroad men" such as Governor James Brown Ray, who in his 1829 message to the legislature had
come out unequivocally for railroads, painting a picture of Indianapolis
as an important rail center with lines radiating in all directions, towns
springing up along the rails every ten miles. He argued that railroads,
unlike canals, would cost less in the long run and could operate 12
months of the year instead of eight or ten. "Canal men" scoffed at Ray
and other supporters of the railroads, called them "cranks," and pointed
out that canal construction would keep money in circulation within the

state, but railroad purchases and profits would go outside Indiana to "foreign" suppliers and investors.

The "railroad men" persisted. In the 1832, 1834 and 1835 sessions of the legislature a total of 18 railroad lines were granted charters and 11 of them listed Indianapolis as their starting point or terminus. The charters, as it turned out, were actually "hunting licenses," as the promoters had little or no capital and the building of the roads was dependent upon their ability to find money for their projects. As a result, many of the roads took forever to complete and some were never built.

The pressure for canals and railroads came from all parts of the state, and the talk, the petitions and the lobbying culminated in "The Mammoth Improvement Bill" which Governor Noah Noble signed into law on January 27, 1836.

The bill was, indeed, mammoth. Put together after a series of deals and compromises, it provided something for every section of Indiana, for every town and city of any size, for every special interest. Even its price tag was mammoth for its time, ten million dollars, which the state planned to raise by floating 25-year Internal Improvement Bonds at interest not to exceed five percent, with the roads, canals, railroads, turnpikes and "their rents and tolls" pledged as security. The cost loomed even larger when set against the state's income of $75,000 annually and a population of some 350,000 people who, for the most part, lacked the common necessities. It was also a time when a dollar a day was considered high wages and laborers earned $10 to $15 a month. Viewed in this harsh light, the bill was a mammoth gamble with the odds stacked against it, but a man made no friends in 1836 by pointing out these unpleasant facts of economic life.

The bill provided for eight major public works projects, and two of these directly affected Indianapolis: the Central Canal, largest and most costly of the projects, designed to serve Muncie and Indianapolis and to connect with the Wabash and Erie "at a suitable point" between Fort Wayne and Logansport; and the Madison Railroad, which would pass through Columbus, Indianapolis and Crawfordsville on its way to Lafayette.

Jubilant residents of Indianapolis, with a canal and a railroad in their future, celebrated passage of the bill with huge bonfires and "brilliant illuminations" and a great deal of dancing in the streets. The town was already feeling the first effect of the new bill. A wave of real estate speculation, which had been touched off the year before in anticipation of the bill's passage, had pushed lot prices sky high, westward toward Missouri Street "where warehouses were to grow thick and mills wake the echoes all night long."

The Internal Improvements program got off to a fast, noisy and bungling start. Everyone wanted his project to start first, and there were squabbles over contracts, wrangles over routes, and scrambles for labor and engineers. Men who wanted a piece of the action hastily formed companies and contracting outfits with limited capital and supplies, and solicited contracts. Labor became scarce, wages went up, thousands of German and Irish immigrants were imported. There was also some dirty work at the crossroads. Dr. Isaac Coe of Indianapolis and Milton Stapp of Madison were among those who learned about it early and at firsthand. Sent East to sell the state's railroad bonds, they accepted bank notes for them, returned to Indianapolis and found the bank's paper worthless. It was a portent of things to come.

The Indianapolis section of the Central Canal, which began at Broad Ripple, was started in the summer of 1836. Its contractor imported hordes of Irish workmen, who came with their soft, musical voices and power-ful shoulders to add color and swagger to the town. The work was hard and the 60-foot-wide canal, six feet deep, was dug with shovels and picks after axemen had cleared the trees and brush. Hard drinkers as well as hard workers, the Irish had an ingrained sense of justice, were quick to take offense, and their brawls and fights became legendary. As the work progressed, lines of workmen's shanties rose on the canal banks to form a series of melancholy silhouettes against the evening sky. Set in the mud and sand and the piles of cleared trees and underbrush, these dreary little "towns" were places of smoky chimneys, gray wash hung on sagging lines, bawling babies and thin, half-naked, dirty-faced children and work-worn women. Only on "Smoky Row," a row of dilapidated rental cabins in town, and "Colored Town" on the outskirts of the donation would one find the same scenes and smells of poverty.

Meanwhile, construction was underway on the Madison Railroad des-tined for Indianapolis and Lafayette. It was a slow and expensive opera-tion and by 1839 only 18 miles of track had been opened to traffic. Help-ing to push up the cost were the iron rails imported from England which cost $60 to $80 a ton by the time they reached the Ohio River port.

In August 1839 the State of Indiana abruptly suspended work on all projects, including the Indianapolis section of the Central Canal and the Madison Railroad. The Internal Improvements program, launched on the high tide of 1835-36 prosperity, was hoist on its own financial petard and the Panic of 1837, which reached its peak in Indiana in 1839. Legis-lators, meeting in special session for 85 days, learned that the state was in debt over $14,000,000, tax collections combined with income from canals and railroads totaled only $106,000, money was scarce, the state's credit was exhausted, and the panic had dried up any further possibilities of new loans. Investigation disclosed a long and disgraceful litany of mismanage-and chicanery. Over two million dollars had found its way into the pockets of state officials and their agents. A New York brokerage house had sold Indiana bonds, turned half the proceeds over to the state and closed its doors, and its owners apparently divided up several millions. Records were inadequate or missing and those found had never been audited. It was a mammoth mess.

To provide immediate operating funds, the legislature authorized the issuance of certificates, or "scrip," backed by the State of Indiana, but the brightly colored notes—known as Red Dog, Blue Dog and White Dog scrip—quickly depreciated until their going value was only 40 cents on the dollar. Early purchasers sustained heavy losses. The legislators also came to the help of debtors suffering from the panic with a series of acts designed to forestall foreclosure and bankruptcies and afford a measure of tax relief. The General Assembly adjourned, however, without solving its overall financial problem—a problem that would prove a burden to the taxpayers for six years and work to the state's discredit for 20 years. Eventually, the state would repudiate its debts, deed half the liability over to its creditors and require the remaining bond holders to exchange their bonds for stocks which might or might not pay interest or dividends.

The panic caused untold suffering in Indianapolis. The Second State Bank of Indiana and its branches suspended specie payments. In the absence of sound money, trade was again conducted by barter. Many small merchants and industries managed to survive on a day-to-day basis, but many were wiped out. Real estate prices plummeted to new lows. Land speculators were generally ruined. The town was filled with unemployed laborers and hungry families. However, foreclosures and bankruptcies were forestalled by the new legislation and the liberality of many creditors.

Only 8.8 miles of the Indianapolis section of the Central Canal were complete when work was halted. Its final cost was $180,000 a mile, nearly a million and a half dollars. Parts of it in the vicinity of Market Street became an open sewer. "Everybody who lived handy," a contemporary writer reported, "threw their old boots, dead cats, ashes and garbage into the canal until it was too offensive to be borne." Eventually the southern portion of the canal was filled and the millrace became the main channel.

Although it would never be connected with the Wabash and Erie or to the other nearby completed sections of the Central Canal, the Indianapolis section of the canal was put to some use. Mills sprang up to take advantage of its water power, although the owners complained volubly because of the frequency with which the canal was shut down and drained so it could be cleaned and repaired. Part of the problem was the soft, shallow banks, which were constantly being undermined by thousands of muskrats. Corn, lumber and occasional loads of hay were transported, and in July 1839 Robert Earl placed a line of canal boats in operation with regular schedules and passage fixed at a dollar. A little excursion packet, the *Silver Bell*, made regular runs and for a time was extremely popular. The little boat, painted silver and complete with tinkling bells, was drawn by silver-gray mules, their harness also decorated with silver. The novelty of a trip on the canal soon wore off, however, and the line suspended operations.

As the year 1839 drew to a close, Governor David Wallace, noting that a growing number of states were setting aside a day of thanks each year, proclaimed Indiana's first and official Thanksgiving Day for November 28 and urged attendance at special church services. It is unrecorded whether those who went to church that day to give thanks avoided walking past or looking in the direction of the canal.

Chapter 6

WAR, POLITICS
AND A PREDICTION

THE HARD TIMES resulting from the Panic of 1837 continued
through the early 1840s. Indicative of the state of affairs in Indianapolis
was an unsuccessful attempt to abolish the town government on the
grounds that the townspeople couldn't afford its cost of nearly $3,000 a
year. But there were hopeful signs. The Second State Bank of Indiana resumed specie payments in 1842 and here and there a merchant or manufacturer reported that business was picking up. Although work was not
resumed on the Central Canal, the state leased the Madison and Indianapolis Railroad to a private company to complete. Under the direction of
the company's chief engineer, Thomas Armstrong Morris of Indianapolis, the tracks crept slowly overland and in 1844 reached Columbus,
only 45 miles away.

In the meantime, there was politics. Indiana had supported Andrew
Jackson and other Democrats at the national level, but at home the voters
were electing National Republicans and Whigs. In 1840 the state went
on a political binge with the renomination of William Henry Harrison as
Whig candidate for President. The sixty-seven-year-old Harrison, although a native of Virginia and in 1840 a resident of Ohio, had deep roots
in Indiana. He had served as Indiana's first territorial governor, leader of
the victorious army at Tippecanoe and brigadier general of the Army of
the Northwest in the War of 1812. The Harrison campaign would long
be remembered for its circus-like atmosphere and demogoguery. Although the general had lived in luxury most of his civilian life, the pio-

neer image builders made him over into the "log cabin and hard cider" candidate, symbol of the common man and the homely virtues. Another slogan, "Tippecanoe and Tyler too," blatantly exploited the general's victory over the last Indian army east of the Mississippi.

The campaign probably excited no more feeling anywhere than in Indianapolis. There were mass meetings, barbecues, speeches, campaign buttons, Harrison songbooks, broadsides, and log cabin breast-pins. A buckeye cabin was built at the corner of Washington and Illinois Streets with free hard cider for thirsty voters. The colorful, noisy parades with their brass bands and flaming torches featured pretty girls waving white handkerchiefs from dugout canoes, oversize latchstrings, and log cabins mounted on ox-drawn wagons.

To stem the rising Harrison tide, Democrats brought Vice-President Richard M. Johnson to town for an "appearance." (It was regarded as undignified for candidates actively to campaign in their own behalf.) Johnson, reputed slayer of the famed Tecumseh at the Battle of the Thames, spoke briefly at an all-day rally in Walnut Grove. Johnson's talk was a mistake. He indicated his favor of Sunday mail deliveries, which were strongly opposed in church-oriented Indianapolis, and, in an apparent effort to offset Harrison's war record, told of "stripping to the buff" at the hotel to show a guest "the scars of five wounds received in the Battle of the Thames"—a statement generally regarded as offensive.

Harrison won the election and Indianapolis Whigs celebrated with parties, bonfires, fireworks and illuminations. A month after his inaugural Harrison was dead of pneumonia, the oldest man to hold the Presidency, the first to die in office. A hushed city suspended business on April 17, 1841, to attend memorial services conducted jointly by Governor Samuel Bigger and the Reverend Beecher.

The Democrats emerged from the campaign with a new symbol, a crowing rooster, which replaced the hickory pole and broom of Jackson days. One of its first appearances was on July 21, 1841, on the front page of the first issue of the *Indiana State Sentinel*, successor to the *Democrat*, which had been purchased by George A. and Jacob Page Chapman. The rooster symbol, which still appears on paper ballots in Indiana, grew out of a letter written to Postmaster William Sebastian, a Democrat, in nearby Greenfield, advising him that "thirty Van Buren men had turned to Harrison in Hancock County" and urging: "Do, for heaven's sake, stir up the democracy. See Chapman, tell him . . . he must CROW; we have much to CROW about." The opened letter was left on a table at the post office, seen and copied by a Harrison man and published in the *Journal*, the state's leading Whig newspaper.

Once the Democrats recovered from their initial embarrassment, they turned the "Crow, Chapman, Crow" to their advantage. Among the first to capitalize on the phrase was John Chapman himself, a Greenfield tavern keeper, candidate for the legislature, a spellbinder of the old school and an expert at crowing. Harrison won the election, but Chapman (no relation of the *Sentinel* publishers) emerged victorious and "Crow, Chapman, Crow" became a part of Indiana folklore.

James K. Polk, a Democrat, became President in 1845 amidst talk of new Western expansion and some real and imagined troubles along the Mexican border that led to a declaration of war against Mexico on May 11, 1846. Less than a month later, 300 volunteers from Marion County—part of Indiana's quota of 3,000 men and three regiments—assembled on the Circle in Indianapolis for a war that men alleged was a trumped-up affair to grab California and New Mexico.

One of the most enthusiastic recruiters was the nineteen-year-old son of a former governor, a student in an Indianapolis law office and a writer of romantic tales in his spare time. His name was Lew Wallace, and the morning after he was commissioned a second lieutenant he opened an office on Washington Street, stuck a flag out the window, hired a fife and drummer to parade up and down the street, and set up a big placard: "For Mexico, Fall In."

While awaiting orders to proceed to Camp Clark at New Albany, the 300 men, mostly farm boys trading the tedium of farm life for the possibility of romantic adventures, drilled for a fortnight in Military Park under Wallace, Captain James B. Drake and First Lieutenant John A. McDougal. Three regiments were formed at Camp Clark. The Indianapolis company under Wallace became part of the First Regiment, with Drake, newly promoted to colonel, in command. Of the three regiments, the First saw no action in the war. The Second and Third were in the crucial battle on the sun-soaked plains of Buena Vista. The Fourth and Fifth Regiments, organized in 1847 and each including a company of Indianapolis men commanded by Lieutenants James McDougal and Edward Lander, saw action at Vera Cruz, Puebla and Mexico City. During the two years of the war, Indiana sent 5,000 men to Mexico, of whom 542 were killed—part of a nation's price for two important new states.

Business generally improved after 1844 and there was a small real estate boom in anticipation of the railroad's coming. Even the hopeless section east of South Street, a mere country lane, and land in Pogue's Run Valley brought good prices. The scrip issued by the legislature in 1839 rose in value.

Indianapolis stores and industries reflected the changing times and the fact that necessities needed no longer to be foregone or made at home. Two large pottery plants turned out decorative pieces as well as "everyday" and fine sets of dishes. Furniture shops and stores offered well-made tables and cupboards and sideboards and bedsteads. Blacksmiths, whose number had grown since the National Road opened, made fireplace andirons, cranes, plowshares and grubbing hoes, and a few repaired rifles and guns. Ready-made clothing was available at Benjamin Orr's. John Hodgkins opened the town's first ice cream parlor. Hodgkins also built the town's first ice house, where cakes of ice were stored in tons of sawdust. Lumber was a big business. Situated in the heart of a wilderness, Indianapolis was shipping the product of its trees to all parts of the nation. The chief demand was for black walnut, and a good tree would bring as much as $100.

In 1848 a smallpox scare swept the town after the death of a traveler at one of the taverns, and a general vaccination was ordered. At the height of the scare, the town contracted to build a hospital. When no new cases of the disease appeared, the citizens protested the tax for the hospital and the town negotiated a settlement with the contractor. Another scare, in 1855, brought renewed demands for a hospital, and one was actually begun on the bank of Fall Creek, but again the work was halted as the scare passed. Dr. Livingston Dunlap, a member of the council, kept the subject alive and eventually it was finished at a cost of $30,000. After it was built, it was put to little use and was finally leased as a "home for friendless women" (a nineteenth-century euphemism to describe a home for prostitutes).

There was another squirrel invasion in 1845, causing thousands of dollars in damage to the corn crop, but far more serious were the floods of 1847. A January thaw and a heavy downpour of rain that lasted several days unleashed the full fury of the White River and Fall and Eagle Creeks. Tons of churning water, which brought the creeks level with the bluffs, carried away homes, ripped deep gullies in the land, tore out canal banks, washed out whole sections of the National Road and inundated others, threatened to carry away the toll bridge on Washington Street, and broke through to the outskirts to flood Indianola (Stringtown). Far worse than the floods of 1828, the town's distress was so great that the legislators extended the deadlines for payment of property taxes and remitted some.

In happier moments there was local art, music, books, the theater and lectures in the courthouse.

Jacob Cox, a tinsmith with a passion for painting, was turning out first-rate landscapes and portraits that would be treasured in another century. T. W. Whitridge, who opened the town's first daguerreotype studio, also painted in his spare time. Eventually he left for New York and even greater fame. Joseph O. Eaton, one of the West's pioneer artists, stayed briefly with Dr. Abner Pope and left behind some of his best and earliest work, including a portrait of the doctor. James G. Gookins, who studied with Cox and later would open a school for painters, completed his first canvases. There was even a small art gallery for exhibition and sale of paintings, run by Dr. Luke Munsell and later by Peter McNaught.

A county library was established in 1844, membership a dollar a year. The state library, established in 1825, which had been confined to a corner of the secretary of state's office, was formally organized and John Cook named the first state librarian in 1841. He was succeeded by Samuel P. Daniels, a tailor and a good Democrat, and in 1845 by John Brown Dillon, who became known as the "Father of Indiana History." Largely self-educated, Dillon had been a printer and a lawyer and published his first book on Indiana's history in 1843.

A dramatic and social event was the formation of the town's first amateur acting group, the Indianapolis Thespian Corps, formed in 1840. Its theater was a former foundry building at the northwest corner of Market and Mississippi Streets, and Jacob Cox built and painted the scenery. Among the moving spirits in the corps were Edward S. Tyler, a bookbinder; James G. Jordon, a law student, and James McCready, a tailor and later mayor of the city. Admission was 25 cents, but merchandise of equal value was often accepted at the door.

The company's first production was a historical drama, *Pocahontas* by Robert Dale Owen, newspaper editor, novelist, champion of women's rights, foe of slavery and son of the Scottish social reformer who had founded the short-lived cooperative colony at New Harmony, Indiana. The play, described by one reviewer as "accurate historically, dreary histrionically," was presented with an all-male cast, since no woman was brave enough to incur the wrath of the puritanical churches or acquire a reputation for being "fast" as the result of appearing in a theatrical performance. A William Wallace played the "sensitive role" of Pocahontas.

The temperance movement was growing and expanding. Besides the already active State Temperance Society, the Sons of Temperance established an Indianapolis lodge in 1845. A fraternal order with a secret handclasp, passwords, ritual and regalia, the Sons preached total abstinence, banned even the drinking of cider and warred against all places where liquor was sold, condemning them out of hand as "liquor hells." A women's auxiliary, the Daughters of Temperance, was formed in 1849, followed by the organization of a junior order, the Cadets of Temperance. The best the dry forces could get from the legislators—who liked a drink themselves after hours and whose closing-day celebrations were becoming a public scandal—was a law that provided for a referendum in which citizens could vote against the licensing of an applicant for a whiskey shop. The law was ignored in Indianapolis and other, larger places and generally proved ineffective.

A second volunteer fire company, the outgrowth of a division of opinion within the Marion Fire, Hose and Protective Association, was formed, with Joseph H. Wright, a merchant and founder of a pork-packing company, as its captain. The new company, The Independent Relief Company, purchased its first engine in November of 1849. During the 1850s a number of other volunteer companies were formed and two companies of boys were also organized. Indianapolis householders were expected to supplement the work of the brave volunteer firemen. Ordinances required each family to keep a fire bucket on hand and to take part in bucket brigades when needed. Families vied with each other in the quality and ornateness of their fire buckets, which occupied a prominent place in most homes.

Membership in a volunteer fire company became a valuable social and economic asset. Volunteer firemen were exempt from city taxes and jury duty, and after ten years of service a fireman could retire with the title of "honorary" and all exemptions. According to a contemporary writer:

No young man could expect political place, business success or social recognition unless he was a member of a fire company. No public demonstration could hope for success unless it found favor with the fire boys who were the aristocrats of everything in sight.

Bitter rivalries sprang up between the fire companies and they jealously competed with one another to be the first to the scene of a conflagration. Coincident with the formation of the fire companies, the town suffered an epidemic of fires, especially in old and vacant buildings. In view of the amazing speed with which some fire companies reached the scene, the suspicion grew that many of the blazes were started by firemen or their friends. The story was told of a fire insurance company that offered a silver trumpet and a silver pitcher to the volunteer companies arriving first or second at the most fires during the year. But so many fires broke out that year, especially in old and isolated houses, that the unhappy insurance company gave up the idea on the apparent grounds it was too sure-fire.

One of the town's biggest fires broke out in the Washington Hall Tavern on a cold afternoon in February 1843. It was some four or five hours before the Marion Company and several bucket brigades brought the flames under control. Classes at the Old Seminary were dismissed for the day and the boys formed one of the lines passing buckets from pumps at the corner of Washington and Meridian Streets in front of Motherhead's drugstore. Even the Reverend Henry Ward Beecher joined in fighting the fire and had his hair frozen to his head.

There was a touch of irony in another of the town's big fires. The building on the Circle that housed the Marion Company fire engine and the town-council rooms on the second floor mysteriously burned to the ground in 1851. Firemen pulled the engine to safety and managed to salvage their clothes and equipment, but the town records were destroyed. Some of the townspeople were unkind enough to hint that the blaze had been of incendiary origin as a movement had been afoot to replace the weather-worn building which had fallen into a state of disrepair. The unembarrassed fire company built a new brick firehouse four years later at New York and Massachusetts Avenue.

In the fall and winter of 1842 a large number of residents of Indianapolis prepared for the end of the world and the Second Coming of Christ. They were called "Millerites" or "Second Adventists," and their trumpeter of doomsday was William Miller, a New York State farmer and student of the Bible. Miller had applied simple arithmetic to his own interpretation of Biblical prophecies and announced that the end of the world would take place between March 21, 1843, and March 21, 1844 (a date he revised later to October 22, 1844).

Miller's doleful prophecies and his exhortations to prepare for the Awful Day swept the Middle West in a revival of religious excitement. Indianapolis, which was to exhibit a tendency toward religious extravagance throughout the years, was fertile ground for the Millerites. Hundreds of townspeople listened to the preaching and bought copies of the *Midnight Cry*, the official organ of the Second Advent. Portents confirmed the belief that the end was near, among them the most brilliant comet of the century.

The lay press and practical jokers had a heyday. But the Millerites ignored the jibes and the jokes, secure in the knowledge they would "go up" to blissful eternal life and that their tormenters would reap only the torments of hell.

Many of the Adventists bought or made white ascension robes. Some sold or gave away their property and canceled all debts owed them. A leading merchant sold his store and inventory and joined the Shakers in Ohio. One gloomy, rainy night a congregation of Millerites were given a tremendous fright. As they sat listening to their preacher describe the fire and lightning that would precede the end of the world, a lurid red glare was seen outside the church windows. The congregation was dismissed and huddled in the drizzling rain to stare uncomprehendingly at a huge red ball of flame and clouds of dense smoke rising from the horizon. Happily, it turned out to be a raging fire in a few ricks of hemp stacked on a riverbank farm on Crawfordsville Road. The strain of waiting was sometimes past endurance. One woman became permanently insane and had to be confined.

On the fateful day the Millerites took their "going up" positions, some

Chapter 7

SCHOOL BELLS AND RAILROAD BELLS

INDIANAPOLIS BECAME a full-fledged city in the spring of 1847, but the adoption of a city charter and the election of the first city officials were overshadowed by the furor raised by a proposal to institute a public school system.

In the 1840s Indiana had no system of public schools. Its constitution of 1816 had been first among the states to promise a school system "wherein tuition shall be gratis and equally open to all," but the fine words had not been supported by any practical means to finance such a system. A predominantly agricultural state, its citizen-farmers preferred to invest money in internal improvements that moved crops to market as opposed to schools that didn't. As a result, the state with the first constitution to promise free schools was listed by the U.S. Census as having the highest rate of illiteracy among the Northern states.

Money, however, was not the entire problem. A large and militant group preferred private and church-controlled schools, and among them were those who saw no reason for educating the poorer classes. A widely held view among farmers was that all a boy needed to know was enough reading and writing and arithmetic to be sure buyers didn't cheat him. Legislators were as divided on the subject as their constituents. There were also tax and operational problems. Some legislators argued that schools were strictly a local responsibility; others charged that under a free school system the more prosperous counties would be robbed of their tax dollars to support schools in poorer counties. Still others contended the state's scattered population and lack of transportation made free schools expensive and therefore unaffordable.

Despite entrenched opposition and sharp differences of opinion, the free school advocates managed to get the issue on the ballot in 1848 and won a 78,532 to 61,887 victory in favor of public schools. They also got a number of bills through the legislature, and the Revised Statutes of 1843 incorporated 20 pages of school laws. But the programs lacked the funds to implement them, and requests for appropriations and the necessary taxes to finance a free school system met with dynamic inaction.

Against this background a bill was introduced in the 1846-47 General Assembly to provide a city charter for Indianapolis. The bill was scheduled for routine passage when Representative S. V. B. Noel from Indianapolis introduced an amendment to establish a system of free schools in the city to be financed by a tax on one-eighth of one percent on the assessment. The anti-school forces rallied to kill the amendment, acrimonious debate broke out, and it became evident the amendment was in very real danger of being lost. A compromise was effected by a second amendment, which provided no school tax could be levied in Indianapolis unless approved by a majority of the voters in the April 24 election.

The Indianapolis charter bill and its amendment passed on February 13, subject to popular vote on March 27. The charter provided for a mayor with veto powers, a councilman from each of the seven wards, authority to appoint city officers and taxing powers not to exceed 15 cents on $100. Indianapolis voters approved the charter at the polls, 449 to 19, and Governor James Whitcomb proclaimed it in force on March 30. It now remained for the new city to elect a mayor and councilmen and to vote yes or no on the levying of a special tax to establish and maintain a free school system.

The ensuing campaign and election commanded attention all over the state. It marked one of the first times the school issue had been joined in a popular election. Arrayed on the side of free schools were most of the city's establishment, including Calvin Fletcher, Samuel Merrill, Dr. Isaac Coe, James Blake and Judge Isaac Blackford, who had been agitating for a school system since the town's beginning. Opposition to the proposal was noisy and well organized and both sides made speeches and personal visits to voters, and distributed literature. As the campaign developed, it appeared certain the free school forces would carry the day, and when the ballots were counted, the victory proved overwhelming, 406 yes and 29 no. Indianapolis had voted its first public school system.

About 500 votes were cast in the city election which swept Samuel Henderson into office as mayor. Henderson, a tavern owner, the town's first postmaster and first president of the original town board of trustees, received no salary in his new post, but the office carried the "jurisdiction of a justice of the peace" and the fees that went with it.

Named to the new city council for two-year terms: Uriah Gates, First Ward; Henry Tatewiler, Second; Cornelius King, Third; Samuel S. Rooker, Fourth; Charles W. Cady, Fifth; Abraham W. Harrison, Sixth; and Henry Wingate, Seventh Ward.

At the first council meeting on May 1, Samuel Rooker was named president and the following appointments were announced: James G. Jordon, secretary, $100 annually; Nathan Lister, treasurer, $50; James Wood, engineer, $300; William Campbell, marshal, fees, and tax collector, $150; Andrew W. Carnahan, city attorney, fees; Jacob B. Filter, street commissioner, $100; David Cox, messenger for the Marion Fire Company, and Jacob Filter, messenger for the Relief Company, $25 each; Sampson Barbee and Jacob Miller, market masters, $50 each; Joshua Black, assessor, paid on a per diem basis; and Benjamin F. Lobaugh, sexton (a ninteenth-century name for undertaker).

Immediately following the election, plans for Indianapolis' first public school went forward. Each of the seven wards became a school district with a trustee in charge. Revenues from the tax, the equivalent of 12½ cents per $100, produced only $6,160 from 1847 to 1850 inclusive, but donations of land and rental property supplemented the carefully husbanded funds, and the trustees performed some minor miracles in establishing a one-story brick schoolhouse in each ward by 1852.

At the start the schools were not wholly free. Because virtually all the available tax funds had to go into land and buildings, parents were charged tuition and these sums went to pay the salaries of the ten teachers. As the building program progressed, tuition fees were reduced, terms extended and more teachers engaged. The new state constitution of 1851 and the school law of 1852 made state funds available for the first time.

In 1853 the accumulations of state funds and a substantial rise in local tax revenues made possible the first free schools in Indianapolis. Opened on April 25 for a two-month session, enrollments immediately soared from 340 to 1,000 pupils. School attendance was not compulsory and this figure represented less than half of the 2,600 children of school age (ages five to twenty-one) in the city.

To comply with the requirements of the new school law, the ward-trustee system was abolished, and the city council appointed a consolidated city board of school trustees consisting of Calvin Fletcher, Henry P. Coburn and Henry F. West. Before the opening of school in September, a system of grades was adopted, and teaching plans and textbooks were made uniform. All grades from primary to intermediate were taught in the same building. The County Seminary was repaired and became the city's first high school, with E. P. Cole as principal.

In April 1854 an enumeration of the school population counted 3,053 children of school age, with 1,160 in school and an average daily attendance of 801 pupils. The high school enrollment, "for lack of proficient children to go higher," was 115 students.

The first superintendent of schools, Silas T. Bowen, head of Bowen, Stewart & Company, booksellers and later publishers, was appointed in 1855. Bowen received a salary of $400 a year and agreed to devote one-third of his time to the schools. He relinquished his post the following year and the trustees appointed George B. Stone as a full-time superintendent at a salary of $1,000 a year. Under Stone's tenure as superintendent, ten new brick schoolhouses were completed, the school year was extended to 39 weeks, school enrollment reached 40 percent of the city's school-age children, and the system employed 30 teachers, most of them women.

At this high point in the growth of the Indianapolis school system the Indiana State Supreme Court stepped in. Supreme Court Judge Alvin P. Hovey had dealt a death blow in 1854 to many Indiana schools by denying the right of townships to levy taxes for school tuition purposes. Then in 1858 Judge Samuel E. Perkins also denied these powers to cities and towns, and agreed with Judge Hovey that local taxation for school purposes violated the "uniform taxation" provisions of the new constitution. The combined decisions spelled the doom of Indiana schools.

The Indianapolis city council went into emergency session, and at the suggestion of the council, citizens' meetings were held in each ward. About $3,000 was raised by popular subscription, but the money soon ran out and the city reluctantly closed its free schools. Some were leased to private schools and others remained vacant and "became hangouts for thieves and strumpets." Except for a dribble of state money in 1860 and 1861 which permitted the schools to open for a single quarter, the schoolhouses remained closed. There was to be no school again until 1862.

The iron rails of Indiana's first steam railroad, the Madison and Indianapolis, which had been inching their way up from Madison for eight years, reached the city in the fall of 1847. The last spike was driven in with appropriate ceremony about nine o'clock the morning of October 1, and a few hours later two excursion trains, with the enormous black stacks of their locomotives belching wood smoke, bells ringing and whistles blowing, came to a clanking stop in clouds of steam at the spanking new railroad station on South and Delaware Streets. It was a momentous occasion. After 27 years in the wilderness, Indianapolis was securely linked by rail to the rest of the world.

Acres of people, most of them dressed in their Sunday best, spilled over the landscape to welcome the trains. A boom of the artillery company's cannon and the sharp, wind-cutting cry of the locomotive whistle brought them surging forward across the end of the tracks and surging hurriedly backward as the "bulgine" and the "steam keers" came closer. Spalding's Circus was in town and the big brass band, led by the nationally known bugler Ned Kendall, mingled with the noise and the chatter of men and women, the whoops and shouts of children, the creak of wagons and the nervous whinnying and frightened snorts of rearing horses.

Governor Whitcomb and members of the legislature were on hand and so was Samuel Henderson and members of the city council and Samuel Merrill, then the new president of the Madison and Indianapolis Railroad. Governor Whitcomb clambered to the top of one of the cars and addressed the crowd, and there were other speeches as the band played and the cannon banged out another charge.

It was all wonderful and exciting, and, unlike the celebrations for the Central Canal and the arrival of the *Robert Hanna*, there would be no disappointment to swallow this time, no dashed hopes on the morrow, no new frustrations. Jubilant men could slap each other on the shoulders and point out that the Madison and Indianapolis was only the beginning—the legislature had chartered other railroads, some 4,000 miles of them—and eventually those iron rails would spread out from Indianapolis in all directions and connect the capital with every part of the nation.

Chief engineer for the Madison Railroad was Thomas Armstrong Morris of Indianapolis, who eventually became one of the Middle West's best-known pioneer railroad engineers. Among other things, Morris had sent his Madison and Indianapolis Railroad tracks up and over the world's steepest railroad incline, extending from Madison to North Madison. The grade was so steep that early locomotives had to be hauled up one side with the aid of eight or ten horses and lowered by cable on the other side. Later an English locomotive was designed, incorporating a pinion gear that worked in a cograil laid in the center of the tracks. It became one of the wonders of the new railroad age.

Getting up and down grades, however, wasn't the only problem. Rails were a continuing source of trouble. Steel and the "T" rails were yet to come, and the iron strips that served as rails wore out rapidly or rusted away. Worse yet, the iron strips often sprang up suddenly like uncoiled snakes as they expanded in the hot summer sun or loosened from the vibrations of the heavy trains. When a "snakehead" was sighted, the train stopped and crews got out and nailed the rail down with heavy sledges. Sometimes they let loose as the train passed over them and ripped through the wooden floors of the coaches, injuring passengers or causing long delays while workmen freed the car.

Trains would often run out of water or firewood between stations and stops had to be made to bail water out of a pond or stream or buy wood from an accommodating woodcutter. Lacking a friendly woodcutter, crew and passengers would get out and chop wood and haul sufficient logs to continue the journey. Also raising havoc with schedules were cows or other farm animals that wandered on the track or curled up on the rails; small boys who yanked down on the stop signal as a joke, and lonely farm housewives who thought nothing of flagging down the train to ask for change of a five-dollar bill—an excuse to chat with crews and passengers.

Passenger coaches were merely boxcars fitted with board seats. The cars were used to ship cattle and hogs on weekdays and cleaned out on weekends for passengers. Henry Ward Beecher, who took the first train out of the city, left this description of a Madison and Indianapolis passenger coach:

> On a wood car rigged with boards across from side to side, went I forth. The car was no car at all, a mere ex tempore wood box, used sometimes without seats for hogs, but with seats for men, of which class I happen to be one. And so at 11 o'clock at night, I arrived at Madison not overproud of riding the first train that ever went from Indianapolis to Madison.

The month following the opening of the Madison and Indianapolis Railroad the *Journal* reported it had "transformed the city's every feature" and commented that "one looking upon the city's crowded thoroughfare and listening to the din and confusion of its commerce, could scarce believe it once had been the 'sweetest village of the plain.' "

The *Journal* could also report in December that corn and wheat prices had doubled and the cost of goods brought into the city was lower. New stores and factories opened. Property values advanced, especially to the south in the vicinity of the railroad station. Within a year 19 new buildings went up east of the station, including a hotel and two brick warehouses. On the west, five warehouses were built, as well as eight houses. Commission and packing houses were established. Business houses, which had formerly been confined to Washington Street, began to spring up in all parts of the city, especially on streets that led to the railroad. South Meridian Street became a wholesaler's row.

Pork packed by Jeremy Mansur and his son, Isaiah, at their plant in Broad Ripple was no longer entrusted to horse and wagon and uncertain roads, but shipped by rail. Hog farmers who annually drove their waddling, grunting lard hogs overland to Cincinnati loaded them in railroad cars. They could now ship any time of the year instead of waiting for winter, when the ground was hard and the streams were frozen.

Less than a year after the first railroad trains pulled into Indianapolis, the first telegraph lines reached the city, from Dayton, Ohio. Known as "O'Reilly's Line" for Henry O'Reilly, who had obtained a franchise from Samuel F. Morse, inventor of the telegraph, the first telegraph message was sent to Richmond on May 12, 1848. The Indiana *Sentinel* published its first wire dispatch on May 24. Offices of the line were on the second floor of the Hubbard Block and in charge of Isaac H. Kiersted, who doubled as operator and manager. Two years later a second line, Wade and Company, came to town, flourished, and merged with O'Reilly's line in 1853, the year before Western Union opened its Indianapolis offices.

In the 1850s the State of Indiana, no longer permitted under its new constitution to engage in such enterprises as canals and railroads, divested itself of its interests in the Madison and Indianapolis Railroad and the Central Canal.

For its share of the railroad which had cost the state nearly two million dollars (before it was leased to a private company to complete) the state finally realized $75,000.

The Central Canal which cost over a million dollars was sold in 1851 for $2,425 to Gould and Jackson who resold it the same year to the Central Canal and Hydraulic Water Works and Manufacturing Company. The canal was a subject of much speculation over the years; it changed hands a number of times and was finally sold to the Indianapolis Water Works, predecessors of the Indianapolis Water Company, for a reported $200,000.

Chapter 8

ALL 'BOARD FOR
PROSPERITY

AT THE END OF HIS TERM as the first mayor of Indianapolis in 1849, Samuel Henderson disposed of his extensive real estate holdings, packed his things and announced he was leaving for California and the gold fields.

Henderson was disenchanted with the city he had served so long and so well. He freely predicted that despite the changes wrought by the Madison and Indianapolis Railroad, Indianapolis would never amount to much and the talk about the city becoming an important railroad center was just that—talk. The disbelieving Henderson departed on the tides of the gold rush, carrying with him the distinction of being one of the worst prophets in the city's history.

Seven more railroads steamed into the city before 1855 and Indianapolis, with eight rail lines, became the center of a giant web of railroads whose main lines radiated out from the city to be interlaced with spurs and short lines that led everywhere. The once insulated capital was linked with such other growing cities as Chicago, Detroit, Cleveland, Cincinnati, Louisville, St. Louis and the lush Eastern markets. And 24 more railroads, some already under construction, were planning routes into the city.

Samuel Henderson's city that wasn't going to amount to much became a booming, busy, bustling railroad city with new stores, residences, hotels, churches and industries going up everywhere—along with real estate prices. Even the formerly despised outlots were "compactly built over" and the city council agreed to annex nearly a hundred lots or tracts outside the original four-mile square. Population soared, climbing from 8,034 in 1850 to 18,611 ten years later. Indianapolis became the state's largest and most important city, surpassing both Madison and New Albany.

On South Illinois Street stood a long, low, steep-roofed brick building with towers and gables and high arched windows that represented a major railroading first, the Indianapolis Union Depot. Here for the first time in America all railroad trains could enter and leave a city from a single central station. It had been conceived and built by Thomas Armstrong Morris and the newly organized Union Railway Company. The tracks had been laid in 1850 and the station formally opened September 30, 1853.

Evidence of the city's new prosperity was everywhere. Some men wore silk hats to work and successful men earned as much as a thousand dollars a year. Well-to-do families "kept a girl" and drove a two-horse carriage or barouche. Most families, even those of modest means, kept a milch cow, chickens and a kitchen garden. Stores were busy and kept open from 6:00 A.M. to 9:00 P.M., six days a week, to catch the transient railroad trade. Among the new stores were Clement Vonnegut's hardware store (in the 1960s, the city's oldest retail outlet); The H. Lieber Company, picture frames and moldings, which maintained a small art gallery; the New York Store, on Washington Street; the newly opened agencies for the Singer and Wheeler and Wilson Sewing Machines; and the Eagle Clothing Company which was setting a retail precedent as a "one-price store" at a time when higgling and haggling over a price was an integral part of shopping. The *Journal* counted four bookstores in the city, "which spoke well for the intelligence and literary taste of our people"; the two largest were the stores of Stewart and Bowen and of Samuel Merrill, the son of the original Samuel Merrill, who had died in 1855.

The city was fast becoming a wholesale and manufacturing center. Little & Company and Schnull & Company, wholesale grocers, made daily shipments by rail to all parts of the state. Henneman & Duzen, wholesale druggists, "traveled" men and took orders from a growing list of drugstores. New industries turned out boxes and staves, wooden butter dishes, railroad cars, wagon wheels, pottery, carriage and buggy wheels, lightning rods, and iron and tin products, including the new cooking stoves. More than 50 steam engines and a dozen foundries were in operation throughout the city. The Eagle Machine Works manufactured the new threshers and separators and Elias C. Atkins' new saw factory, which he had moved from Cleveland to take advantage of Indianapolis' railroads, was fast becoming one of the state's largest industries. The 1860 census placed the value of products manufactured in Indianapolis at $890,470 and local factories employed 587 "hands." There was another sign of the city's industrial growth. Game was becoming less plentiful and fishermen were complaining that wastes dumped into the White River and other streams were killing off the fish.

Labor unions were beginning to appear. Among the first to organize were the city's shoemakers, who campaigned for a uniform wage and divided shops into "society shops" (union) and "non-society" shops (non-union or "scab"), the latter "to be regarded as unworthy of the respect of any mechanic or well meaning members of the public." In June of 1850 a group of artisans, newly formed into the Mechanics Mutual Protections, paraded through the city streets and held their first state convention at Masonic Hall. Their stated objectives were increased wages, improved educational opportunities, better understanding between employer and employee, "protection against pecuniary distress during sickness of its members and to extend care and relief to their destitute families."

Travelers arriving in the city had a choice of more than a dozen hotels, including the Occidental, Washington Hall, Palmer House, Capital House, Duncan House, Carlisle House, Tremont House, the Farmers' Hotel and the Oriental designed by Francis Costigan. Most lavish of the hostelries was Hervey Bates' new hotel, The Bates House, at the corner of Illinois and Washington Streets (which he would later sell to Henry Claypool for $160,000). It boasted the city's first built-in bathtubs made of tin and wood. Part of the city's history was built into David Macy's new Macy House: it incorporated materials from the governor's house on the Circle, which he had purchased at auction for $665 and torn down.

At night some homes and streets were lighted with the new gaslights. The Indianapolis Gas & Coke Company, chartered by the city in 1851 with David V. Culley as president, was providing gaslights for 116 residences two years later and extending its original 7,000 feet of gas pipe all over the city. Street lights were confined to a section of Washington Street and a few adjoining streets where property owners were willing to pay for the lamps and posts. A proposal to levy a special tax for street lighting was defeated in the election of 1852 but approved in 1859, and the following year Indianapolis installed several miles of street lights, four to a block.

As a result of a state craze for plank roads—actually corduroy roads that used smooth planks instead of logs—part of the National Road and sections of the Michigan Road were planked. Other plank roads were built in the vicinity of the city, some of them toll roads built by private companies. Although slippery when wet and subject to warping and rapid deterioration, they provided a smooth ride during good weather and their promoters hailed them as a faster and more efficient way to move crops to the railroad sidings. City streets, however, remained in generally deplorable condition and the Circle was an eyesore, a treeless expanse where cows grazed and hogs rooted in the crumbling basement of the former governor's mansion.

Out on the northeastern border of the city was North Western Christian University, a single building in Gothic style on a 25-acre campus with plans to establish "departments or colleges in every branch of liberal and professional education" and "to educate and prepare suitable teachers for the common schools of the country." Sponsored by the Disciples of Christ, the university opened its doors November 1, 1855. It was also unique: it was one of the first colleges or universities in America to admit students "without regard to sex, race or color."

The moving force behind the new university was Ovid Butler, a retired Indianapolis attorney, and a group of dedicated Disciples. Butler, the first president of the board of trustees and for whom the university would later be named, was a native of New York and the son of the Reverend Chauncey Butler, first pastor of the Indianapolis Disciples of Christ Church. He had been a schoolteacher in Shelbyville and, at different times, a law partner of Calvin Fletcher, Simon Yandes and Horatio Newcomb. A gentle, modest man with deep religious convictions, he retired from the practice of law because of ill health and spent the remainder of his life fighting slavery and forwarding the interests of the university and his church. His Butler University would become one of the few denominational institutions founded in Indiana before 1850 to survive and expand into the present.

Other church-sponsored schools provided education at the elementary level. Besides the city's first Catholic school—St. John's, conducted by the Sisters of Providence and built at the corner of Tennessee and Georgia Streets—there were two German-English schools, one private and one church-supported. The Indianapolis Young Ladies' Institute, opened in 1858 on the northeast corner of Pennsylvania and Michigan Streets, was under the auspices of the Baptist Church.

The Indianapolis Post Office, a transient for nearly 40 years according to the whim of politics and postmasters, moved to a new, permanent building on the southeast corner of Market and Pennsylvania Streets, once the site of the city's first blacksmith shop. Started in 1857, it was finished three years later and its upper floors housed the federal courts and national offices.

Four other public buildings reflected the city's and state's concern for the less fortunate. The Orphan's Home, built in 1855 at the corner of Tennessee and Fifth Streets, was a project of the Indianapolis Benevolent Society. The other three buildings were state institutions: the Deaf and

Dumb School, the Asylum for the Blind and the Hospital for the Insane, the latter located at Mt. Jackson on land purchased from Nathaniel and Sarah Bolton.

Two large downtown buildings that housed the Grand Lodges of the Masons and the Odd Fellows were symbolic of the city's new stature. The Masons had been founded in Madison in 1818 and the Odd Fellows in New Albany in 1835, and for many years both had maintained their state headquarters in Madison. In the 1850s both lodges, apparently in recognition of shifting population and the growing importance of Indianapolis, moved to the capital city.

The three-story Odd Fellows Building at the northeast corner of Pennsylvania and Washington Streets was a handsome structure topped with an elongated dome. A feature of the Masonic Hall, designed by J. M. Willis of Indianapolis and completed in 1850 at the corner of Washington and Tennessee Streets (now Capitol Avenue), was a spacious hall for public use. The hall was a focal point for virtually all of the city's important meetings, lectures, debates and concerts.

As it would continue to be throughout history, Indianapolis was a city of churches. About a dozen new edifices rose in the downtown area during the 1850s, some to serve expanding congregations, others to serve dissenting members of older churches. Nearly all maintained Sunday schools and it was estimated that two-thirds of all Indianapolis children attended church school on Sunday.

The churches, especially the Presbyterians, continued to lay a heavy and repressive hand on community life. They vigorously campaigned against dancing, cardplaying, horse racing, theatergoing, fairs, circuses, croquet, ballplaying, drinking and use of tobacco. Sunday in Indianapolis was observed with puritanical strictness, and if one dared flout the church rules, there was secular law: an 1855 legislative act reminiscent of New England's "Blue Laws" that imposed fines for persons quarreling, rioting, fishing, hunting or engaging in common labor on the Sabbath, "works of charity or necessity excepted." An English visitor, A. M. Murray, reported that on Sunday in Indianapolis, "no trains start, letters do not go, nor are they received, so that a father, mother, husband or wife may be in extremity and have no means of communicating their farewells or last wishes if Sunday intervenes. Surely this is making man subordinate to the Sabbath—not the Sabbath to the man."

A common sight on Sunday was a procession of men and women making their way to the river or the canal to be baptized by immersion. The east and west sides of the White River at the Old Ferry was a particularly popular spot as there was "a stepping off" place. Some churches also used the canal at Washington Street near the Kentucky Avenue bridge. Negro churches used the canal west of the Georgia Street bridge. Baptism by immersion was abandoned, however, in favor of "sprinkling or pouring" as the river and the canal became fouled with waste.

The sudden and spectacular changes in the city placed a strain on its still new municipal government. Everything had happened too fast. Less than ten years before, the first mayor and city council had presided over a small country town with only a few thousand inhabitants; now, in the 1850s, their former village was grappling with all the problems of a major urban center: taxes, new streets, maintenance, lighting, water, sanitation, police and fire protection. Statistics told part of the story. The first city budget, in 1847, had been $4,000; by 1860 it had increased 20 times, to $87,262, and still failed to meet the city's growing needs.

It was not enough that the problems had descended upon the city fathers virtually en masse, but a large segment of the citizenry resisted many of the proposed improvements. Some of this was understandable. Residents of the city were used to doing what they "damned well pleased," subscribed to the theory that the less government the better, and paid little or nothing in the way of taxes. Fiercely individualistic, they viewed most of the proposed changes and improvements as an encroachment upon their freedom and independence that could cost them hard-earned money in the bargain. They firmly opposed the formation of an organized, paid police department and assessments for street lights and sidewalks, and they voted against any and all proposals to increase the basic city tax limit from 15 cents on a hundred dollars in order to carry out a number of city improvements.

Streets, however, were regarded in a different light. A succession of city administrations carried out a regular program of street improvements, and by the mid-1850s most of the streets in the mile square were improved, a few main thoroughfares were boulderized, and the city was in debt for $15,000.

As a result of its street-improvement debt, the city was involved in its first municipal scandal. In 1856 the city council approved a $30,000 bond issue to pay off the $15,000 it owed and provide funds for further improvements. A local bank cashier was appointed the city's agent, and he speedily sold the bonds to a reputable New York brokerage firm and disappeared with the proceeds. It was generally reported in Indianapolis that the cashier had used the money to bet on an election which would have made him a rich man—if he had won.

Less serious, although it provoked more widespread anger and directly affected more people, was the city's first attempt at numbering streets. The man engaged to do the work was careful and accurate, but he numbered only those lots on which houses had been built and neglected to number vacant lots and lots where houses were under construction. The embarrassed council ordered the work to be redone on the Philadelphia Plan, 50 numbers to a block, and for months irate householders all over the city were engaged in painting out old numbers and painting in new ones.

In 1853 the Indianapolis city government adopted the general charter law of 1851 in place of the original city charter with its limited taxing power. The new charter also provided for the election of all city officials, made the mayor president of the Board of Councilmen, increased the number of councilmen to two from each ward and established one-year terms for elected officials. The terms were increased to two years in 1857, with half the council seats to be vacated each year, and in 1859 another amendment set the terms at four years.

Councilmen continued to receive $24 a year, but the salary of the mayor was set at $600 and later raised to $800. The city treasurer, the only fee office, was paid four percent of current and six percent of delinquent tax collections. Under the new charter tax rates were increased and in 1859 were established at 60 cents on a hundred dollars, four times the original rate.

One of the most controversial issues in Indianapolis in the 1850s was a proposal to establish a regular, paid police department. On the surface Indianapolis was under the strict influence of its churches and their puritanical standards of conduct, but at another level, Indianapolis was a "wide-open town." Saloons were everywhere, gambling and prostitution flourished, fights and brawls were common, and the city appeared to have more than its share of thieves, robbers, burglars and pickpockets. Crime and vice in themselves were not new in the city; what was new was the extent to which they had grown since the advent of the railroads. The city's unprecedented prosperity had attracted hordes of undesirables who nightly preyed on the city's permanent and transient population.

The increasing rate of crime and vice resulted in continued pressure on the city council to establish a police department. Churches, newspapers and the nineteenth-century equivalent of the establishment favored the proposal, but most citizens were opposed on the grounds that a police force would pose a threat to personal freedom and add to the already rising cost of government. Some of the strongest opposition came from the city's expanding German population. The freedom-loving Germans, joined by the city's Irish population, feared the inauguration of a police system would only mean a repetition of the kind of police and political tyranny they had run away from in Europe.

Although Indianapolis had had town constables in an earlier day and a city marshal in the 1840s and 1850s, most men acted as their own police force and courts. A man who discovered he had been cheated at cards or robbed by a prostitute settled the matter personally or called upon a group of friends to help. Escorting the transgressor out of town, sometimes on a rail, was a common method of disposing of such matters, but there were also cases of beatings, tarring and feathering, and dunkings in the river or canal.

Personal and collective police action was sometimes a form of diversion. Indianapolis' volunteer firemen frequently got together of an evening and conducted raids on a row of brothels on East Washington Street near the creek and another cluster of houses on West Street.

The police issue came to a head during the administration of Mayor James McCready and the passage of a city ordinance establishing a regular, paid department of 14 men, two from each of the city's wards. Jefferson Springsteen was appointed "Captain of the Watch," patrols were established, and the city fathers promised that henceforth Indianapolis would be a city of law and order.

All might have gone well for the new police force if a series of events, including the state election of 1854, had not conspired against them. In the election, a fusion party, the People's party (forerunner of the modern Republican party), captured control of the statehouse.

Among the first acts of the new legislature in 1855 was the passage of a state prohibition law. Patterned after the Maine "bone-dry" law, which had been passed in 11 other states, the new legislation prohibited the manufacture of whiskey except for medicinal purposes and then only with the permission of the county agent.

Indianapolis ministers and temperance leaders were jubilant, but a large segment of the population viewed the prohibition law with anger and dismay. The city's German population were particularly incensed, since the new law deprived them of their beer.

When prohibition went into effect in late June, many of the German saloons and beer gardens remained open in defiance of the law, and the police force closed the saloons and arrested the owners. The angry Germans vigorously opposed the action of the police, and a series of riots culminated in the police shooting and wounding several German citizens in a melee on East Washington Street.

Two of the first saloonkeepers arrested and imprisoned under the new law, Roderick Beebe and William Hermann, filed appeals with the State Supreme Court. The court heard arguments in the Beebe case but adjourned for the summer, postponing a decision until the fall term. Hermann's lawyers appealed to Supreme Court Judge Samuel E. Perkins for a writ of habeas corpus to release Hermann from the county jail. Judge Perkins, a Democrat whose opposition to the prohibition bill was well known, released Hermann on the grounds that the law was unconstitutional in that it was "destructive of property rights of manufacturers, sellers and consumers"—a decision the court upheld in the Beebe case in November.

Indianapolis saloons and beer gardens immediately reopened, but the leaders of the German community were in no mood for celebrating. Although victorious in their fight against prohibition, the Germans were embittered over the findings of a public meeting which upheld the action of the police during the "beer riots." As a result of German pressure, abetted by other citizens opposed to the cost of a police force, the city council not only abolished the year-old police department on December 17, 1855, but eliminated the deputy assigned to the city marshal's office. The city marshal, George W. Pitts, remained as the city's lone symbol of law and order.

This victory was short-lived. Indianapolis, as one writer described it, was "riotous and unsafe," and a second police force of ten men was created a month later, January 21, 1856, with Jesse Van Blaricum as captain. Following the spring election, the force was dismissed and Jefferson Springsteen, former police captain and now the new city marshal, was empowered to appoint one officer from each ward, with C. G. Warner as captain.

The police department, as in our times, was affected by the pressures of local politics and special interest groups. In the first seven years of the new police department, eight different men were captains.

A particularly vexing problem of the changing city was the increasing number of volunteer fire fighting companies and their rising costs. Originally the volunteers were concerned citizens organized for mutual protection against fire. Costs had been slight and confined to repairing hoses or the occasional repainting of the apparatus, and these chores had been carried out by a $50-a-year fire messenger appointed by the council. In the 1850s, however, the volunteers had become, in effect, unpaid employees of the city who, in lieu of wages, clamored for larger outlays in equipment, firehouses and uniforms and special appropriations for parades and picnics.

Despite mounting appropriations for the volunteer firemen, there was no perceptible improvement in their ability to extinguish or control a fire. The basic problem was a lack of cooperation. Firemen were intensely loyal to their companies, the companies were fiercely independent and the rivalry between companies was bitter. As a result, there was more confusion than working hose lines at the scene of a conflagration.

To remedy this situation the city council in 1853 passed an ordinance designed to give the city full control over its expensive and independent fire fighters. The ordinance placed all of the companies under the authority of a chief engineer and two assistants and provided that companies which failed to cooperate would lose their annual appropriations. Joseph Little was appointed the first chief and B. R. Sulgrove and William King were named assistants.

Three years later the firemen reacted to the city council's control of their affairs by forming the Volunteer Firemen's Association "to enable them to exert their power more effectively and countercheck the despotism of the purse in the hands of the council." The association consisted of two delegates from each of the volunteer fire companies, who met regularly at the hall of the Relief Company on Meridian Street. The association chose as their president B. R. Sulgrove, formerly first assistant to the fire engineer, a leading editor who would later write a popular history of Indianapolis.

The association quickly grew in strength and political power. Gaining the recognition of the council as representatives of the volunteer firemen, the association virtually became its legislative wing. No fire-company appropriations were made without the association's recommendation or approval, and all actions that affected the general interests of the volunteers were subject to its supervision. Firemen began to act together in elections—a formidable bloc of over 400 votes—and they were conceded the office of city clerk. As the firemen's political "clout" increased, taxpayers began to complain of the firemen's exorbitant demands and the councilmen became more and more unhappy over the usurpation of their power. Earlier proposals for installing a regular, paid department and one of the new horse-drawn steam engines were revived.

But factional strife, unmanageable jealousies, internal struggles over policies, procedures and appropriations, and bitter fights over the presidency were tearing the association apart. The climax came with the election of a new chief fire engineer in 1858, Joseph W. Davis, a man of positive opinions and deep-seated prejudices, qualities that create both firm friends and sworn enemies. His partisan policies so divided the firemen that it became obvious their power as a union had been broken.

Efforts to restore harmony the following year failed, and at the urging of taxpayers and newspapers, the city council in August 1859 voted to establish the city's first regular, paid fire department and to purchase a steam fire apparatus which, as the chief of the Cincinnati fire department remarked, could "neither drink whiskey nor throw brick-bats." A horse-drawn Lee and Larned rotary pump engine was purchased in October and delivered the following March. A hot dispute was waged over its location, but it was finally placed in the brick firehouse of the Westerns on the south side of Washington Street. In August 1860 a third-class Latta was purchased and placed in the Marion Firehouse on Massachusetts Avenue, and in October a Seneca Falls was added and stationed in the Union Firehouse on South Street.

Joseph W. Davis became the chief engineer of the new, paid company. The six members appointed to the new fire department were Frank Glazier, Charles Curtis, and Daniel Glazier (and later G. M. Bishop) as engineers in charge of the new steam apparatus; William W. Darnell, hook and ladder company; and Charles Richmond and William Sherwood, who were placed in charge of two hand engines.

Chapter 9

POETRY, PANIC, BANKS

INDIANAPOLIS WAS THE SITE of the first Indiana State Fair on October 20, 21 and 22 of 1852. Staged under the auspices of the newly organized State Board of Agriculture, the fair drew an estimated attendance of 30,000 persons to Military Park on West Street. Fair visitors saw demonstrations of new farm machinery and watched the horse and ox pulling contests. For women there were new conveniences: a hand-cranked washing machine and the new cooking stoves. A midway offered a giant and a giantess, real grizzly bears and a great sea dog.

In succeeding years the fair was held in Lafayette, Madison, Indianapolis and New Albany, but in 1860 the board decided upon Indianapolis as a permanent site for the fair, and it purchased a 36-acre tract, Henderson's Grove, at what is now Nineteenth and Alabama Streets, just outside the mile square.

Over a dozen new newspapers were started in the 1850s but, with only a few notable exceptions, failed to offer any real competition for the entrenched *Journal* and *Sentinel*, which were now publishing daily except Sunday. Two of the successful papers were the weekly *Volksblatt*, the first German-language paper in the city, and the *Locomotive*, started in 1847.

The *Locomotive* was based upon a successful formula: local news. Newspapers of the day were generally partisan party organs which limited their columns to politics and national news and issues. The *Loco-*

motive, however, devoted itself exclusively to the happier and deceptively inconsequential side of the human comedy. It printed church and club news, engagements, weddings, births, and personality sketches; it reported goings and comings, and wrote glowingly of the city's progress. The little newspaper ignored politics and issues, but it was not above carrying special features such as a description of the drunken orgy of the expiring 1851 legislature, "an annual disgrace for a dozen years."

In July 1861 the *Locomotive* purchased the *Sentinel* and combined the papers under the *Sentinel* banner. The *Sentinel* had started life in 1830 as the *Democrat*, under Alexander F. Morrison, who, in the same year, purchased the *Gazette*, Indianapolis' first newspaper, and consolidated them under the *Democrat* banner. In 1841 he had sold the paper to the Chapmans, who had given it its current name and converted it to a daily, the first in the city.

Although all newspapers were morning editions, no attempt had been made prior to 1852 to carry overnight news. Papers went to press about sundown or as soon as the day's type had been set and locked in the forms. Monday editions were printed on Saturday. Two events changed all this. On the night of a big fire at the Eagle Machine Works, J. A. McNeeley, city editor of the *Journal*, dropped into the office, stopped the press and inserted a five-line bulletin reporting the fire and its probable loss. Its appearance the next morning was a phenomenon of local journalism. The *Journal* followed up this success by covering city-council meetings and publishing their proceedings the next morning.

A new sophistication appeared in the city's concert and lecture programs in the courthouse and the new Masonic Hall. Classical music and opera vied for audiences along with minstrel shows and band concerts. Among the more important serious musical highlights were two appearances of the famed Ole Bull, the Norwegian violin virtuoso, and Madame Anna Bishop and M. Boscha, who presented the city's first program of selections from the operas. Most of the lecturers who appeared in the 1850s were sponsored by the Young Men's Christian Association, organized in 1854, and the Young Men's Literary Society. Temperance was still a popular lecture subject, but audiences also heard of other issues of the day from such giants as Ralph Waldo Emerson, Horace Greeley, the Reverend Theodore Parker, Edward Everett, and a former resident, the famous Reverend Henry Ward Beecher. There was also a touch of spice on local platforms in the person of Lola Montez, the actress, who made three appearances at Masonic Hall under auspices other than that of the Y.M.C.A. Less spicy were the lecture appearances of Lucy Stone, feminist and women's-rights leader, who for her first Indianapolis lecture appeared in the new bloomer costume, "Turkish pantaloons" worn with a skirt reaching just below the knee. Miss Stone also demonstrated her famous independence. She was scheduled to talk at eight o'clock, but the audience began clapping and stamping for her to appear some 20 minutes before. Miss Stone appeared on the platform, looked at her watch, upbraided the audience for calling her out before her scheduled time, retired and reappeared on the stroke of eight. A newspaper editor in his next issue called her an "impertinent minx."

Indianapolis was a center for many musical activities. The city played host to its first convention of music teachers and choir directors. The Maennerchor, founded in 1854, entertained a state convention of German Singing Societies and, later, a Saengerfest of all North American Saengerbunds. Two state conventions of brass bands were held under the management of George B. Downie, leader of the Indianapolis Band. The city's Germans boasted a number of good bands, ranging from the "oompah, oompah" type, to those which played the classics.

Touring circuses regarded Indianapolis as a "good show town." Although condemned by the churches as "devices of the devil," William R. Holloway reported that "despite weather, mud or money, a circus in Indianapolis would fill all its seats." Among the early wagon shows that played to packed houses were G. A. Spalding's (later Spalding & Rogers), G. F. Bailey's (later Barnum & Bailey's) and the Sand's Nathan & Company American Circus.

A traveling company in 1854 presented the first Indianapolis production of *Uncle Tom's Cabin*. Packed houses hissed the villainous Simon Legree, held their breath as Eliza crossed the ice a step ahead of the panting bloodhounds; even brave men sobbed as Little Eva died and ascended to heaven with the help of a creaking windlass. The show, a combination of unabashed melodrama and bathos, plus an afterpiece and singing and dancing specialties between the acts, became an Indianapolis favorite as it did everywhere in the North.

The same year the city saw its first *Uncle Tom* show, a troupe of touring Shakespearean actors presented *Romeo and Juliet* at the Athenaeum, a new theater managed by W. F. "Yankee" Robinson upstairs over a former distillery at the corner of Maryland and Meridian Streets. It was the city's first look at the Bard and it had one feature that delighted the men and shocked the church people no end: Kate Denin, who played star-crossed Juliet, essayed the role in black tights that displayed her considerable charms to the fullest extent.

In 1858 Valentine Butsch built the city's first theater, the Metropolitan, which would later become the Park. It boasted 1,500 seats and stood at the corner of Washington and Tennessee Streets, a favorite location for circuses. Following design plans of the times, the theater occupied the second and third floors, and the ground floor was rented out to stores. The first season's offerings ran the gamut from operas to Sallie St. Clair, described as a leader of the "naked school" of actresses. The first season was not highly successful, and when the management proposed a benefit for the local Widows and Orphans Society, the offer not only was spurned but drew the indignant fire of the churches.

National fame came to poetess Sarah T. Bolton of Indianapolis with the publication in 1854 of "Paddle Your Own Canoe," a seven-stanza ode to self-sufficiency. Like Finley's "Hoosier's Nest," the piece was first published as a carrier's address and achieved the same kind of over-night acclaim by being clipped and reprinted by newspaper editors across the country. It was translated into eight languages and, when set to music, became a best seller. The verses had a background. Mrs. Bolton's husband, Nathaniel, founder of the town's first newspaper and former editor of the *Journal*, was appointed State Librarian in 1851, when the librarian's duties also included keeping the statehouse and its grounds in good order. Among the problems that came up was a recep-tion for governors of adjoining states in whose honor new carpets had been ordered for the hall of the House of Representatives and the Senate chamber. Mrs. Bolton, after searching in vain for someone to take on the difficult task of fitting, cutting and sewing the carpets, decided to do the job herself. As she worked, the verses formed in her mind. Set down on paper, they became, as one reviewer put it, a "magnificent battle hymn of the victorious army of successful workers in every age and every land." Thousands of people could recite the last eight lines, which, even today, have a ring to them:

> *Nothing great is lightly won,*
> *Nothing won is lost;*
> *Every good deed nobly done*
> *Will repay the cost.*
> *Leave to heaven in humble trust*
> *All you will to do;*
> *But if you succeed you must*
> *Paddle your own canoe.*

Nathaniel, after serving as clerk of the U.S. Senate, was appointed American Consul to Geneva in 1855. For the next four years the Boltons lived and traveled in Europe until Nathaniel became critically ill and they returned to Indianapolis. Following Nathaniel's death, Mrs. Bolton lived for many years at "Elm Croft" in Irvington and later at "Beech Bank," a 55-acre tract of rolling land about five miles southeast of the city. She died in the summer of 1893, leaving behind several slim volumes of her collected works and the title "Pioneer Poet Laureate."

The newly completed Masonic Hall, with its gaslit chandeliers and red-upholstered chairs, provided the setting for Indiana's second constitutional convention, authorized by the Democratic legislature of 1849-50. Generally the new constitution adhered to Jeffersonian principles and mirrored the rising spirit of Jacksonian Democracy in the state. It gave more power to the people and imposed new limits on government by increasing the number of offices subject to election, providing for more frequent elections and prohibiting legislation on many local and special subjects. For example, only the legislature could grant divorces before 1851. It also required that each law passed by the General Assembly concern itself with only one subject, thus ending the "undemocratic" practice of enacting hidden legislation by attaching riders to popular bills.

To preclude the possibility of another internal-improvements fiasco, the state was prohibited from becoming a stockholder in any bank, corporation or association and denied the right to incur any debt "except to meet casual deficits in the revenue; to pay the interest on the state debt, to repel invasion or suppress insurrection."

Voting rights of white male citizens were expanded to include "foreigners who had been in the United States one year and in the state six months immediately before any election, and who shall have declared under oath their intention to become citizens." There was, however, no welcome mat for Negroes. Under Article 13, they were prohibited from entering the state and those who were already residents were encouraged to move out. The question of rights for women, the subject of a small but growing militant movement in the 1850s, remained on dead center. Its lone symbol of women's progress was an 1847 legislative act, hailed as liberal for its day, which permitted married women to devise property and control real estate. Robert Dale Owen, who would champion the cause of women's rights throughout his life, sought to supplement these rights by extending them to include personal property and to write both laws into the constitution. His proposals went down under a barrage of oratory. The attitude of the convention may have been expressed in the comment by one legislator that women had "all the rights which the Bible designed them to have in this Christian land of ours."

There was victory for the free school advocates in Article 8 of the new constitution. It provided for a free public school system, established a common school fund and set up the office of state superintendent of public instruction—provisions which would be later implemented with the free public school law of 1852.

Among the direct results of the new constitution were two banking laws, the free banking act of 1852 and an act authorizing a charter for the Third State Bank of Indiana. Both had a tremendous impact on the economy of Indianapolis and the state.

The bank charter act stemmed from the fact that the State of Indiana, which owned half the stock in the Second State Bank, must now divest itself of its interest in order to comply with the new constitution. This posed a problem for the officers of the bank. They could wind up the affairs of the institution and close its doors, thus paving the way for other banks, or they could reorganize it as a private bank. After much discussion, the officers decided to close the bank.

Meanwhile, a group of the bank's principal investors decided to seek a renewal of the charter and worked quietly behind the scenes in the election of 1854 to elect men who could be counted on to vote their way in the forthcoming legislature. The investors chose their men wisely and well. In the closing days of the legislature the bill to charter a new bank not only passed, but was passed again over the angry veto of Governor Wright.

Two years later Governor Wright, in his message to the legislature, charged that the bank act and the events that followed constituted a "dark page of fraud." "Books for the subscription of stock," he charged, "were kept open but a few minutes and were then only accessible to parties to the fraud; in other instances they were opened in out-of-the-way places, known only to a few; and in scarcely any instance, was full and free opportunity given, for citizens generally to subscribe." The governor also charged that a majority of the stock had been subscribed by a favored group, few of them bankers, who immediately sold their stock to bankers at a premium. A legislative committee confirmed most of the governor's charges. In Indianapolis, for instance, the subscription books had been open for only 15 minutes and most of the stock bought and sold to W. C. DePauw at a substantial profit. Politicians from both parties, named as commissioners in the bank charter, had realized thousands of dollars from the transactions.

Although conceived in sin and for a time lacking in public confidence, the new bank and its 17 branch offices proved sound. It was one of the very few banks in the nation that did not suspend specie payments during the Panic of 1857. Most of its stock was in the hands of the original stockholders and its policies remained generally the same. The main office continued in Indianapolis, with Hugh McCulloch as president and Volney T. Malott as manager of the local branch. McCulloch had been manager of the Fort Wayne branch of the former Second State Bank and would go on from Indianapolis to become Comptroller of the Currency and, for a time, Secretary of the Treasury under Lincoln.

While the soundness of the new state bank contributed to Indianapolis' economy, the free banking law with its series of banking and money crises, combined with the Panic of 1857, delivered a jolt to the city's rocketing prosperity.

The free banking system, fathered by an 1852 legislative act and reluctantly signed by Governor Wright, a hard-money man, grew out of longtime dissatisfaction with the Second State Bank of Indiana. Its conservative policies—careful but substantial loans to hog and grain buyers and a $200 limit for individuals—had made it sound and profitable, but laid it open to charges of failing to provide sufficient capital for the state's swiftly expanding economy.

The new law was liberal. Under its terms a bank was required to have a minimum capitalization of $50,000, which could consist of U.S. bonds or Indiana bonds or those of other states, and to maintain a reserve of specie (coin or bullion) amounting to 12 percent of the bank's capital. Once these requirements were met, the bank could start issuing its own paper money or bank notes up to the full amount of its capitalization. Failure to redeem in specie at any time could lead to the bank's immediate closing by the state auditor's office. Six months after the law went into operation, 15 free banks were opened in the state, and by the end of 1855, 91 had been opened, five of them in Indianapolis.

It immediately became apparent that the new law was an open invitation to dishonest men and speculators and the establishment of "wildcat" banks (banks located in remote places inhabited only by wildcats). A common practice was for a speculator to make a small cash down payment on $50,000 or more in bonds of one of the several states, print a batch of handsomely engraved paper money, call on the state auditor, turn over his unpaid-for bonds, select a name for his bank, designate an out-of-the-way location and receive a charter as well as authority to issue the bank notes as legal currency. The new banker would then use the paper money to purchase property, make loans, trade it for other money or circulate it in other profitable ways. As soon as the money was disposed of, the banker "would depart for some distant part of the Union, secure in the knowledge that holders of his bank notes would have no means of demanding their redemption!"

The legislature turned a deaf ear to the pleas of Governor Wright to tighten the banking laws, and the number of banks continued to increase, along with the unrestricted issuance of currency. In contrast to the conservative State Bank of Indiana, with an estimated circulation of seven million dollars in its own notes and those of out-of-state banks, the free banks quickly ran their circulation past the ten-million-dollar mark, issuing more than six million dollars in a six-month period. Paper money began to depreciate and much of it turned out to be worthless. Many banks, unable to redeem their notes in specie, were forced to close their doors. Sometimes a "run" on a bank was forced by a rival bank presenting a large number of notes and a demand to be paid in specie.

Free banks played havoc with Indianapolis' growing business and industry. The city was flooded with worthless "wildcat" money or money that could only be turned over at a substantial discount. Creditors, businessmen and wage earners seldom knew the value of the bank notes in their pocket until they were evaluated by a banker, who, according to William Holloway, "would decide this was 'good' and that one worth 'eighty or ninety' and the other 'he couldn't say,' and the roll [of bills] was divided and preserved or got rid of accordingly." Worse yet, these judgments "varied every day or two; the 'good' went to 'ninety' and the 'uncertain' of one week came up to 'fifty' the next."

To remedy the situation, a convention of free bankers met in Indianapolis in January 1855 to determine the condition of the various banks and to classify and establish the value of their notes. Some of the free banks were honestly managed and backed by adequate security, but the failure of 51 banks in the first three years of the new law had made all free banks and their currency suspect. Unfortunately the new classifications were based on unreliable data, and the holders of the bank notes had to continue calling upon their banker or broker for an opinion. The *Journal*, as a public service, printed a list of the different bank classifications and their day-to-day changes—a list which "was consulted as constantly as the Union Depot time-table."

The Panic of 1857 wiped out the last of Indianapolis' five free banks and virtually destroyed business in the capital city. Stores were devoid of customers, industries were forced to shut down, new enterprises were paralyzed, and building came to a halt, leaving many structures half-finished. Suffering was acute and it was generally agreed the city's distress was greater than that which followed the Panic of 1837.

Nature also took a hand to add to the city's woes. Temperatures in the hard winter of 1856 dropped to 25 degrees below zero during January, and in the spring of 1858 heavy rains brought flood waters to the lower part of the city, inundating houses, damaging hundreds of acres of rich bottom farmland, washing away bridges, and sufficiently weakening a Central Railroad bridge to cause a locomotive to plunge through into the churning waters below.

Chapter 10

FAREWELL TO UNION

NOWHERE IN AMERICA was a city or a state more tragically divided by the issues of freedom and slavery, union and disunion than Indianapolis and Indiana in the 1850s. In a very real sense the city and the state were the divided nation in microcosm.

Indianapolis stood at the crossroads of America, a major railroad center where East and West and North and South met, ideologically and geographically. It was the capital and principal city of a politically important free state, a state often characterized as the most southern of the Northern states and courted by North and South. The city's population was a sectional mix. Men from the South rubbed elbows with neighbors who had come from New York, Ohio and the New England states, and with a growing number of German and Irish immigrants. Each brought to Indianapolis his sectional and native loyalties, politics and prejudices. Despite this diversity of backgrounds, devotion to the Union was strong, a devotion reflected in the newspaper editorials and speeches of the day. Citizens of Indiana generally supported the Compromise of 1850, denounced the extremists, North and South, and urged acceptance of the harsh and onerous Fugitive Slave Law as the price of one nation indivisible.

Although Negroes in Indianapolis and Indiana were not bereft of friends or sympathy for their situation, the general attitude in the city and state was anti-Negro. Black men were not permitted to vote, serve on juries or in the militia, give testimony in court against a white man or

send their children to public schools. Extreme penalties were in force
for intermarriage of whites and Negroes. Article 13 of the 1851 constitution provided that "no Negro or mulatto were to come into the state"
and provided fines up to $500 for anyone who encouraged them to
come or employed them.

In framing the constitutional provision, geography, prejudice and
simple economics had outweighed moral or humanitarian considerations.
Indiana bordered on the Southern tier of slave-holding states, and in
common with Ohio and Illinois, where equally restrictive black codes
were in effect, the state feared an influx of free Negroes who would
compete for jobs and drive down already prevailing low wage rates.

As a publishing center, Indianapolis was the birthplace of newspapers
in support of every position on the slavery question. The first of the
antislavery newspapers, *The Indiana Freeman,* edited and published by
Henry DePuy, was started in 1848, supporting the short-lived Liberty
party, and it viewed slavery as a moral issue. Regarded as a radical sheet
and its editors as "troublemakers," the newspaper's office on Washington
Street was often threatened with violence, and DePuy and his friends
spent many a night barricaded in the office. The first of the free-soil
papers, *The Free Soil Democrat,* appeared the same year. The *Democrat*
was for "Free Soil, Free States and Free Men" and was sponsored by
Ovid Butler, founder of Butler University. More radical in tone was
the antislavery *Western Presage* of 1857, which was fiery and short-
lived, and the *Indiana American,* published by the Reverend T. A. Goodwin, which was fiery and successful. To oppose the moderate and Democratic views of the German-language *Volksblatt,* Theodore Heischler
launched the antislavery *Freie Presse,* the first of a number of German-
language antislavery and free-soil papers.

Not all men were content merely to denounce slavery with fiery
words. Many dedicated Indianans, mostly Quakers, acted as "conductors" or "stationmasters" for the "Underground Railroad" that was
secretly ferrying escaping slaves across the Ohio River, through Indiana
to Canada and freedom. Indianapolis was a key station of the railroad's
central route, which started at four points on the Ohio, converged at
Salem, moved north to Columbus and thence to the 385-acre Washington Township farm of Hiram Bacon, the first and largest cheese-dairy
farm in Marion County.

There was other evidence of the city's growing sympathy for the
Negro, a sympathy often translated into action following the passage
of the Fugitive Slave Law. One of the first slaves captured under the
law was spirited from the city jail during the night by antislavery men,
but was recaptured the following day and returned to Kentucky.

In the case of John Freeman, citizens were more successful. Freeman was the owner of a small but successful whitewashing business, a resident of the city for ten years, well known and respected by the white community. Indianapolis was shocked one afternoon in May 1853 when it learned that Freeman had been seized by a U.S. marshal under the Fugitive Slave Law on the claim of Pleasant Ellington, a Missouri planter, who alleged the Negro was his escaped slave. As the marshal hurried Freeman before a U.S. commissioner, prominent local attorneys rallied to his defense, and an angry mob filled the streets.

The commissioner refused to release Freeman despite strong arguments by his attorneys that the Negro was a free man, a native of Georgia, and in no way resembled the escaped slave. Caught between the arguments of Freeman's attorneys and a street filled with men determined that Freeman would not be taken South, the commissioner reluctantly agreed to a stay of proceedings. Freeman was remanded to jail, where he had to employ guards to prevent his being kidnapped by proslavery men.

The case attracted widespread attention and some of Indiana's best legal talent provided counsel, obtaining proof of Freeman's status and locating the real fugitive. In August, three months after his arrest, Freeman was released. Jubilant citizens celebrated with a mass meeting at Masonic Hall, but for Freeman the victory had a hollow ring. He had regained his freedom, but he had spent nine weeks in jail, had been subjected to numerous indignities, and his savings had been wiped out. He was even cheated of revenge. Ellington, indicted for perjury, fled the city before the warrant could be served, and a suit for damages came to naught.

The Freeman case was indicative of the growing repugnance for the Fugitive Slave Law, engendered in no small measure by the publication of *Uncle Tom's Cabin* in 1852. Mrs. Stowe's thesis that slavery was contrary to all Christian principles was also dividing the churches. Many denominations had sought to avoid the issue, but it was a moral question that struck at the very tenets of Christianity, and churches found themselves embroiled. Presbyterians were split into Old and New Schools, partly over slavery, and Indianapolis Methodist churches joined the newly organized Northern Conference as the result of a division of the church into Northern and Southern Conferences. Even the antislavery Society of Friends (Quakers) were quarreling and dividing over methods of accomplishing their goal of ending human bondage.

Politics, however, produced most of the tumult and turmoil of the 1850s. Problems of city and state were overshadowed by national issues, and Indianapolis, a center for most of the political activity, was kept in an almost continuous state of excitement.

The decade opened with the Democratic party in control of the state and nation. The Democrats had responded to the threat of the new Free Soil party by embracing many of its principles. Following the passage of the Compromise of 1850, however, Indiana Democrats no longer displayed Free Soil tendencies. Party leaders generally believed the Compromise had united the nation and laid the slavery agitation to rest. In the election of 1852, which was dominated by national issues, the Democrats won a sweeping two-to-one victory over the Whigs, winning control of the legislature and the Congressional delegation. The election marked the demise of the Whig party, but the Free Soil party, which had polled only 3,000 votes, reorganized under the banner of the Free Soil Democratic Association, with Ovid Butler as president.

In 1854, as the Kansas-Nebraska Act ripped and tore at the fabric of the Democratic party, the association called for all those opposed to the Kansas-Nebraska Act to join with them in fighting for its repeal. The result was a convention in Indianapolis, called by Jacob P. Chapman in his new Free Soil newspaper, *The Chanticleer*, and the formation of a new party, the People's party, which in 1856 would formally become the Republican party. The new party had chosen a right moment in history. Democrats were divided over the Kansas-Nebraska Act. Many lifelong members were leaving the party, while still others, because of their refusal to support the party's state convention platform endorsing the act, were being read out. Equally disturbing for many Indiana Democrats was their party's position on temperance, a critical political issue of the 1850s. Democrats, in effect, had given the back of their hand to the powerful temperance forces and their demands for legislation of the Maine type which would make the state bone-dry. The People's party platform offered a sharp contrast, incorporating a strong temperance plank and calling for immediate restoration of the Missouri Compromise.

Political campaigns based on moral issues are usually bitter and the campaign that followed was no exception. The People's party, upholding the banner of righteousness, cast their opponents on the side of sin, slavery and strong drink. On election day the forces of right had their reward. The People's party elected its state ticket by some 13,000 votes, elected nine of 11 Congressional candidates and won control of the state House of Representatives, although the Democrats controlled the Senate by two votes.

Kansas overshadowed all issues in the state election campaign of 1856. North and South were pouring settlers into the troubled territory and violence flared. The North was angered at the attempt to extend slavery into Kansas and the South was inflamed because, contrary to a backstage understanding, the Free Soilers were attempting to wrest the territory from them. Indianapolis was a base for Free Democrats, Free Soilers and the Kansas Aid Society, and men like Calvin Fletcher and Ovid Butler helped them to raise funds to purchase arms and equip settlers for Kansas. Indiana ranked third in providing new settlers, including nearly fifty men from Indianapolis.

At the opening of the People's party convention in Indianapolis a mock raid was staged by a group of men disguised as Missouri Border Ruffians. The raid brought tremendous applause and cheers, and the convention lost no time in adopting platform planks that opposed the extension of slavery into the territories and demanded the immediate admission of Kansas as a free state. Although now aligned with the rising new Republican party, the People's party decided to continue under its original name and, reflecting growing Whig influence, elected John Defrees of Indianapolis as state chairman. For governor the party nominated Oliver P. Morton, a thirty-two-year-old attorney from Wayne County, a former Democrat who had bolted the party on the Kansas issue.

Despite the Kansas issue, the Democrats elected Ashbel B. Willard by some 6,000 votes after a bitter campaign and an election that brought widespread charges of fraud. Democrats also elected their state ticket, picked up four new seats in Congress and won control of the state House of Representatives, although the People's party controlled the Senate by virtue of two holdover Know Nothings they had supported in 1854.

A little before sundown on May 29, 1860, a violent storm struck Indianapolis. It was accompanied by a tornado that ripped across the south end of the city, snapped and uprooted trees and twisted the Virginia Avenue residence of Gardner Goldsmith halfway round on its foundation. Other and more destructive winds were already blowing across a troubled land. Dissension had ripped asunder the Democratic party and the outlook was ominous. The party had managed to keep the nation together with concession and compromise, but now it was hopelessly divided over slavery and the candidacy of Stephen A. Douglas. The split came at a time when the new Republican party was in its ascendancy, and Southern men in and out of Congress were saying that if the Republicans won the election in the fall, the South would leave the Union.

The Democratic party's state convention in Indianapolis had indicated which way the wind was blowing. Pro-Douglas men had emerged with a slate of delegates pledged to the "Little Giant" after a tumultuous and bitter fight that marked the defeat of the powerful forces of Jesse D. Bright, arch foe of Douglas and the man who for years had exercised tight control over the state Democratic party. The defeat left party wounds that were deep and festering, and Bright vowed to campaign against Douglas if he was nominated.

In May divided Democrats met in national convention at Charleston with Douglas as the leading candidate of the Northern wing of the party. Indiana's delegates stuck with Douglas during 57 fruitless ballots before the convention adjourned in confusion. Meeting again at Baltimore in June, the Douglas men speedily nominated their hero. Inflamed Southern Democrats staged a rival convention, nailed together a platform favoring extension of slavery into the territories and annexation of Cuba, and nominated John T. Breckinridge of Kentucky for President.

While Democrats were fighting and dividing, the Republicans, scenting victory in the turbulent wind, were wheeling and dealing and building platforms and tickets with middle-of-the-road planks and candidates. In the view of many party leaders, Republicans had too often laid themselves open to charges of "radicalism" and "abolitionism." If the party was to win in the fall, it required an image that bespoke moderation and included appeals to the many and diverse elements of the American electorate.

Indiana Republicans at their state convention in Indianapolis followed this line of reasoning. The party platform incorporated the conservative views of Democrats and Whigs. To oppose the popular Thomas A. Hendricks, the Democratic nominee for governor, the Republicans chose Harry S. Lane of Crawfordsville, a former Whig and regarded as a "sound man." Lane and Oliver P. Morton, the candidate for lieutenant governor, had been the leading contenders for the gubernatorial nomination, but it was agreed that if the Republicans won the legislature, Lane would be named to Graham Fitch's seat in the U. S. Senate and Morton would automatically become governor.

Indiana delegates to the Republican national convention in Chicago had been uninstructed, but their leaders, Lane, Morton and Defrees, were openly hostile to the nomination of William H. Seward, the favorite. Exploiting the delegation's anti-Seward feeling, Lincoln's hardworking campaign managers met with the Indianans in an all-night session and emerged with an agreement that Indiana would vote as a solid block for Lincoln on the first ballot. Part of the understanding that clinched the deal was the promise that Caleb B. Smith of Indianapolis would be appointed Secretary of the Interior. On the third ballot the prairie lawyer, railsplitter and middle-of-the-road candidate became the party's standard bearer.

Indiana Republicans were pleased with their choice. Lincoln appeared to be uncommitted to any policy beyond the preservation of the Union and he was also a former Hoosier. He had spent his formative years at

Pigeon Creek, Spencer County, coming to Indiana in the year of state-hood and leaving as a strapping young man to find his destiny in Illinois law and politics.

Indiana was regarded as vital to the plans of all four parties in the campaign of 1860, and Indianapolis, as the capital and principal city of a key state, was a focal point for much of the feverish campaigning.

Republicans were particularly desirous of capturing Indiana. The state had 13 electoral votes, and only three Northern states, New York, Pennsylvania and Ohio, had more. Indiana would also elect a governor in October, and a Republican victory could have both real and psycholog-ical effects on the Presidential balloting. For Indiana Republicans a seat in the U. S. Senate was at stake as well as an opportunity to redistrict the state and thus assure Republican domination for years to come.

Excitement mounted as Republicans and Democrats poured money and speakers into Indiana. Among the party's most effective campaigners was German-born Carl Schurz, friend and confidant of Lincoln and a writer and scholar. He visited Indianapolis and other parts of the state to sway German voters and win over German newspapers. His efforts were generally crowned with success. Of the state's eight German-language newspapers, only Indianapolis' *Volksblatt* supported Douglas and popular sovereignty.

Indianapolis also saw something new in a Presidential campaign: the appearance of a Presidential candidate, Stephen A. Douglas, at a mon-ster Democratic rally at the old fairgrounds. It had been traditionally re-garded as undignified for a Presidential candidate to campaign on his own behalf, but Douglas had boldly broken with the past. His speech in Indianapolis was a forerunner of the modern barnstorming campaign.

The Douglas meeting was only one of scores of rallies and torchlight parades during the summer and fall. Republicans, blessed with a substan-tial campaign fund, spent money with a lavish hand. Buttons, badges, bunting and banners extolling the virtues of "Honest Abe" and "The Railsplitter" were everywhere. Uniformed marching groups known as the "Rail Maulers" and the "Wide Awakes" were organized. One Re-publican parade was a monster day and night affair which drew so many viewers it could hardly move along the streets.

In the October state election Republicans scored an overwhelming victory. The Lane-Morton ticket was elected and the Republican party captured both houses of the legislature and seven Congressional seats. The election returns were significant. For the first time in 17 years the Democrats had failed to elect a governor, and unless the strong Republi-can tide could be stemmed in November, the state's 13 electoral votes would be lost to the party for the first time in 20 years.

To stave off disaster in November, defeated and desperate Democrats made a switch in strategy. Their newspapers and orators joined in warning the voters that the election of a "sectional party" could only destroy the Union and perhaps bring on a civil war. Voters were apparently inclined to dismiss the dire predictions as more election-year bluff, for Lincoln won the election and carried the state by more than 23,000 votes.

In December of 1860 the warnings of the Democratic campaigners proved to be more than election oratory. South Carolina seceded from the Union, and in the weeks and months that followed, ten other Southern states followed her over the precipice.

One of the most positive reactions to South Carolina's action came from Lieutenant Governor-elect Morton in an address at a victory celebration in Masonic Hall on November 22. South Carolina was then preparing to meet in convention and formally secede from the Union, and Democrats and Republicans alike were talking concession, conciliation and compromise.

Morton saw it differently. Taking over the podium from other speakers who had expressed conciliatory views, Morton declared that secession was an unlawful and "revolutionary" act and the President had no choice but to put down the rebellion. As for taking up arms, he asserted that "if it was worth a bloody struggle to establish the nation, it is worth one to preserve it." Morton's speech made him a national and controversial figure.

In January of 1861 and in keeping with their preelection agreement, Lane was named by the Republican legislature to a U.S. Senate seat and Morton became Indiana's fourteenth chief executive. The new post in no way changed Morton's position. In his first public address after taking office he denounced secession as "treason" and called upon all loyal men to close ranks and support the Union. The following month he had an opportunity to exchange views with President-elect Lincoln as he stopped in Indianapolis on his way to Washington for his March 4 inaugural.

President-elect Abraham Lincoln came to Indianapolis on February 11, 1861. His flag-bedecked Wabash train arrived in the city at sundown and halted at the East Washington Street railroad crossing at Missouri to a star-spangled greeting from a crowd of 30,000. After greetings by a welcoming committee headed by Governor Morton, members of the legislature, county officials, Mayor Samuel D. Maxwell and the city council, Lincoln spoke to Indianapolis and the nation:

I will only say that to the salvation of the Union, there needs but one single thing—the hearts of people like yours. [*Applause*] When the people rise in behalf of the Union and the liberties of this country, truly may it be said, "The gates of hell cannot prevail against them." [*Renewed applause*] In all trying positions in which I shall be placed, and doubtless I shall be placed in many such, my reliance shall be upon you and the people of the United States and

I wish you to remember, now and forever, that it is your business, and not mine; that if the Union of these states and the liberties of this people shall be lost, it is but little to any one man of fifty-two years of age, but a great deal to the thirty millions of people who inhabit these United States and to their posterity in all coming time. It is your business to rise up and preserve the Union and liberty for yourselves, and not for me. I appeal to you again to constantly bear in mind that not with politicians, not with Presidents, not with office seekers, but with you is the question: Shall the Union and shall the liberties of this country be preserved to the latest generations? [*Cheers and applause*]

The Lincoln party then entered a handsome flag-draped carriage drawn by four plumed white horses—part of a procession that included two bands, several companies of soldiers, the fire department, state, city and county officials, and "hundreds of carriages and thousands of citizens on foot and on horseback" that escorted the Presidential party to the Bates House, where they would stay the night. In the parlor of the Bates House that evening there was a grand reception for the President-elect and the halls and the stairways of the hotel swirled with people come to shake hands with the nation's next President. Outside the hotel masses of people jammed the intersection of Washington and Illinois Streets and Lincoln appeared on the hotel balcony and spoke briefly.

In March, in keeping with the bargain made for him at the Chicago convention, Lincoln appointed Caleb B. Smith as Secretary of the Interior, a post that Smith would hold until 1863, when he would resign to take a federal judgeship. Smith, a lawyer, newspaper publisher and railroad president, had been a state representative and a member of the U.S. House of Representatives. John Defrees, former publisher of the *Journal* and first state chairman of the original People's party, was named Government Printer, a post he would hold during the Lincoln, Johnson and Grant administrations.

On the morning of April 12, 1861, Indianapolis awakened to learn that in the cold gray dawn at Charleston Harbor, South Carolina, Confederate batteries had fired on the Union garrison stationed at Fort Sumter. Federal troops under the command of Major Robert Anderson had returned their fire an hour and a half later.

The city closed its stores, shops and factories. Thousands jammed the areas in front of newspaper offices waiting for bulletins, and hushed crowds milled in the streets. The telegraph clicked ominously all day and far into the night.

The morning of the following day, Saturday the thirteenth, brought only news that the bombardment was continuing. The Indianapolis *Sentinel*, the state's most powerful Democratic organ, announced the news with a headline written in bitter partisanship:

THE IRREPRESSIBLE CONFLICT INAUGURATED
CIVIL STRIFE COMMENCED IN CHARLESTON HARBOR
THE ABOLITION WAR OF SEWARD, LINCOLN AND COMPANY

The abolition and disunion administration have attempted the coercion of
the Confederate States. Such are the first fruits of Republicanism—and the
end no one can foresee.

That night a mass meeting overflowed the courthouse, moved to the
Metropolitan Theater and spilled over into the Masonic Hall and into
the streets. Governor Morton and leaders of both the Democratic and
Republican parties spoke. Resolutions were adopted supporting Lincoln,
declaring: "We unite as one man to repel all treasonable assaults upon the
Government, its people and citizens in every department of the Union—
peaceably, if we can, forcibly if we must." As it neared ten o'clock, Ebenezer Dumont, a veteran of the Mexican War and chairman of the meeting, stepped to the center of the Metropolitan stage and waved for
silence. "My friends," he said in a solemn voice, "I have just been advised
that Fort Sumter has surrendered. The Stars and Stripes have been hauled
down."

Chapter II

WARTIME CAPITAL

ALL DAY SUNDAY, April 15, 1861, Indianapolis streets echoed to the beat of fife and drum as the recruiting of troops began. Ministers dispensed with regular sermons and offered prayers for the divided nation and its President. Governor Morton dispatched a telegram to President Lincoln: "On behalf of the State of Indiana, I tender you for the defense of the nation, and to uphold the authority of the government, ten thousand men."

On Monday Indianapolis was a city gripped in the fever and excitement of war. A holiday air prevailed. Flags flew everywhere, brass bands played, marching fifers and drummers kept up their deafening beat, uniformed horsemen rode up and down on official errands. Incoming trains disgorged hundreds of gangling, fuzzy-chinned young men—the first of the volunteers. Newsboys hawked the latest war extra. In the quiet of many bedrooms, men tried on their old Mexican War uniforms and tested their saber blades. Captain Frank Shoup, commander of the Indianapolis Independent Zouaves, an artillery officer and graduate of West Point, quietly left the city for Charleston, South Carolina. He was one of many who would leave to join the Confederate Army and fight against former comrades.

The early-morning telegraph brought the news that Lincoln had called for 75,000 three-month volunteers to quell the "insurrection." Indiana's quota was six regiments, or nearly 5,000 men. Colonel Lew Wallace, already busily recruiting for his Zouave Regiment, was appointed adjutant general. The new fairgrounds was designated Camp Morton, the old fairgrounds Camp Sullivan; the horse barns were hastily converted to barracks. Governor Morton appointed his old friend Isaiah Mansur, owner of the city's largest pork-packing plant, to head the state commissary and arrange for the feeding of the growing number of troops in the city. Thomas A. Morris of pioneer railroad fame was appointed quartermaster general.

Among the first military companies to respond to Governor Morton's call for volunteers were the city's National Guards, City Grays, Independent Zouaves and Zouave Guards. Six regiments were formally organized: the Sixth through the Eleventh, the numbering following after the five regiments formed during the Mexican War. The Seventh was under the command of Colonel Ebenezer Dumont of Indianapolis. By Wednesday most of the volunteers were assembled at Camp Morton, and Indianapolis began to resemble an armed camp.

In the initial flush of war excitement, Indianapolis and Indiana appeared unified for the first time in more than a decade. Party lines were obliterated. Meeting in special session on April 24, the state legislature, which only weeks before had been embroiled in bitter partisan debate, closed ranks in response to a plea from Governor Morton. Legislators gave Morton wartime powers, divided appointive offices between the two parties, appropriated $1,600,000 for military purposes, and authorized a two-million-dollar bond issue for defense of the state and nation. The Indianapolis City Council met, passed patriotic resolutions and appropriated $10,000 for war purposes. The Indianapolis *Sentinel*, the voice of the Democratic party, which on April 15 had suggested the North let her erring sister "go in peace," was asserting in May, "There is no choice in the matter. The government must be sustained."

Volunteers continued to stream into the city. Within a week after Sumter, 12,000 troops were camped in Indianapolis and more were on the way. The original six regiments were organized into the Indiana Brigade under Thomas A. Morris, who had resigned as quartermaster to take command. Lew Wallace asked for a field command and, coincident with the mustering of Indiana's regiments into federal service, resigned as adjutant to take command of the Eleventh Zouave Regiment.

Indianapolis took special pride in the Eleventh Regiment, which included four companies of city volunteers. The best-disciplined of the troops, it was the first to be organized and the first to leave the city. It was also the most colorful. Its members wore the exotic uniform of the French Zouave fighting forces: a short blue jacket trimmed in scarlet and gold, scarlet baggy trousers, white leggings and tassled, fezlike scarlet and gold hats. The regiment's leave-taking on May 8 was pure theater. As the troops were assembled on the statehouse lawn prior to their march to Union Depot, the ladies of the city presented Colonel Wallace with a magnificent silk flag sewn by their own hands. At the conclusion of his acceptance speech, Wallace held the flag high, bade his men kneel and take a solemn oath never to disgrace the regimental colors and to "remember Buena Vista"—a reference to the Mexican War and charges of cowardice brought against an Indiana regiment by Jefferson Davis, now President of the Confederate States of America.

The Eleventh was sent to Evansville to guard the Ohio River, moved to Cumberland, Maryland, and distinguished itself by marching 46 miles in less than 24 hours to stage a dramatic raid on Romney, Virginia. In June at Maryland a mounted squad skirmished with a band of Rebel cavalry, and John C. Hollenbeck of Company B was killed—the first Indianapolis soldier to die for the Union.

Colonel George B. McClellan came to Indianapolis on May 24 to review Indiana troops on a large common north of the fairgrounds. A few days later Indiana's Sixth to Tenth Regiments were on their way overland to drive the Rebels out of western Virginia in the first battles of the war. Brigadier General Thomas A. Morris was appointed commander of all federal forces in western Virginia and is generally credited with drawing up the plans for the campaign, but the dashing and flamboyant McClellan took both the credit and the headlines.

Indianapolis was a city of soldiers, a place for mustering in and mustering out, for organization and reorganization, for marching and drilling and reviews and ceremonies. More army camps were established to accommodate the new soldiers who arrived daily in the city. Before war's end, Indianapolis would have 24 camps in operation, including the state's largest, Camp Carrington, situated between the Canal and Fall Creek, near Fifteenth and Missouri Streets.

Indianapolis' small police department—uniformed for the first time in 1862 and increased to seven day men and 18 night patrolmen a year later —was hard-pressed to cope with the great numbers of thieves, gamblers, rowdies and camp followers who had come into the city to prey on the men in uniform. Disorderly and disreputable places were everywhere. Merchants hired a private police force to supplement the efforts of local police after burglars broke into D. J. Callinan's store and took $8,000. Prostitution was rampant. The problem eventually became so serious and the jails so overcrowded with the play-for-pay ladies that the city council appropriated funds for building a house of refuge "to secure some alleviation of the evil and some chance of making punishment effectual toward reform."

Touring shows, including minstrels, came to town to entertain the troops. The Metropolitan Theater, closed after two unprofitable seasons, reopened and its shows played to packed houses for the duration. Among the performers who came to town was a noted actor who would play one of history's most infamous roles—John Wilkes Booth.

The war brought unprecedented prosperity, inflation and privation. Silver money was scarce, treasury notes depreciated and gold climbed to new highs. Labor shortages developed and wages climbed. Profits were handsome, particularly for those engaged in furnishing supplies. Business property on Washington Street valued at $400 to $500 a front foot in 1861 went to $1,000 a front foot. Clothing prices were generally 60 percent higher. A private's pay of $13 a month was worth less than $9 in inflated currency.

In early 1862 Camp Morton was designated as one of four Northern prisoner-of-war camps, and on February 22 the trains brought the first Confederate prisoners—3,700 young men, mostly sick, who had been captured at Forts Donelson and Henry in Tennessee by troops of the then relatively unknown Ulysses S. Grant. The Rebel prisoners spent their first night in Indianapolis sleeping on the floor of Union Depot, a mass of groaning, coughing, pain-twisted humanity. The next day local doctors mobilized to provide aid, prescribed for 500 men, and converted the old Athenaeum Theater and all four floors of Blackford's building into hospitals. Men and women of Indianapolis, touched by the plight of the prisoners, provided volunteer nursing service, food, writing materials, clothing and hospital supplies. Despite their efforts, a contemporary writer reported, "Hardly an hour passed for the first five days that a death did not occur, and the motality continued for a month or more until the [cold] weather moderated." In all, 1,600 men would die at Camp Morton, over ten percent of the 15,000 men interned during the war years.

An Indianapolis inventor, Dr. Richard Gatling, came forward with a revolutionary new weapon: a hand-cranked rapid-fire gun with ten revolving barrels that fired over 250 shots a minute. Gatling patented the weapon in November 1862. The gun was immediately adopted by the navy and used with some small success on federal gunboats which plied the Ohio and Mississippi Rivers. The army's experience was less successful. The new weapon gave a great deal of trouble and was not formally adopted until 1866.

Gatling, a native of North Carolina, had come to Indianapolis in 1854, married Jemima Sanders and was about to market a new patented steam plow when the Civil War broke out. His new gun was manufactured in his Indianapolis plant and a corporation was formed to market it, with Washington Houston Talbott, owner of an Indianapolis book and jewelry business and a former president of the Indiana and Illinois Central Railroad, as president of the new company. Talbott spent much time abroad demonstrating the gun to European powers.

In the first year of the war 54 regiments, the Sixth through Fifty-ninth, three cavalry regiments and 12 artillery batteries were formed. Through the efforts of August Willich of Indianapolis, an all-German regiment, the Thirty-second, was formed. There was also a green-capped all-Irish regiment, the Thirty-fifth, which was consolidated with the Sixty-first or Second Irish Regiment in 1862. The following year, and not without controversy, the Twenty-eighth Regiment, U.S. Colored Troops, was organized. The troops encamped at Camp Fremont, east of Virginia Street, and were commanded by Colonel Charles Russell.

At the outset, volunteers regarded the war as a kind of national picnic and they rushed to be a part of it, often because everybody else was going, and even more often to exchange the awful tedium of farm, bench, stable, store or pork-packing plant for the Great Adventure. They lined up at recruiting stations in Indianapolis in a holiday mood, laughing, pushing, joking, and they departed the city still men on a holiday, only perhaps feeling a little more proud and heroic as they received a picture-book send-off.

But the Great Adventure lost all aspects of a picnic in the cruelest and most personal of all American wars. Some of the disillusioned Indiana boys simply went home—2,300 of them up to December of 1862. Letters from friends and relatives politically adverse to the war urged desertion and promised protection. Others deserted to return to their families, who were often in dire straits as the result of inflation. To underscore the seriousness of desertion in wartime, the first military execution of the war was carried out at Camp Burnside on Tinker Street (Seventh Street) in the summer of 1862. Robert Gay was taken to Henderson's orchard and executed by a firing squad as he stood blindfolded in front of his own pine coffin.

As the war expanded, casualty lists mounted and recruiting lagged, a system of bounties was instituted to provide an incentive for enlisting: at first, $300 cash on the barrel head, but before war's end, nearly $1,000 in benefits before leaving for camp. The larger sum represented the scarcity of manpower as well as inflationary pressures. War appropriations of the Indianapolis city council totaled nearly a million dollars, most of it for payment of bounties, and city taxes were hiked to $1.50 and later to $1.75 per hundred.

The bounty system led to many abuses. Towns and cities, competing with one another to fill quotas, increased their bounty payments and often filled their rolls with men of doubtful character. A new profession, bounty jumping, was born: men who would enlist, collect their bounty and immediately desert. Some men would try this several times, as in the case of three bounty jumpers who were executed, as a warning to others, by a firing squad at Camp Burnside in 1864. Parades of arrested bounty jumpers were not an unusual sight in Indianapolis, and in November of 1864 a band of 150 were marched through the streets with placards hung around their necks.

An even more profitable business, and legal as well, was that of the bounty broker. Under the unpopular draft law, a drafted man was permitted to hire a substitute, and the brokers specialized in providing such men. They also cooperated with recruiting officers and towns and cities in meeting quotas, and their advertisements appeared regularly in state newspapers. A typical advertisement appearing in the Indianapolis *Daily Sentinel* and *Daily Journal* in 1864 suggested: "If you want a Good Sound Man to Represent You in the field, you can get him at a Reasonable Price, by applying at our Office, Northwest Corner, opposite Union Depot."

As the war progressed, the plight of soldiers' families came to the fore. The Indianapolis city council helped with several appropriations—the first, $400 for firewood—and the Sanitary Commission provided additional help. Days were often set aside for private contributions, and on the appointed day processions of wagons loaded with flour, wood, potatoes, meats, vegetables and fruits would rumble through the streets of Indianapolis and other Indiana towns and cities. Contributing often became a kind of contest between generous farmers, and "wagons carrying five and even ten cords of wood and others with mountains of food were not infrequent sights."

Conscription Acts passed by Congress in 1862 and 1863 provided for the drafting of able-bodied men whenever necessary to fill troop quotas. The draft proved even more unpopular than in our own time, and attempts to enforce its provisions resulted in disorder and violence. Two draft officials were reported killed in Rush County, another in Sullivan County, and in still others draft officials were harassed, sometimes mobbed, frequently run out of the county. So many men took their families "visiting" on draft enrollment day that a system of passes was instituted to prevent draftees from leaving the state.

Indianapolis had no trouble in meeting its initial troop quotas, but in the summer of 1864 "citizens had to bestir themselves to avoid a draft." The city's fall quota was 1,258 men, and the best that could be produced was 800 men and $40,000 in bounty money which had been raised at a number of citizens' meetings. To offset the deficit in men and money, "enrolled men" on draft lists came up with $8,000 for substitutes, and the city council made two appropriations of $92,000 and $40,000. Thus at a cost of $180,000 the quota was met without drafting city men.

The city also had to "bestir" itself in meeting another and final call for troops in 1865. Unable to meet its quota of over 2,000 men and with only $147,000 in bounty funds, the city council, acting on a petition from Indianapolis citizens, authorized a $400,000 bond issue. The bonds went unsold in New York, but local banks loaned the city $100,000 at 12 percent interest. City officials also secured approval from Washington to draft men by wards, and as the deadline neared, it appeared certain Indianapolis would meet its quota. At this moment someone discovered that a clerk in the War Office had made an error in establishing credits for Indianapolis volunteers and the quota was actually filled with hundreds of men to spare. Alternately angry and jubilant city officials and citizens went about unscrambling the resulting manpower and financial mess.

Chapter 12

OLIVER P. MORTON, WAR GOVERNOR

I N THE MONTHS that followed Sumter, the war effort in Indiana became centered in one man, Oliver P. Morton, the passionate and positive chunk of a man who occupied the governor's office in Indianapolis. He regarded himself as the war's personal proprietor and the symbol of Union in Indiana, and he wielded raw, naked power with force, energy and determination for the winning of one and the restoration of the other and, more often than not, for the greater glory of Oliver P. Morton and the Republican party.

The first native son to become governor, Morton was born at Salisbury, August 4, 1823, the son of a country innkeeper, who named him after the famed hero of the Battle of Lake Erie, Commodore Oliver Perry. Following his mother's death, he spent most of his boyhood in Ohio and Centerville, Indiana. He clerked briefly for an apothecary, learned the hatter's trade and attended Ohio's Miami University, where he was described as an indifferent student but a brilliant debater. Leaving college, he read law in the office of John S. Newman of Centerville, married Lucinda M. Burbank, and in 1847 became a member of the Wayne County Bar.

Biographers agree that Morton was no expert in preparing briefs, but in a courtroom before a judge or addressing a jury he was "irresistible." A massive young man with flashing eyes, coarse black hair and a bullhorn of a voice, Morton regarded the law as a form of personal combat; he gained a reputation as a fighter and winner and attracted attention and drew crowds whenever he appeared in court. Morton's law practice grew, profitable railroad litigation came his way, and he prospered. In the 1850s he entered politics.

Morton started out as an orthodox Democrat who condemned radicalism, supported the Compromise of 1850 and campaigned for the Northern Bourbon Franklin Pierce. In 1854, his orthodoxy shattered by the Kansas-Nebraska Act, Morton joined the newly formed People's party, served as a delegate to the 1856 Republican national convention and ran unsuccessfully for governor on the People's party-Republican ticket. In the spring of 1860 he opposed the nomination of Seward, but by fall the once moderate Morton had become a sufficiently radical Republican to be in the vanguard of those calling for force against the seceding states.

As wartime governor, Morton presided over a strategically important but tragically divided state, and in Morton's defense it could be said a strong man and an iron hand were needed. Indiana's vast network of railroads and enormous production of hogs, corn and wheat were vital to the war. But it was a state where more people of Southern ancestry and Southern sympathies lived than in any other free state, and as a consequence, the war divided families and split lifelong friendships and political parties.

A law partner had once said of Morton that "he never did things halfway," and as Indiana's governor drove the state deeply into the war, he proved the accuracy of the judgment. Combining the qualities of a human dynamo with a genius for organization, he bulldozed his way over all opposition, slashed red tape and ignored all legalities as he raised money, recruited troops, purchased arms and supplies. In a time when recruiting was left up to the states and Washington was ill-prepared to furnish sufficient arms or equipment, Morton saw that Indiana raised more than its quota of troops, and he got them armed and equipped. He sent agents to Europe, to Canada and the East to purchase cannon and quantities of the new Enfield rifle. When Wallace's Eleventh Regiment needed uniforms, he purchased the entire output of Giesendorff's Indianapolis woolen mill and mobilized the ladies of the city to convert the wool into uniforms. Morton also personally inspected camps, checked the food, listened to soldiers' complaints, organized the Indiana Legion for the defense of the state and arranged for their instruction at Camp Burnside in Indianapolis.

Morton's solicitude for Hoosier troops did not end when they left the state. The campaign in West Virginia was an early example. Learning that Indiana troops were shivering in the cold nights of the West Virginia mountains, Morton harassed the federal quartermaster in Indianapolis until he requisitioned several thousand overcoats. When the coats went astray, Morton purchased 29,000 overcoats through his New York agent and sent them posthaste to the front.

Morton, who was never satisfied that anyone was doing enough for Indiana troops, organized the State Sanitary Commission in 1862 "to render all possible relief to our soldiers, especially those sick or wounded, whether in transit, in hospitals or on the battlefield." For director Morton chose William Hannaman of Indianapolis, a partner with Jacob Scudder in a drugstore and a flaxseed oil factory and long identified with charitable and benevolent organizations. Agents were attached to all Indiana troop units, sanitary stores shipped to them for distribution, and doctors and volunteer nurses dispatched whenever needed. Throughout the war thousands of wounded and sick Indiana men were brought home by train and by steamboat through efforts of commission agents. These dedicated men also distributed food, clothing, wine, whiskey, soap, bedding, tobacco, writing paper and books to Indiana troops. They wrote letters, furnished legal aid, forwarded battle souvenirs, arranged transportation for furloughed or discharged soldiers, attended the dying, kept death and grave records and sent home the belongings of those who died. On the home front the commission was organized into a network of auxiliaries and societies, with Indianapolis as a warehousing and shipping point for all supplies. Public appeals, meetings, newspaper publicity and Sanitary Fairs brought contributions of money and merchandise that totaled, statewide, some $5,200,000 before the war was over.

Morton's concern for Indiana troops also resulted in establishing the Soldiers' Home in Indianapolis, a large transient hotel with free accommodations for the thousands of soldiers who daily passed through the city to and from the camps or the fronts. At the beginning of the war state agents had met the trains and provided supplies, cared for the sick or arranged for accommodations in local hotels. This system, however, was expensive and inconvenient, and at Morton's suggestion a large tent city was established on vacant ground south of the depot. In 1862 the governor resolved to establish a more permanent home and Quartermaster Asahel Stone selected a grove on the west side of West Street, north of the Vandalia Railroad, where temporary but comfortable frame buildings were erected to provide free accommodations for 1,800 persons and up to 8,000 meals a day. Hospital facilities were also provided. In 1863 the Ladies' Home for the care of soldiers' wives and children was opened near Union Depot, with accommodations for 100 persons.

Much of what Morton did was highly irregular, transcended state functions and embroiled him with federal purchasing officials and the U. S. Sanitary Commission. Quartermasters protested that competition for arms pushed up prices and encouraged speculation, but Morton retorted he was merely cutting "red tape," charged the federal government with paying insufficient attention to the needs of Indiana troops, and went right on purchasing arms and supplies. He also tangled with the U. S.

Sanitary Commission and commanders in the field over clothing allotments and furloughs, and when he failed to get satisfaction, he went over their heads and appealed directly to Lincoln.

Morton's constant embroilment with the federal government underscored an issue of the war. One of the things the conflict was all about was the matter of state and federal powers, and it was obvious the issue was being settled in favor of a strong central government. But Morton was exercising, as a U. S. Sanitary Commissioner put it when it became evident the Indiana Sanitary Commission was going to act as a separate entity, "the obnoxious heresy of state sovereignty."

Morton's ardor and energies were not confined to Indiana. He regularly fired off telegrams or paid personal visits to Washington voicing his impatience over the progress of the war, and kept up a voluminous correspondence with commanders and private soldiers in the field, key Washington officials and other governors. He openly interfered in the affairs of Kentucky, which had voted to remain neutral. Morton sought, with marked success, to bring that torn and unhappy state within the sphere of his influence and move it over to the Union side. In the fall of 1862, when Confederates invaded Kentucky and ran up a quick string of victories, Morton raised troops, borrowed money on his own and rushed green troops across the Ohio River, to be slaughtered at Perryville and Richmond and captured en masse at Munfordville. Morton personally visited the state to watch—and interfere—as Major General Don Carlos Buell drove the Rebels out of Kentucky. He blamed Buell for the disaster to Indiana's troops and had the satisfaction of seeing Buell relieved of his command.

Morton met his first formidable challenge in the election of 1862, an election that mixed politics with war and revealed the poignant division within the state.

The war was going badly in the fall of 1862. Discontent was widespread, and opposition, which had been underground since Sumter, was boldly asserting itself. In Indiana the casualty lists were tragically long and lengthening daily. A growing number of Indianans were confined in Confederate prisons. Indianapolis families had firsthand testimony on squalid conditions in the infamous Libby Prison at Richmond. Colonel Abel D. Streight of Indanapolis and 108 fellow prisoners had escaped by digging a tunnel under the prison wall to the street and eventually finding their way into the Union lines. The popular Lew Wallace was without a command. In southern Indiana the counties along the Ohio River lived in constant fear of Confederate raids. Desertion was becoming common.

Against this backdrop Democrats and Republicans campaigned for votes. When Lincoln issued his preliminary Emancipation Proclamation virtually on the the eve of election, the Democrats gleefully exploited the state's Negrophobia by raising the twin specters of abolitionism and Negro equality. It was not just a war to end the Union, Democrats could proclaim, but a war to free the Negroes, who, they predicted, would pour into the free states following victory.

Republicans, on the defensive early in the campaign, retaliated by attempting to brand their opponents as disloyal and involved in treasonous activities. To support their charges, they circulated a federal grand jury report on the Knights of the Golden Circle, a secret, oath-bound society with an estimated membership of over 15,000. The grand jury report had found the organization "probably treasonable," but Republican attacks became more exaggerated and frightening as their party's position weakened. Democrats replied that the Knights existed only in the fertile imagination of Republicans and were quick to point out that the empaneling marshal was a Republican, the jury had been made up entirely of Republicans and Morton had been active in producing witnesses.

Democrats won a not surprising victory on October 14. They elected their state officers by more than 9,000 votes, won seven of 11 Congressional seats and captured control of both houses of the Indiana General Assembly. Governor Morton promptly wired Lincoln that he feared the new "Copperhead" legislature was planning passage of "a joint resolution to acknowledge the Southern Confederacy and urge the Northwest to dissolve all constitutional relations with the New England states."

The divided and Democratic-dominated General Assembly convened in January and gave the lie to Morton's charges by proving sufficiently loyal. Although a few "Peace Democrats" introduced a batch of resolutions calling for compromise or an armistice, these died in committee, and the legislative majority adopted a resolution declaring for preservation of the Union and branding the Rebels as "traitors." But the discontent with the conduct of the war was an opportunity to restore the glory of the Democratic party, and old-fashioned power politics became the order of the day as they set out to accomplish their goal.

Most of the session was devoted to condemnation of Lincoln, Morton, the Emancipation Proclamation, the usurpation of power by Republicans and the loss of constitutional liberties. The legislature halls rang with cries of "despot," "tyrant," "dictator." Democrats refused to sit still for Morton's message to the legislature and Republicans refused to meet in joint session to name U. S. Senators. When Republicans finally capitulated, the Democratic majority named Thomas A. Hendricks and David Turpie to the U. S. Senate. Then the Democratic majority settled down methodically to strip Morton of his power and to gerrymander the state. The Republicans, to prevent a quorum, removed themselves to Madison, where they were prepared to escape across the Ohio River into Kentucky if they were threatened with arrest—all apparently with the approval of Morton, who made no effort to call them back.

The Republican bolt paralyzed the legislature and it finally adjourned. As no appropration bills had been passed, the Democrats were confident that Morton would call them into special session as provided for under the state constitution. But Morton simply took over the state government and ran it single-handedly for the next two years.

Democrats raged over Morton's seizure of the state government. Orators and editorial writers called him a usurper and compared him with Julius Caesar, Cromwell and Charles I, and for good reason. The positive and passionate Morton was setting up a virtual dictatorship in the spring of 1863.

The army, in the persons of a former Hoosier, General Ambrose E. Burnside of the Department of Ohio, and General Milo S. Hascall of the Indiana district with headquarters in Indianapolis, was prepared to go even further, but to Morton's credit, he talked the army out of declaring martial law and protested many of the arrests the army was making in Indiana. There is no evidence, however, that Morton protested the army orders that anyone who spoke or wrote against the government's conduct of the war "would be tried as spies or traitors." The order resulted in a wave of selected arrests and the suppression of many state newspapers. The Democratic *Sentinel* in Indianapolis was threatened several times, once by a band of soldiers, but it was neither suppressed nor wrecked.

To Democratic charges that Morton was attempting to destroy freedom of speech and press, Morton answered he was suppressing treason and fighting "Copperheads." For evidence, there was a secret, oathbound organization, the Sons of Liberty, made up of Democrats who were allegedly plotting to take over the state by force of arms and remove it from the Union. The Sons of Liberty (successors of the Knights of the Golden Circle) was a real organization, but much of what Morton and others said about it was unreal, including its numbers and its ability to cause trouble. But the story enabled Morton to consolidate and expand his power base and create the impression that all Democrats were traitors.

To counteract the "menace" of the secret Sons of Liberty, Morton encouraged the organization of Union Clubs and Union Leagues, which were formed along strict Republican lines. These secret organizations were furnished arms and regularly drilled and marched in preparation for the uprising whch was always just around the corner. Democrats charged this was further evidence of Morton's "despotism," that talk of an armed insurrection was a Republican "nightmare," and it all added up to another attempt to intimidate them. But Republicans continued to insist that an armed uprising, aided and abetted by Democrats, was in the making.

The Sons of Liberty must have been one of the most spied-on secret organizations in history. Virtually all of its lodges contained undercover agents of Morton or the army. In 1863 Morton was informed that the society was planning an uprising in Indianapolis with the avowed purpose of taking over the state governement. The date of the uprising, May 20, was, significantly, the same day a statewide Democratic convention was to be held in the city. On the appointed day Indianapolis bristled with soldiers. The convention hall was heavily guarded by soldiers with glistening steel bayonets in place. Several Democrats never reached the convention hall as they were arrested for carrying concealed weapons and hauled off to military jails.

Despite the armed soldiers about the hall, the Democratic convention went bravely and defiantly forward. Speaker after speaker, many obviously "Peace Democrats," attacked Morton and Lincoln for their usurpation of constitutional powers, but there was no mention of revolution or resort to arms. The soldiers, who had come expecting action, became bored and by late afternoon were openly baiting the speakers with cries of "Copperhead." Matters came to a head during a speech by Senator Thomas A. Hendricks. The soldiers took umbrage at something he said and started moving toward the speaker's rostrum with cocked rifles and fixed bayonets. Congressman Daniel Vorhees of Terre Haute, the meeting chairman, immediately adjourned the meeting and Democrats scrambled to get out of the hall.

What followed was part chaos, part comic opera. Soldiers harassed the fleeing conventioneers to Union Depot. As a waiting train began to pull out, a shot was fired and the troops were galvanized into action. Cavalrymen rode ahead, boarded the locomotive and stopped the train. Soldiers boarded the cars and began methodically searching each passenger, including the women, for weapons. A second train was halted behind the first and boarded by other troops and searched. Genuinely frightened, passengers surrendered their guns and knives—in all some 500 weapons, according to one account—while others opened the coach windows and hurled their weapons into the black waters of Pogue's Run which wound alongside the tracks.

This little *opéra-bouffe* provided more grist for the Republican propaganda mill. Overlooking the fact that a good Democrat visiting Indianapolis might well be armed in self-defense, Republicans gleefully displayed the collected weapons as evidence of Democratic disloyalty and treasonable plots.

In January the Republicans convened at Indianapolis and, in clear violation of the state constitution, nominated Morton for a second term. Morton, in his acceptance speech, set the campaign theme. He indicated that he regarded the Democratic party as synonymous with treason, denounced the actions of the "disloyal" legislature of 1863, condemned "peace at any price" Democrats and called for continued and vigorous prosecution of the war. Democrats postponed their convention from January to July 12 on the premise that they could exploit growing dissatisfaction with the war. Moderates dominated the convention, but a clutch of "Peace Democrats" and actually disloyal party members proved militant and vociferous and supported Lambdin P. Milligan, a Huntington lawyer, for the gubernatorial nomination. Milligan lost the nomination to Joseph E. McDonald, a Crawfordsville attorney and personal friend of Morton. The moderate party platform contained nothing revolutionary or subversive and concentrated most of its fire on Lincoln and Morton for suppression of liberty of speech and press.

In the campaign that followed, Republicans continued to stigmatize their Democratic opponents as disloyal and revived the stories of secret organizations plotting to undermine the war effort. The Indianapolis *Journal*, which had earlier urged all Democrats "with any semblance of patriotism left" to leave the party of "Copperheads," furnished further evidence of party disloyalty with an exposé on July 30 of the Sons of Liberty. More alarming was a story relayed to Morton by a secret agent of a new plot for an uprising in Indianapolis on August 16, 1864.

As reported by the agent, the plot was a revival of the earlier scheme to seize the government arsenal and release and arm the Confederate prisoners at Camp Morton. Early in the game, J. J. Bingham, editor of the Indianapolis *Sentinel* and chairman of the Democratic state central committee, got wind that something was up and, with the Democratic candidate for governor, saw that Harrison H. Dodd, a printer and leader of the Sons of Liberty, called off the scheme.

Morton may or may not have learned the plot was canceled or he may not have taken any of it seriously. In any event, it was not until four days after the proposed uprising that he acted. A Provost Guard under General Alvin P. Hovey raided Dodd's printing plant and found 400 navy revolvers and 135,000 rounds of ammunition. They also seized the Great Seal of the Sons of Liberty and a list of members which, to the great glee of Republicans, contained the names of many prominent Democrats. Dodd escaped, but when he attempted to slink back into the city two weeks later, he was arrested and charged with treason. When Dodd escaped from prison during his trial, Morton posted a $1,000 reward for his recapture and a military court found the Indianapolis printer guilty *in absentia* and sentenced him to hang. Ever suspicious Democrats charged the escape had been planned by Morton and carried out by his minions.

Close on the heels of the Dodd case there were new sensations. Virtually on the eve of the October state election military authorities announced the arrest of Dr. William A. Bowles, the alleged military head of the Sons of Liberty; Stephen Horsey, publisher of the Paoli *Eagle;* Milligan, the unsuccessful candidate for the gubernatorial nomination; Andrew Humphrey, a former legislator from Greene County; and Horace Heffren and Bingham of the *Sentinel.* Except for Heffren and Bingham, who were freed upon turning state's evidence, all were brought before a military commission and charged with treason. The arrests, coming just before election and including their state central chairman, were viewed by outraged Democrats as politically motivated.

The trials were conducted by a military commission in Indianapolis shortly before the November national election. Witnesses charged that the four defendants were part of a grand conspiracy to take over Indiana and forge it into a Northwest Confederacy. Bowles, Horsey and Milligan were found guilty and sentenced to be hanged. Humphrey was sentenced to hard labor for the duration of the war. The executions, scheduled for May 19, 1865, were postponed pending an appeal to the U. S. Supreme Court. In what has become one of the great bulwarks of American civil liberty, *ex parte* Milligan, the court decided April 3, 1866, that the trial by a military commission was illegal, since the civil courts were open and functioning. "Martial law," the court held, "cannot arise from a *threatened* invasion. The necessity must be actual and present; the invasion real, such as effectually closes the courts and deposes the civil administration."

As a result of the decision the four men were released. Although subject to trial in a civil court, no action was taken. There were even rumors abroad that Morton had helped the four men to obtain their freedom and there is some evidence that perhaps he did. Milligan later successfully sued the arresting officer, General Hovey, and the jury awarded him damages of $5.

The arrests and trials, however, had served their purpose. In October Morton was swept into office on the Republican-Union ticket by over 20,000 votes and the party won control of the legislature and captured eight of 11 Congressional seats. In November President Lincoln carried the state by a similar margin.

Chapter 13

DEATH OF
A PRESIDENT

INDIANAPOLIS WAS thrown into panic in July 1863 as John Hunt
Morgan and 2,500 Rebel cavalrymen crossed the Ohio River in captured
steamboats, made a lightning sweep through southern Indiana and headed
for the capital.

It was generally believed that Morgan planned to take the city, seize
the arsenal, free the prisoners at Camp Morton and blow up the city's
railroads and bridges. Troops were immediately alerted, stores closed,
and home guard units formed. Some of the banks sent away their specie.
University Square became a drill ground and an assembly point.

Within a matter of hours Morton had troops on the way to the front
and issued an appeal for men to defend the city. Within two days over
20,000 patriotic but untrained home guards, armed with an assortment
of weapons, were ready and eager to repel the raiders. The number
quickly swelled to 65,000. Morton dispatched Lew Wallace, home on
leave, to assist General Edward H. Hobson, already in hot pursuit of
the Rebels.

Morgan's lightning strike was losing some of its zing. Help from
Southern sympathizers in Indiana had failed to materialize and his too
few troops were getting out of control. Indiana's shops and stores,
crammed with merchandise, were proving too great an attraction and
Morgan's men had become more interested in pillaging and looting than
in military objectives. To add to his woes, Indiana troops and local
militia were rapidly closing in. About nine miles the other side of Sey-

mour he wheeled his horsemen eastward to Vernon and Versailles and crossed into Ohio after burning Whitewater Bridge behind him.

Elsewhere the war moved desperately forward. Lincoln found a new general-in-chief, the cigar-smoking, whiskey-drinking Ulysses S. Grant, a man who knew how to fight a meat-grinder kind of war, and he drove single-mindedly toward Richmond. The wholesale sacrifice of lives and the brutal hammer blows paid off: in April of 1865 the Indianapolis *Sentinel* and the *Journal* could report the capture of Richmond and the surrender of Lee and his tattered army at Appomattox Courthouse. Indianapolis and the nation celebrated far into the night with bonfires and illuminations, fireworks and cannon salutes.

The statistics of Indiana in the Civil War were impressive and chilling. Of all the free states, Indiana had given a higher percentage of men of military age, 74.3 percent, than any other except Delaware, with 74.8 percent. In numbers, nearly 200,000 men left home to march and fight in 129 infantry regiments, 13 cavalry regiments and three companies, one heavy-artillery regiment and 26 batteries of light artillery. Men from Indianapolis and Marion County served in 39 regiments. Many Indiana women served as volunteer nurses, some of them at the front. Among them were Catharine Merrill, Mrs. John Coburn, Bettie Bates, Mrs. Calvin Fletcher, Jr., Mrs. Jane Graydon and Mrs. J. L. Ketcham of Indianapolis. Indiana troops were involved in virtually every important battle of the war. Indiana men fought in the first battles of the war in the hills of West Virginia, 1861, and they fought in the last battle of the war, at Palmetto Ranch, Texas, May 13, 1865, a month after Appomattox. Death claimed 25,028 Hoosier men, including 17,758 who died of disease. In addition to the dead, there were untold thousands who came home maimed or suffering from war wounds or disease.

Shortly after receiving the news of Appomattox, Governor Morton proclaimed April 20 as a day of public thanksgiving and prayer, but the proposed celebration never took place. On the night of Good Friday, April 14, Abraham Lincoln was the victim of an assassin's bullet as he sat in a box at Ford's Theater in Washington.

Indianapolis read the news in black-bordered extras of the *Journal* and the *Sentinel*, and, in the words of a contemporary writer, "Never within the history of the city had such excitement existed." Many men and women openly sobbed. Others, stunned by the news, were grieved beyond words or tears. The loss, as in our times following the murders of President Kennedy, Senator Robert F. Kennedy and Martin Luther King, was incredible, shocking and personal. By noon the entire city was suffused with mourning. Stores and businesses closed for the day. Men and women aimlessly walked the almost silent streets and talked in hushed tones.

By midafternoon there were rumors of impending trouble. Grief in many cases had turned to angry resentment directed against those known to have opposed the war or reported to be Southern sympathizers. Morton, fearing attempts on lives and property, quietly moved soldiers to strategic points in the city.

Morton and Senator Thomas A. Hendricks headed the delegation from Indiana that attended the martyred President's funeral in the nation's capital. A former Indianapolis pastor, the Reverend Phineas Gurley, preached the funeral address. Now of the New York Avenue Church of Washington, D. C., the Reverend Gurley had served as pastor of the First Presbyterian Church of Indianapolis from 1840 to 1849, when the church was on the Circle. He had been present at Lincoln's deathbed as a friend of the family and Mrs. Lincoln's pastor. And he had agreed to accompany the Lincoln family on the long, sad journey to Springfield, where the President would be buried.

The funeral train of seven black cars festooned with mourning crepe left Washington on April 21, retracing the route Lincoln had taken on his way to his first inaugural. At three o'clock in the morning on April 30 the "black train" arrived in Richmond, Indiana, where it was met by Morton and Hendricks at the head of an official delegation that took charge of the train during its stay in the Hoosier state. It was cold and raining in Indianapolis when the train pulled into Union Depot. Thousands of wet and whispering people, many of whom had waited all night, met the seven black cars. In the half-light of a gray dawn the coffin was removed from its special armor-plated car to a waiting catafalque and borne through the city's black-draped streets to the statehouse, where all that was mortal of Abraham Lincoln would lie in state.

All day and into the night people filed into the statehouse in solemn lines, over 100,000 of them, to gaze for the last time on the former boy from Spencer County who had touched glory and saved a Union. They stood patiently in the cold and the wind and the rain waiting to enter the south door of the statehouse, their long lines sometimes extending several blocks up rainswept Washington Street. Distinguished visitors came from all parts of the state and from Ohio and Kentucky to pay their last respects and view the haggard face still discolored by the assassin's bullet. Among those who came was the venerable Colonel James Blake, for 40 years leader of the city's Sunday schools, who led a procession of 5,000 Sunday school children in white starched shirts and dresses.

Of the many thousands who gathered at the station to watch the funeral train pull out, only a few knew that the black train carried another and smaller coffin. Twelve-year-old Willie Lincoln, dead these past two years and kept in a Washington vault until the family returned to Springfield, was also going home.

Chapter 14

"CHANGE WAS OVER ALL"

MARCHING FROM Union Depot to be mustered out, Indiana soldiers moved through a transformed city. Old Indianapolis landmarks were gone—replaced by block-long warehouses, palatial stores, shops and banks. Horsecars plied the streets. New residences fanned out north and east from the city's center and hundreds more were going up, as well as new factories and business blocks.

To the south and west, clustered along the railroad tracks, were the city's new and expanding industries—pork-packing plants, cotton and woolen mills, foundries, glassworks, wagon shops, saw works, wheel works, paper mills, buggy and wagon shops and factories for pumps, starch, varnish, pianos and sewing machines. A new rolling mill, the city's second, turned out 18 iron wheels a day. The Woodburn "Sarvin Wheel" Company made the first wagon spokes by machinery west of the Alleghenies. Kingan & Company, Limited, was the world's largest packer of pork. Founded by two brothers from Belfast, Ireland, its sprawling plants on 15 acres of ground specialized in pork products prepared in the English style for export to the British Isles. The firm was the first to slaughter hogs in summer as the result of an "artificial cooling process" invented by George Stockman of Indianapolis. The primitive refrigeration system ended seasonal slumps and eliminated shutdowns in warm weather. Farmers could now drive their waddling lard hogs down Kentucky Avenue to the Kingan plant in July as well as in January, traditionally the peak month for slaughtering.

The city's tax list, set at $10,700,000 in 1860, had doubled by 1865, and ten million dollars more was added in 1870. City expenses were $854,391, ten times more than five years before. In the more normal year of 1870 expenses would be listed at $405,000. The city's streets, neglected and dirty, were being paved—nine miles in all, along with 18 miles of sidewalks. Gaslights were installed on three more miles of city streets.

Six national banks were operating, including the First National, founded in 1863 by William H. English and Associates—the first national bank to be established after passage of the National Currency Act in the same year. (Only two of the banks, the Merchants National Bank and the Indiana National, were destined to survive into our own times.) Folks called banker Volney Malott Indiana's "Ice King." He had gained control of the ice plants on northern Indiana lakes, and with the cooperation of the Indianapolis, Peru and Chicago Railroad, owned by his brother-in-law David Macy, he enjoyed virtual monopoly.

Behind the smoke and the noise, the crowded stores and shops, the horsecars and the smells were hard statistics to confirm the big change. Manufacturing investment, set at $647,650 in 1860, had risen to $8,420,614 in 1870; and the number of "hands" employed increased from 587 to 5,929. Both manufacturers and employees were part of the city's growing population: 48,244 in 1870 to compare with 18,611 in 1860.

But statistics did not reflect all the changes. J. H. Holliday in his *Indianapolis and the Civil War* perhaps best described the others:

The war had brought sorrow to many households and broken up many others. . . . Old friendships and social relations had been severed by death and by estrangement through differing opinions. The alteration in circumstances made a difference, for many large fortunes had been made and other families impoverished. There was more luxurious living and ostentation. . . . Both morality and religion were affected. Hundreds of young men had become addicted to intemperance and the general moral tone had been lowered. Extravagance had increased in many things and was driving out the former simplicity. Change was over all.

The changing city was reaching out everywhere, spilling over into Waterloo, Kinderhook, Cotton Town, Stringtown, Germantown. New suburbs were rising—Brightwood, Belmont, Haughville, Mt. Jackson and the fashionable Irvington and Woodruff Place.

Irvington, named for Washington Irving and incorporated in 1873, was a place of curving drives and beautiful homes planned and platted by Jacob B. Julian and Sylvester Johnson. Hogs were not permitted to run at large and lot owners agreed never to kill a bird within the town. Irvington was also the new home of Butler University. Woodruff Place was originally an 80-acre tract known as "Dark Wood" which James O. Woodruff of New York had purchased for $240,000 and turned into a residential park. In the 1870s it was resplendent with "$20,000 mansions," handsome drives, statuary and elegant fountains.

For contrast there were the first of the city's slums, and Bucktown, in and around Indiana Avenue, where the free Negro population was concentrated. To the west, in Plainfield, stood the new House of Refuge for Boys, and east of the National Road, the Reformatory School for Females. The Home for Friendless Women on Tennessee Street aimed to reform prostitutes and care for other "unhappy females." Neglected or abandoned children were bound out as apprentices or sent to the newly built Marion County Poor Farm. At the corner of Tennessee and Fifth Streets the Orphan's Home, operated by the Indianapolis Benevolent Society, cared for 35 children. Northwest of the city was the Indianapolis Home for Colored Children, new in 1870 and headed by William Hadley as president.

The city's schools, reopened during the war, were vastly improving under Professor A. C. Shortridge, who had resigned his post at North Western Christian University to accept the job of superintendent of schools. Two new school buildings were built, new teachers were hired and the high school was reorganized, with William A. Bell as principal. The high school was located in the former Second Presbyterian Church building on the Circle at Market Street and it opened with 28 students. Shortridge organized a training school for teachers and inaugurated a night school in 1867. Following the dedication of a new schoolhouse on the corner of Michigan and Blackford Streets, the old Fourth Ward schoolhouse on Market was assigned to colored children in anticipation of legislation providing for their education.

Indianapolis took special pride in its rejuvenated school system and, although normally sensitive about tax increases, gladly raised school taxes to 25¢ on $100 and 50¢ on each poll. Shortridge's salary was doubled, to $2,000, and the city's 39 teachers placed on a new salary scale, $400 to $625 per year. The high school principal's salary was set at $1,250. In 1870 the school system reported 4,734 pupils enrolled in 12 elementary schools in 9 districts—the populous fourth, fifth and sixth districts boasting two schools each.

Besides the public schools, Roman Catholics maintained six parochial schools, three for boys and three for girls; three German Protestant churches operated parochial schools; and two private German English schools were flourishing. A business college offered the longest title in town—The Indianapolis Practical Business, Military and Lecture College.

Readers could borrow books from four libraries, including the new Indianapolis Public Library, opened April 8, 1873, with Charles Evans as librarian, the city's first free library. Housed originally in the high

Indianapolis, when the capital came. One of four pictures painted by Thomas B. Glessing, an Indianapolis artist, representing scenes of the very early days of the capital. These pictures were purely fiction, as Glessing came to Indianapolis long after its founding.

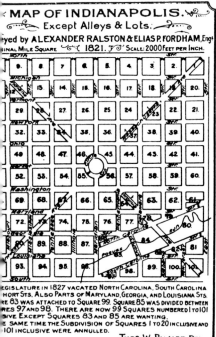

MAP OF INDIANAPOLIS.
Except Alleys & Lots.
eyed by ALEXANDER RALSTON & ELIAS P. FORDHAM, Engs
INAL MILE SQUARE 1821. Scale: 2000 Feet per Inch.

EGISLATURE IN 1827 VACATED NORTH CAROLINA, SOUTH CAROLINA
HORT STS. ALSO PARTS OF MARYLAND, GEORGIA, AND LOUISIANA STS.
RE 83 WAS ATTACHED TO SQUARE 99. SQUARE 85 WAS DIVIDED BETWEEN
RES 97 AND 98. THERE ARE NOW 99 SQUARES NUMBERED 1 TO 101
SIVE EXCEPT SQUARES 83 AND 85 ARE WANTING.
E SAME TIME THE SUBDIVISION OF SQUARES 1 TO 20 INCLUSIVE AND
101 INCLUSIVE WERE ANNULLED.

THOS. W. PALMER, DEL.

The original mile-square plan of Indianapolis.

Street Scenes

Pennsylvania Street north of Washington, 18

Washington and Delaware Streets, 1880.

West Market as seen from the Monument, 19

Washington and Illinois Streets, 1906.

Oliver P. Morton, Civil War governor.

Benjamin Harrison, 23rd President of the United States.

Kin Hubbard's famous Abe Martin of Brown County.

Four Indiana writers: front row (*l. to r.*), George Ade and Booth Tarkington; back row, James Whitcomb Riley and Meredith Nicholson.

Indianapolis, Transportation Capital

The world's largest traction terminal in the day when Indianapolis was the interurban capital of the world.

Start of the first 500-Mile Race at Indianapolis, 1911.

The Indianapolis 500 today.

The English Theater and Hotel
the Circle, 1948.

Clowes Memorial Hall, Butler U
versity, home of the Indianapo
Symphony Orchestra.

Monument Circle,
1970.

Mayor Richard G. Lugar greets President Nixon as the President's Urban Affairs Committee meets in Indianapolis.

The City-County Building houses the new consolidated city government.

Aerial view of Indianapolis, 1970.

school building, it was moved to the *Sentinel* building in 1875 and to its own building, the former Alvord block, at the corner of Pennsylvania and Ohio Streets, in 1880.

The Street Railway Company, whose rolling stock consisted of horse-cars (actually drawn by mules), was chartered in 1863 after a bitter fight between rival companies. The winning company, the Citizens Railway Company, was plagued by wartime shortages, but in June of 1864 Mayor John Caven proudly drove the first car down Illinois Street to Union Depot. Besides running north and south on Illinois, tracks also ran up and down Pennsylvania. Both streets connected to the main line that ran east and west on Washington Street. A single track turned at West Street and ran north to the old state-fair grounds on Morton Place, northwest of Nineteenth Street and Central Avenue.

Cars were originally drawn by a pair of horses or mules and manned by a driver and a conductor, but to cut expenses, single-horse cars were introduced and the conductor was eliminated. Fares were deposited in a glass box at the front of the car and it was the duty of the driver to see that the number of nickels and passengers came out even—and to watch for slugs and buttons. On Pennsylvania Street at St. Joseph there was a turntable for the cars, and in front of Charles Mayer's Washington Street store, a transfer car. At the Union Depot a large, deep tunnel was built under the tracks and a pair of mules were stationed at each end to assist in pulling the cars back up to street level.

Schedules were frequently upset by stray cows which found the tracks a convenient place to nap. An extra fare was charged for large wash baskets or big packages. Snow and ice presented special problems, as sometimes the cars slid off the icy tracks. Inside the cars straw was spread on the floor to keep passengers' feet warm and dry. Later the company furnished a small iron stove and coal scuttle, but it was up to the passengers to throw on the coal and keep the fire going.

The Indianapolis City Hospital, on the bank of Fall Creek at the end of Indiana Avenue, was unique as the only publicly supported hospital in the state at a time when most people regarded hospitals as "pest houses," a place of confinement only for those with infectious diseases. Built in 1859, the hospital had lain vacant and unused until the Civil War, when it was converted into a U. S. military hospital and placed in the charge of Dr. John M. Kitchen and Dr. P. H. Jameson. After the war Dr. Kitchen urged it be put to use for the citizens of Indianapolis, and the city council responded by appropriating funds to renovate and equip the building, and it opened as a charity institution in 1866 with a capacity of 75 patients with Dr. G. V. Woollen as superintendent.

Dr. Kitchen and Dr. John S. Bobbs of the Marion County Medical

Association organized the new Indiana Medical College, housed in a four-story building on Delaware Street on the west side of the Courthouse Square. Dr. Bobbs was the college's first president, and upon his death a bequest of $2,000 was used to establish a dispensary for city poor in the college building.

As befitted a growing city, a new 250-acre cemetery, Crown Hill, the site of the former Martin Williams farm, was dedicated in the spring of 1865 by former U. S. Senator Albert S. White. The Crown Hill Cemetery Association, founded in 1864 with James M. Ray as president, had bought the land for $51,500, and F. W. Chislett had laid it out. It already glistened with marble pillars and columns and some people vowed they would be buried nowhere else.

The firing of the cannon at the U. S. Arsenal each daybreak signaled Indianapolis households to be astir. Mail was delivered downtown four times daily. Real estate was booming. Over a million dollars in real estate transfers were recorded in 1860, but by 1870 they passed the five-million mark. A public bathhouse was opened downtown. Lamplighters made nightly rounds to light the gas lamps for business houses on Washington, Illinois and Meridian Streets.

Music and art were gaining new appreciation. The Choral Union, formed in 1870, and its friendly rival, the Harmonic Society, presented opera, cantatas, "grand concerts" and glees. The Matinee Musicale, founded by Mrs. A. G. Cox, held May festivals and brought great musical artists to Indianapolis.

A group of Indianapolis artists set up an informal studio in an upper story of the statehouse. Among them were Jacob Cox, dean of local artists, John W. Love, who liked to experiment with new forms, B. S. Hayes, unsurpassed in his painting of animals, and William Merritt Chase, student of Hayes, son of a shoe-store proprietor and destined for fame. Gookins, an early Cox student, and Love opened the Love-Gookins art school in 11 rooms of the upper story of a building at the corner of Pennsylvania and Court Streets. Nearly 50 students enrolled, including T. C. Steele, J. Ottis Adams, August Metzner, Samuel Richards and William Forsyth, all of whom would later form the Hoosier Colony at the Royal Academy in Munich. Steele would achieve lasting fame in his native Indiana and Forsyth would win national recognition.

The theater was in good health in a changing climate. Valentine Butsch, who had made a fortune with his Metropolitan during the war, bought the unfinished Miller block, finished it and in the fall of 1868 opened a 2,500-seat theater, the Academy of Music. Among its early attractions was the famous actor Joseph Jefferson in his hit play, *Rip Van Winkle*. Butsch leased the Metropolitan and it continued as the city's second-largest theater, presenting touring minstrels, variety shows and stock melodramas.

The Indiana State Fair went to Fort Wayne in 1865 and played Terre Haute in 1867, its last appearance out of Indianapolis. Tragedy struck at the 1869 fair. An overheated boiler in a steam engine exploded into a dense crowd, killing or wounding nearly a hundred persons. A shocked city raised funds to help the injured and furnish aid to families of the dead.

Honors came to the brilliant Catharine Merrill, thirty-one years old, a teacher and the daughter of Colonel Samuel Merrill, the bookseller. At the behest of Governor Morton she had written a two-volume record, *The Indiana Soldier in the War of the Union,* to supplement the detailed reports of Adjutant General Terrell. In 1869 she was named to the Demia Butler Chair as professor of literature at North Western Christian University (Butler) and became the second woman in the nation to attain a college professorship.

Other women were in the news—the members of the Women's Rights Association, who were crusading for the right to vote, a campaign given new impetus with the enfranchisement of Negroes. Among the leading suffragists was Miss May Wright Sewall of Indianapolis, cultural, social and reform leader, head of the Classical School for Girls, a community leader in Indianapolis for 40 years. She was active in the Rights Association and was a charter member of the Indianapolis Suffrage Society founded by Captain and Mrs. Horace McKay and Miss Laura Doonan in 1872.

National speakers in the suffrage movement came to Indianapolis to spread the doctrine of equal rights—Susan B. Anthony, Elizabeth Cady Stanton, Belva Lockwood, Harriet Beecher Stowe, Julia Ward Howe and Mrs. David (Zerelda) Wallace, mother of Lew Wallace, president of the Equal Suffrage Society and vice-president of the National Woman Suffrage Committee. Bills giving the vote to women were introduced in the legislature with great regularity, and were treated favorably, but they never managed to pass.

Dozens of women's clubs sprang up in the city following the formation of the Indianapolis Woman's Club, a "literary club," at the home of Mrs. Martha Nicholson McKay. Its incorporators included Miss Sewall, Margaret Chislett, Harriet M. Foster, Helen B. Holman, Elizabeth V. Pierce, Carrie F. Milligan and Mary N. Walcott. The Young Women's Christian Association was organized as an auxiliary of the Y.M.C.A. Its objectives were to secure homes and employment for friendless women and to visit and care for the sick.

Indianapolis women were active in revived and expanded postwar temperance movements, among them the Ladies' White Ribbon Clubs and the Women's Christian Temperance Association. Some of the ladies personally called on the city's saloonkeepers, asking them to sign pledges promising to cease their evil business. For those who refused, the

women offered prayers—sometimes kneeling in the sawdust of the bar-
room floor.

Although the legislature failed to enact prohibition, it passed the
"Baxter Law" in 1873, which provided that an application to sell liquor
must be accompanied by a petition bearing the signatures of a majority
of the voters in the ward or township. In addition, the applicant had to
post a $3,000 bond, and both saloonkeeper and building owner were
liable for any injury to customers resulting from the sale of intoxicants.
The law drew a storm of protest, particularly from the city's Germans,
and in 1875 the legislature gave the county commissioners sole authority
to license liquor dealers.

Begrimed wage earners who had worked ten or 12 hours a day, six days
a week, for two or three dollars a day were now joining unions and working for increased pay, sick benefits and the eight-hour day. Indianapolis
was a headquarters for many unions, while others, including the rising
Knights of Labor, maintained their largest and strongest locals in the
city. Among the unions were the Indianapolis Typographical Union,
established in 1852, those of the blacksmiths and machinists, cigarmakers,
shoemakers, iron molders and puddlers, tin and coppersmiths, coach
makers, stone cutters, bricklayers, sheet-iron workers and coopers. There
were also locals of the Brotherhood of Locomotive Engineers and there
was talk of forming a brotherhood of firemen.

The unions were organized along craft lines and were often fiercely
independent of each other. They also lacked the membership, money
or muscle to win the dozens of strikes called during and after the war.
Employers broke most strikes by importing strikebreakers or resorting
to friendly courts.

One of the city's early labor leaders was John Fehrenbatch, a member
of the Machinists' and Blacksmiths' Union and their international president in 1870. Fehrenbatch campaigned for the eight-hour day, and following the Workingman's Convention in Indianapolis in 1865, which
he was instrumental in staging, Eight-Hour Leagues were formed all
over the state. The movement gained sufficient momentum to become
a political issue, and both parties supported the shorter day in their
campaign platforms of 1866. But the bills proposing the eight-hour day
died in legislative committee, the graveyard of labor proposals.

The affinity of the Irish for politics was reflected in city elections of
the 1860s and 1870s. An Irishman and Republican, John Caven, won the
office of mayor in 1863 and 1865. Caven was a native of Pennsylvania, the
son of immigrant parents, self-educated, a resident of the city since 1845
and a member of the law firm of Smith and Yandes. He was probably
the most popular and most beloved of all the city's mayors and he served

more terms than any other, five in all, winning reelection in 1875 and for two additional terms. While he was out of office, the voters elected another Irishman and Republican for two terms, General Dan McCauley, a bookbinder and Civil War hero. McCauley was succeeded by yet another Irishman, Thomas Mitchell, the first Democrat to win the mayoralty after the Civil War. Mitchell was a native of Kentucky and a well-known attorney who later would become the Marion County prosecutor.

The city's Irish helped provide a footnote to U. S. history: the abortive attempt of the Fenian Brotherhood to seize Canada as part of an overall plan to help Ireland regain its independence from Great Britain. A large sum of money was subscribed by one of the two rival Fenian lodges in Indianapolis and 150 men were armed and equipped under the command of Captain James Haggerty. The men marched off in May 1866 and, with a few hundred other Fenians, invaded Canada from Buffalo, New York. The Fenian troops were routed in an engagement at Lake Erie, and the Grant administration rushed General Meade to Canada and ordered the arrest of all who had taken part.

Among the new business ventures launched in the 1870s was one that was destined to play a major role in the city's history—the small pharmaceutical company of Colonel Eli Lilly at 15 West Street, opened May 10, 1876, with a staff of three, including the colonel's fourteen-year-old son, Josiah. The firm had $1,400 in cash assets and the good will of August Kiefer, a wholesale druggist who had promised to buy Lilly's products and introduce him to other potential customers. Colonel Lilly had learned the trade of a pharmaceutical chemist and at twenty-two years of age had opened his own drugstore, which he promptly closed a few months later to answer Lincoln's call for volunteers. He had served with distinction and, as commander of the Eighteenth Artillery, was credited with firing the first shell on the advancing army of General Bragg at Chickamauga.

The little firm prospered from the beginning. Within two years it was moved to larger quarters on Meridian Street, and Josiah, as general superintendent, directed the work of 30 hands. Ten years later the firm occupied a three-story building on McCarty Street, employed 100 hands and "traveled" 12 salesmen.

On Washington Street, Lyman S. Ayres took over the management of the "One-Price, Systematic, Wide-Awake" Trade Palace of R. N. Smith & Company then housed at 28 Washington Street. It was the city's largest dry goods store in 1872, and the changeover marked the beginning of the famous L. S. Ayres Department Store—in the 1970s a giant merchandising chain with two major department stores in Indianapolis, others throughout the state and a rapidly multiplying chain of Ayr-Way Discount Department Stores.

As the city entered the 1870s, newsboys hawked five daily newspapers on street corners: the *Journal*, the *Sentinel*, the *Daily Commercial*, the German-language *Daily Telegraph* (launched by the *Freie Presse*) and the city's first successful afternoon newspaper, the *Indianapolis Evening News*, which marked its one hundredth birthday in 1969.

The *News* was the brainchild of John H. Holliday, a twenty-three-year-old reporter on the *Sentinel*. Although every attempt to launch an afternoon paper had ended in failure, the ambitious Holliday believed the time was ripe for a good two-cent evening newspaper. He confided his plans to Richard J. Bright, the *Sentinel* publisher, who apparently had no fear of the new paper encroaching on his morning territory. Bright offered Holliday editorial space in the *Sentinel* building and agreed to print the new paper on the *Sentinel* presses.

The success of the well-edited *News* caused the newly launched *Daily Mirror* to fold, but it was later revived and consolidated with the weekly *Town Talk*, which became the city's first weekly literary paper. Nine other weeklies were also published in the city, among them three in German, the *Journal of Commerce* and a Sunday school paper, *The Little Sower*. Of the 14 monthlies published in Indianapolis, two were musical papers, *Benham's Musical Review* and *Willard's Musical Visitor*.

Murder and murder trials occupied many of the newspaper headlines. Among the most sensational was the trial of Nancy E. Clem, her brother, Silas W. Hartman, and William J. Abrams for the murder of Jacob Young and his wife. The Youngs were found dead of gunshot wounds on the bank of White River near Cold Springs. Investigation revealed mysterious money transactions between Mrs. Clem and Young and the arrests followed. Mrs. Clem was tried and sentenced to life imprisonment, her brother committed suicide in jail, and Abrams served a penitentiary term. Mrs. Clem, however, secured a series of new trials and kept the case in the courts for years.

The first hangings in the city took place in 1879, the dubious honors going to John Achey, who had killed his gambling partner, and William Merrick, convicted for the death of a young schoolteacher. Merrick was charged with seducing and marrying the teacher, taking her buggy riding after the marriage and compelling her to drink a poisoned liquor. Merrick drove the dead teacher and her newborn baby several miles, then buried both under a pile of logs.

There was also the unfolding story of the Reno Gang, four brothers from Rockford and their ruthless band of robbers and cutthroats who were credited with being the first men ever to rob a train. In a pattern to be followed in endless dime novels and Western movies, the gang boarded an Ohio and Mississippi train at the Seymour station on October 6, 1866, made their way to the express car, smashed down the door, emptied a small safe of some $16,000 and, as the train reached a prearranged spot where the rest of the gang were waiting, shoved the big safe out the open door. Before the gang could manage to open the safe, however, a hard-riding posse galloped into view and the gang fled.

A second robbery followed, in December 1867; then the desperadoes struck out for new territory, appearing a few weeks later in Iowa, where in two quick and carefully planned raids they got off with nearly $26,000 taken at gunpoint from two county treasurers. A month later, after being captured and escaping, the gang pulled its biggest and most daring robbery—the famous Marshfield train robbery on May 12, 1868, which netted the gang $90,000.

The robbery created a national sensation. Pinkerton men were assigned en masse to the case, and a railroad engineer's tip led to the eventual capture and vigilante hanging of six members of the gang.

Meanwhile, the hunt continued for the three Reno brothers and a Charles Anderson. Simeon and William Reno were captured in Indianapolis, Frank Reno and Anderson in Canada. All four were eventually locked in separate cells on the second floor of the New Albany jail. But their cases, like the others, ended not in court but at the end of a vigilante's rope.

The issue of reconstruction dominated Indiana politics, and Oliver P. Morton, his wartime actions vindicated by the 1865 Republican legislature, continued to dominate the state and his party. Following the legislative session, he had been stricken with paralysis from the waist down, but the crippling blow in no way diminished his ability to wield absolute power.

Morton, for the second time in his career, made a political about-face. Following Lincoln's death, he had embraced the moderate views of President Andrew Johnson and opposed Negro suffrage, but it was not long before he joined the Radical Republicans and became a passionate supporter of Negro suffrage. Named to the U. S. Senate in 1867, he joined the group of Radical Reconstructionists who produced one of American history's most tragic eras.

After joining the Radicals, Morton directed much of his invective against President Johnson and was blamed for being the force behind the shameful treatment of the President in Indianapolis in September 1866.

Johnson had come to the capital city as a part of a planned speaking tour designed to win friends for his alleged "soft" policy toward the South, to explain his veto of the Fourteenth Amendment and to urge the election of congressmen who would support his views.

Johnson's tour had gone badly in some cities and Indianapolis was

no exception. For days before his visit Republican leaders, led by the
Indianapolis *Daily Journal*, fed anti-Johnson feeling. Johnson's day in
the city started with an insult. Although greeted by a brass band and a
small but friendly escort to the Bates House, there was no official welcoming committee; Morton was conveniently out of town and Indianapolis city officials pointedly stayed away. By nightfall a hostile crowd
had gathered around the hotel and when Johnson appeared on the
balcony and started his speech he was greeted with groans and hisses. In
other cities Johnson had responded to similar treatment with "give 'em
hell" speeches, but now he angrily turned on his heel and retired from
the balcony.

A riot between pro- and anti-Johnson elements broke out as pro-
Johnson Democrats attempted to organize a torchlight parade. Shots
were fired, several men were wounded and one man, later identified as
a Republican, was killed. It required troops and the entire Indianapolis
police force to bring order finally and clear the streets. The next morning an Indianapolis newspaper charged that the riot had been "carefully
staged" by Radical Republicans and that "rumors of a disturbance had
been rife throughout the day."

Not unexpectedly, the Republicans won the 1866 election. The state
ticket was elected by 14,000 votes; the party won both houses of the
legislature and eight of the state's 11 Congressional seats. Morton could
take much of the credit for the victory. In his role as "The Soldiers'
Friend," he had met all homecoming troops with speeches and ceremonies, organized a statewide veterans' rally at Indianapolis and taken a
major role in the organizing of the Grand Army of the Republic, a Union
veterans organization designed to obtain benefits for returning soldiers
and the widows and orphans of the Union dead.

The G.A.R. was formally organized as a national organization in Decatur, Illinois, in April 1866, but its taproot was in Indianapolis. As early
as 1865 a G.A.R. post had been established in the city, purportedly the
first full-fledged post in the U. S., with Morton and General Robert S.
Foster as its moving spirits. Morton and Foster attended the Decatur
meeting and were instrumental in bringing the first national G.A.R. encampment to Indianapolis, in November 1866. For two days the flag-
bedecked city echoed to the sounds of military bands, parading soldiers
and patriotic oratory. Morton was everywhere on his crutches and in his
wheelchair. From the encampment came a long list of G.A.R. demands,
from soldier preference in federal appointments to lavish pension raids on
the U. S. Treasury.

The ex-soldier vote was cultivated by both parties in the 1868 state and
national elections in which racism, reconstruction and Negro suffrage,

the Fifteenth Amendment, played a major role. Republicans specialized in bloody-shirt slogans such as "Vote as you shot," "Scratch a Democrat, find a Rebel," and "The party that saved a nation, should rule it." Democrats who played up white supremacy and the dangers inherent in the Negro vote organized veterans into "The White Boys in Blue" and Republicans came up with "Fighting Boys in Blue."

The Democrats again nominated U. S. Senator Thomas A. Hendricks for governor and the Republicans named Conrad Baker, who had succeeded to the governorship after Morton's appointment to the U. S. Senate. Baker had been a colonel in the First Indiana Cavalry at the outbreak of the war, but in 1864 had been ordered to Indianapolis by the Secretary of War, where he served as assistant provost marshal for Indiana and superintendent of volunteer recruiting. The 1868 campaign repeated earlier campaigns, with the Republicans charging the Democrats with treason and the Democrats emphasizing white supremacy. Democrats opposed the right of the federal government to interfere with suffrage in the states and declared the Negro vote would serve to perpetuate the Radical hold on the nation. Republicans countered by pointing out their platforms declared that in the "loyal states" the matter of determining who should vote belonged to the states.

Each party charged the other with plans to steal the election, and when Baker won in October by 961 votes, Democratic cries of "fraud" were heard all over the state. Republicans also won control of both houses of the legislature and took seven of 11 Congressional seats. In November Ulysses S. Grant was elected President by over 9,000 votes and Indiana had its first Vice-President, Schuyler Colfax, a former South Bend newspaper publisher and leader of the Radicals in Congress.

There was high drama in the 1869 legislature and a new demonstration of the powers of Oliver P. Morton. One of the leaders in obtaining passage of the Fifteenth Amendment, Morton was determined to see to it that the amendment would be ratified by the states, particularly his native Indiana. But Democratic members of the legislature resigned en masse to halt its ratification, preventing a quorum. Governor Baker promptly called for a special election and the resigned Democrats were renominated and reelected.

Called into a special legislative session, the Democrats again resigned—this time confident that ratification was doomed. But Oliver P. Morton, who had arrived on the early-morning train, sent word to the Republican leaders to declare a recess and to meet with him at once. At the meeting Morton explained that, in point of law, a quorum meant two-thirds of the members who were in the house, and therefore those remaining comprised the legislature and represented a quorum. The legislature reconvened, Morton saw to it that the doors were locked, and while he looked on, grim and determined, Indiana ratified the Fifteenth Amendment. There was, of course, an immediate outcry from the Democrats and some Republicans that the action was illegal, but the vote was certified in Washington, and Indiana was counted among the states ratifying the critical amendment.

Chapter 15

GREENBACKS AND BREAD

THE POSTWAR BOOM in Indianapolis and the nation exploded in September 1873, touched off by the stunning news of the failure of the New York banking house of Jay Cooke & Company. The failure set off a chain reaction in a nation overextended in wild speculation in mining, manufacturing, railroading and grain farming. Large and small businesses went down like falling dominoes, nearly 1,000 in Indiana from 1873 to 1876 with a value of over 14 million dollars. History called it the Panic of 1873, a cruel depression that lasted for nearly a decade and brought unemployment, riots, strikes, new political parties and new alignments.

Indianapolis, as a rising industrial power, felt the impact of the Panic almost at once. Some banks closed their doors and those that remained open placed limits on the amount they would pay out. A number of firms, some marginal operations, others presumably solid, went bankrupt. Others followed as banks called in notes or mortgages. Money became scarce. The city, without operating funds during the initial banking crisis, paid its employees in warrants. Some factories paid workers in scrip; others, partly in notes, partly in cash. The pork-packing plants, usually busy in cold weather, slashed payrolls and announced they would not take on any more hands. Manufacturers held a series of meetings and decided against taking concerted action to cut payrolls or reduce wages, but individual firms could and did. Workingmen responded by striking, but the strikes were of short duration. It was better to work for lower wages than to lose their jobs to strikebreakers and go hungry.

Unemployed and hungry men walked Indianapolis streets looking for work. Union meetings and workingmen's meetings called for a program of public works to furnish jobs and alleviate the suffering. The city, county and state responded by taking on men to work on the streets and roads. The city council, on the plea of the city's charitable organizations, appropriated $2,000 for direct relief, but refused to appoint a relief commissioner to administer the funds. The measure was passed over strong opposition. The *Journal* characterized direct relief as "wrong in principle" and "demoralizing in practice"—original phrases then.

Farmers were particularly hard hit. Their depression had started in 1865, with the end of the Civil War. Farm prices had immediately plummeted; hog prices, tied to corn quotations, slipped to new lows. The National Grange of the Patrons of Husbandry, originally a social and educational organization with Masonic-like rituals and degrees, became a new political influence, a social and economic force. To fight monopolistic farm machinery manufacturers, the Grange began cooperative purchasing. It fought for lowered railroad rates and regulation of the railroads, and denounced high interest rates, the cost of government, corruption, special favors to railroads and monetary reform. The Grange grew in power and influence. In 1874, two years after formation of the first Indiana Grange, the Patrons of Husbandry were organized into 3,000 locals with 60,000 members.

As conditions worsened, farmers, wage earners and businessmen became convinced that the solution was the printing of greenbacks, as opposed to the policy of redeeming the depreciating Civil War paper currency in gold. Greenbackers, as they were called, advocated a generous printing of money to be supported by bonds deposited in the U. S. Treasury. "Hard money" men such as William H. English, president of Indianapolis' First National Bank, argued that no nation could prosper unless its currency was backed by gold, but "soft money" or "cheap money" men countered that such a currency was inadequate to meet the needs of an expanding nation or develop the wealth of the country.

Leaders of the Indiana Greenback movement were Ezra O. Olleman, popularly known as E.O., the strong-willed and "hotheaded" editor and publisher of the Grange's official voice, the *Indiana Farmer* (formerly the *North Western Farmer*), and James Buchanan, an attorney and editor and publisher of a new Greenback weekly, the *Indianapolis Sun*. Olleman, among the first actively to expound Greenbackism in Indiana, was a self-educated man and an avid reader, an unsuccessful politician and a farmer.

Olleman and Buchanan, and to some extent Buchanan's brother, Thomas, were prime movers behind a series of mass meetings at Masonic Hall attended by workers, farmers and businessmen urging currency reform. Thomas D. Kingan, president of the world's largest pork-packing plant, presided at the final key sessions out of which grew a series of resolutions called the "Indiana Plan," later to be incorporated in the platform of the Greenback party. Although patterned after ideas originally offered by Olleman, the resolutions which comprised the plan were introduced by Buchanan and generally credited to him. The plan blamed the 1873 panic on "insufficient money" and declared it was the duty of Congress, not the banks, to furnish an adequate currency that "could be increased or diminished as business necessities required." Special government bonds paying three percent interest could be deposited in the U. S. Treasury and exchanged for legal tender notes. Accrued interest on the bonds would go to the government, but the owner could redeem the bonds at any time in legal tender notes. Banks and hard money men immediately opposed the plan on the grounds it was "inflationary" and "dangerous." The Indiana *Sentinel* found the plan reeking of "financial heresy," but workingmen and their unions endorsed the plan at a mass meeting in Indianapolis.

Meanwhile, President Grant vetoed a measure passed by Congress which would have expanded paper currency from $382 million to $400 million. The veto had an immediate reaction in Indiana. The Greenbackers met in a "Tenth of June Convention" in 1874 at Indianapolis and formed a third party, the Independent party. The convention marked the beginning of the national Greenback party and, in a sense, the Populist party, which would grow out of the Greenback movement. In August the new party held its state convention in Indianapolis and nominated a full slate of candidates for Congress and state offices. The convention, which often resembled a revival meeting, approved the Indiana Plan; denounced monopolies in transportation, manufacturing, commerce and grain; called for lowered taxes, reduced government spending, and a revision of real estate assessments; and endorsed the temperance movement.

Although the Democrats won the October state election, beating the Republicans by 17,000 votes, eight of the 13 new Democratic Congressmen were avowed Greenback men. Democrats controlled the state House of Representatives and could name the new U. S. Senator in a joint session, but the Independents, with five Senate seats and eight in the House, would hold a balance of power on close votes.

Exultant over their showing, Olleman and the Buchanan brothers called for a convention to be held in Indianapolis on November 25, 1874, to form a national third party. The convention served as a prelude to a meeting in Cleveland on March 11, 1875, where the National Independent Greenback party was formed, with Olleman as chairman of the executive committee and Thomas Buchanan secretary. Buchanan's *Sun* also became the official party organ. The state convention of the Indiana Greenback party met in Indianapolis in February 1876 and nominated former Congressman Franklin Landers, a Democratic maverick, for governor and Anson Wolcott, a former Republican, for lieutenant governor.

In May the first Presidential convention of the Independent National Greenback party was held in Indianapolis. Between 300 and 500 attended and the *Journal* reported the crowd as "neither large nor enthusiastic but it embraced some earnest and intelligent men as well as some of a different sort." For President the party nominated Peter Cooper of New York, an inventor, manufacturer and philanthropist. Olleman emerged from the convention as a member of the executive committee. Buchanan retained his post as secretary.

National attention was now focused on Indianapolis and Indiana. The conventions, the proliferation of Greenback Clubs, and the speeches of Olleman and the editorials of Buchanan—all these promised much for the new party. Nineteenth-century political experts agreed that the success or failure of the party now depended upon what happened in its birthplace.

From the beginning, the Greenback party was torn between combining with one or the other of the established major parties or standing on its own as an independent party. Although warned by one of its leaders, Judge Henry W. Harrington, to "make no combinations with disaffected members of either of the old political parties, or else you have gone by the board," it apparently couldn't resist the Democrats. Even before the Greenbackers' state convention there were charges by the Indianapolis *Journal* of a "corrupt bargain" struck by leaders of the Independents and the Democrats. The newspaper alleged that Landers was to obtain both the Independent and Democratic nominations "at the right price" and that the Independent convention would be stage-managed by Democrats.

Landers, the candidate of the Independent party, did try to obtain the Democratic nomination at the party's state convention, but was defeated by John D. "Blue Jeans" Williams in a three-way race. He then resigned as the Independent candidate, and party leaders hastily chose Anson Wolcott, candidate for lieutenant governor, as his successor. Landers' resignation brought a renewal of charges of "collusion," "sell-out" and "deals" and created more turmoil and confusion within a party already the target for ridicule and abuse.

There were still more breakers ahead for the Greenbackers. Six days before the October 10 election, Wolcott submitted his resignation as candidate for governor. In a letter of resignation to Olleman he stoutly maintained his support of Greenback principles, but declared it was futile to campaign when so many voters remained loyal to the old parties.

Olleman withheld the letter from Greenback party leaders, but the Republican *Journal* gleefully printed its text the next day and revived new charges that there had been a "sell-out." Buchanan and other party leaders called a rump meeting of the state committee and selected Judge Henry W. Harrington as Wolcott's successor.

The Republican nominee for governor, Godlove S. Orth, withdrew early in the campaign, and his successor was Benjamin Harrison, forty-three years old, a Civil War brigadier general, former Supreme Court reporter, grandson of William Henry Harrison, and a successful Indianapolis lawyer specializing in railroad litigation. Harrison was branded the "kid glove candidate" in retaliation for Republican jibes directed at Williams' rural clothes and manners.

The election results were divided between the major parties. Williams won the governorship by 5,000 votes, but Republicans garnered nine of the 13 Congressional seats and control of the state House of Representatives. In the state Senate, Democrats counted 25 votes, Republicans 24 and Greenbacks one. As for the Greenback party, the election was a fiasco. They polled fewer than 13,000 votes. In November their Presidential candidate failed to poll 10,000 votes.

In September of 1875, John Caven, the mayor of Indianapolis, went out walking. His walk took him along the old abandoned west embankment of the White River, and from the Vandalia Road he pushed his way through weeds higher than his head and waded across a shallow place in the river which proved deeper than he had guessed. He sat down on the east bank and waited for the sun to dry his clothes. As he looked around, studying the landscape, he was struck with an idea. At home that night in his bachelor's quarters, he put the concept down on paper and added it to a plan he was developing for a Greater Indianapolis.

In July 1876 he presented to the city council his master plan to attract new industries and provide jobs for the city's unemployed. Central to Caven's highly imaginative and practical plan was a belt line railroad and stockyards. The belt line would connect with all rail lines entering the city, encircle Indianapolis, and, in Caven's view, serve as an attraction to new industries. Within two years 14 miles of single or double track were running three-fourths of the way around the city. Coincident with the construction of the belt line, the Indianapolis stockyards started operations on November 12, 1877, two miles southwest of the city. The stockyards became one of the largest in the nation, and in its first 20 years hog sales alone averaged over a million a year.

Caven also faced another kind of railroad problem during his last three terms in office, a wave of railroad strikes that engulfed the state. The most serious of the strikes occurred in 1877 and paralyzed all transportation throughout Indiana except for mail cars. Caven, whom the workingmen regarded as a friend, personally visited the Union Depot where huge crowds were gathered and met with union leaders. He exacted a promise that there would be no trouble and, on the suggestion of union heads, closed all the city's saloons. Caven joined with Governor Williams in refusing to call for troops and incurred the wrath of many of the city and state newspapers and railroad owners. Fifteen of the strikers were arrested and brought before a federal district court charged with contempt. Mayor Caven personally testified in behalf of one of the men and the man was acquitted. The other fourteen served jail sentences of three months.

In June of the same years Indianapolis was threatened with a bread riot. Hundreds of unemployed and hungry men assembled on the statehouse lawn. Mayor Caven hurried to the scene, and, as he told the story later:

I requested those who were willing to pledge themselves to preserve the peace and obey my orders in putting down any disturbance to hold up the right hand, and every hand went up. There were men there who, together with their families, had not tasted food for two days, and I told them they should not go to bed hungry that night, and invited the crowd to go with me, and we first went over to Simpson's bakery, south from the State House. He happened to have a large quantity of bread on hand. I commenced handing out six loaves to each one as the hungry crowd passed by, and the supply was soon gone. We then went to Taggart's, on South Meridian, but could not obtain admission, and from there to Bryce's bakery, on South Street, the hungry crowd following. Mr. Bryce was in bed, but got up when I told him what I wanted and directed the crowd to pass the door. Mr. Bryce handed me the loaves, and I handed them to the men, giving six to each; but as the pile became smaller, we reduced the number to five, and then to four and three, and then to two, and I invited those who only received two and three to wait, and if we could give them more we would; and they came again and we gave them all the bread in the bakery and succeeded in supplying them all. . . . I told the men to go to the Beatty Farm in the morning and they would find work. About 2 P.M. the next day I went there and about three hundred men were at work, many of them the hungry men from the night before . . . and it seemed as if the Belt Road [then under construction] . . . had thus providentially come to the rescue.

Chapter 16

OH, THOSE GOLDEN
YEARS

OLDER RESIDENTS of Indianapolis, looking back on the 1880s and 1890s, called them the "golden years" and said Indianapolis was the best of all places to be. To Claude Bowers, an author and political leader, the period was the "city's springtime." Recalling his Indianapolis boyhood, Bowers described the city as a place where people lived "normal lives," where there was no "pushing or shoving" and men found time in the evening "to read the *News* and to stroll across velvety lawns to their neighbors' to exchange views of what they read."

A new city had been built since the Panic of 1873, glossy, shiny as a new tintype and charming as an old picture book. Handsome new brick and stone buildings were everywhere—like the Lombard, Windsor, Majestic, Fitzgerald, Thorpe, Stevenson, Ingalls and the Indiana Trust buildings—and the new club buildings, the Propylaeum, the Y.M.C.A., the Commercial Club and Das Deutsche Haus. Residents and visitors sang the praises of the city's fine hotels, elegant restaurants and celebrated bars—the new 500-room Denison with indoor plumbing, the Grand, the English, the Spencer, the Normandie, the remodeled Bates House, Shaffer's Restaurant (the "Delmonico's of the West") and the Circle Park with its gold-leafed ceiling. Even the Circle, so long neglected and scraggly, was neatly landscaped, its grass and graveled walks dominated by Franklin Simmons' statue of Oliver P. Morton, dead since 1877.

On Washington Street was the new Marion County Courthouse,

completed in 1876, a three-story Renaissance-style stone building with a mansard roof, a 97-foot tower and clock, and two 28-foot-high pavilions at each end. There was much disagreement over its esthetics, some saying the front had too much "gingerbread," others criticizing its "bewildering array of colors in the halls."

Reaching out from the Circle were the fashionable streets—Meridian, Delaware, Pennsylvania—where the rich and the famous lived, in mansions set far back from the street behind iron fences, well-trimmed lawns and gardens guarded by that nineteenth-century status symbol, an iron deer. On other streets were the brick and frame houses of businessmen and other upper-middle-income families—spacious homes with cupolas, jigsaw scrollwork and wide porches, shaded lawns, neatly trimmed hedges, white picket fences, and stables out back. On still other streets were row upon row of small and boxlike workingmen's cottages of frame and clapboard, roses climbing over the front porch.

Side by side with older and remodeled stores, new retailers filled their windows with new products, gadgets and fashions: H. P. Wasson, Baldwin & Miller, Sloan's Drug Store, Kahn Tailoring, George J. Marott's Shoe Store, and the new When Department Store, John T. Brush, proprietor, which gave every boy a baseball and bat with the purchase of a suit and paid railway fares of customers up to 100 miles away. Charles Mayer's emporium and the expanding L. S. Ayres featured "cash railway systems" that sped your money across the store on wires and sped back with your change. Among the several city bookstores was the third-largest in the nation, the firm of Bowen-Merrill Company on Washington Street, under the management of William C. Bobbs, John J. Curtis and William Elvin. The new firm, which traced its beginning back to Samuel Merrill's little bookshop in 1838, represented a consolidation of the Bowen-Stewart house and Merrill, Meigs and Company in 1888.

Although a part of Indianapolis was fashionable and sophisticated and another sinful and gaudy, for most people Indianapolis was a large country town where "everybody knew everybody else." The country town atmosphere was most in evidence on Saturday nights, when stores stayed open and the farmers came to town. The brightly lighted streets were jammed with horses and wagons; the sidewalks thronged with families, buying, visiting, gossiping, while a band played from the balcony of the When Store.

But the city was also a metropolis of some 20 square miles with 35,000 homes, businesses and factories, 175 churches, 500 grocery stores, a city budget nudging the million-dollar mark, and a bonded indebtedness already well over that figure. Eleven hundred factories furnished employment for 25,000 hands and turned out diversified finished products valued at 70 million dollars. Three hundred jobbing houses traveled over 1,000 "drummers," and their invoices totaled 45 million dollars annually. Sixteen railroad lines came into the city, and trainmen counted 150 arrivals and departures a day. Seven daily newspapers, two printed in German, and the Sunday *Times* brought the news to thousands of doorsteps. Commission brokers read the *Indianapolis Daily Live Stock Journal* published at the busy, booming stockyard.

In population Indianapolis was twice the size of Evansville, the state's second-largest city. A movement from farm to city was swelling the population; restless young people were moving to Indianapolis and its bright lights, and more Irish, Germans and Negroes were coming. In 1890, 70 years after its founding, Indianapolis counted 105,000 inhabitants.

Industries, attracted by the railroads and plentiful supplies of gas and coal, swelled city payrolls. Thomas J. Madden & Company was the city's largest manufacturer of furniture; the Indianapolis Manufacturing Company, the world's largest manufacturer of baby carriages. Out on Parry Avenue near the Vandalia Railroad was the world's largest cart-, wagon- and carriage-making plant, the Parry Manufacturing Company. President of the company was David Maclean Parry, a former $10-a-week clerk in a general store at Laurel. He had bought a small carriage shop at Rushville and converted the firm's production to the manufacture of a low cost two-wheel cart for farmers, an immediate success. Moving to Indianapolis in 1884, the firm soon set an all-time production record of 1,000 carts a day and in 1890 began making four-wheelers— surries, piano-box buggies, phaetons, buckboards, spring wagons, and others—at the rate of 350 a day.

To boost the new city was a new Commercial Club, predecessor of today's Chamber of Commerce, founded in 1890 by William Fortune, a newspaperman, and Colonel Eli Lilly, the pharmaceutical manufacturer and the club's first president. From a group of 28 it grew to a membership of 1,000, and the club erected a handsome eight-story stone-front building on the southwest corner of Meridian and Pearl Streets. Its officers included David M. Parry, first vice-president; A. C. Ayres, second vice-president; Evans Woollen, secretary; and A. B. Gates, treasurer. It campaigned for a new city charter, street improvements, a University of Indianapolis, a park system and an improved sewer system, and it sought to bring conventions to the city.

The new capitol building, completed October 2, 1888, was one of the few buildings in the country to be built within its original appropriation ($2,000,000). Its construction had been voted after winds tore off the roof of the old statehouse and the ceiling fell in, one month before the 1877 legislature convened. Edwin May of Indianapolis was the architect and he created the three-story neo-Roman building of oolitic limestone in the shape of a Greek cross and topped with a copper-covered dome 75 feet in diameter.

Construction of the new Union Depot underscored Indianapolis' importance as a major national rail center. The old depot had long been crowded and worn out from the estimated 25,000 passengers passing through the station each week. The new structure was a showplace, with its lofty tower and clock, spacious waiting rooms and modern offices for railroad executives on the upper floors.

Tomlinson's Hall on Market Street was a new site for conventions, political rallies, lectures, balls and the annual Flower Mission Fair. The hall, with its 5,000-seat capacity, resulted from a bequest of $200,000 in the will of public-spirited Stephen D. Tomlinson. The hall site also became a marketing center for the city's housewives as the ground floor of Tomlinson's housed an extensive fresh vegetable market and the new $30,000 City Market adjoined it on the east.

On the northwest side of the Circle, curving gracefully with its wide arc, were two handsome buildings long remembered with affection by several generations of Hoosiers, the English Opera House and the English Hotel. Conceived as a memorial to the English family, the buildings were planned and built by William H. English, a successful businessman, Democratic Congressman and candidate for Vice-President in 1880. English spared no expense on the two buildings and they were among the glittering showplaces of the Middle West.

The magnificent Opera House, with its beautiful carved woodwork and great gas chandeliers, opened September 27, 1880, to an enthusiastic and fashionable audience. Its opening bill was Lawrence Barrett's *Hamlet*, followed the next week by the "divine Sarah" Bernhardt in her famous *Camille*. Under the management of Henry Dickson and George Talbot, English's also brought the best of opera, ballet, music and lectures to the city. The Opera House became a center for hundreds of important local events, including the annual May Festival, moved from Tomlinson's Hall. When the theater was torn down in 1949, the city mourned its passing as it would an old friend's.

Equally glittering and lavish was the English Hotel. Completed in 1884, its stone front incorporated a series of stone medallions, executed in bas relief, of George Rogers Clark, early governors of the state and members of the English family. The lobby was perhaps the most ornate in the West, a place of elegantly framed mirrors, marble floors and a broad marble staircase. A second section of the hotel, extending south to Market Street, was built by Will English after his father's death in 1896.

After the opening of the English Theater, Dickson's Grand Opera House (the Grand) was forced to hustle for attractions. It booked minstrel shows and revues featuring dozens of bare-limbed young ladies, and it brought in Lotta Crabtree in a road version of *The Black Crook*, generally credited as the first musical comedy. It ran afoul of the law with *Matt Morgan's Art Exhibition*, which featured a number of well-formed and scantily attired young ladies. The police raided the show and hustled the management and ladies off in a paddy wagon.

The Park was a home for stock companies, admission ten, twenty, and thirty cents, and specialized in comedies and melodramas such as the *Two Orphans* and *East Lynne*. Among its big productions was *Blue Jeans*, a New York success and the work of an Indianapolis playwright, Joseph Arthur, the son of a local minister. Arthur had been stage struck since he saw his first play at the old Metropolitan and after serving in the Civil War, traveling with a circus and attending college for a year, he set out to be a writer. His first play, produced in Indianapolis, was a failure, but three years later his *Great Encounter* was a New York hit. He followed it with two melodramas, *The Still Alarm* and *Blue Jeans*, both featuring special scenic or mechanical effects. *Blue Jeans*, which opened for a long New York run in 1890, had all the elements of first-rate melodrama: a rural setting (Rising Sun, Indiana), a beautiful heroine from the poor farm, a rich, handsome hero, and a pair of jealous rivals. The climax of the play came when the hero was placed on a slow-moving belt that carried him toward the whirring teeth of a giant buzz saw, but as audiences gasped and women turned away, the brave heroine appeared in the nick of time to stop the saw.

Drama on canvas was offered at the Cyclorama on Market Street, an enormous round building, its interior walls circled by an equally enormous canvas depicting the Battle of Gettysburg, life size, which gave the viewer the effect of standing in the center of the battle. When the city tired of the Battle, the owners tore down the building and installed a zoo which enjoyed a brief life.

The Indiana State Fair moved to its present site in 1892. The old fairgrounds, "Camp Morton," had proved too small and there was no room for expansion, as the city had grown up around it. After much controversy and a court suit, the Board of Agriculture purchased the 214-acre Voss farm on the edge of the town, fronting on what is now Thirty-eighth Street. A feature of the new fair layout was a "mile horse track" and grandstand where such great pacers as Indiana's famed Dan Patch would set records in the early years of the next century.

Indianapolis' public school system was growing and expanding. In 1895 45 grade schools and two high schools were in operation, including Shortridge High School, named in honor of the man who had given so much to the city schools. New in the school system was a manual training school named after Professor Charles E. Emmerich and opened through the efforts of John P. Frenzel, banker and for 14 years a member of the Board of School Commissioners; and Mrs. May Wright Sewall's Classical School for Girls, which opened in 1882 on North Pennsylvania Street.

Young medical students attended Butler University, or the Medical College of Indiana at the corner of Market and Senate, or the Central College of Physicians and Surgeons. Men prepared for law at the new Indiana Law School and by "reading" with established firms, and in the summer of 1894 Indiana Dental College opened its new buildings to students. Indianapolis Business University, established 1886, was a consolidation of the Indianapolis Business College and Bryant and Stratton.

The Indianapolis Water Company, successor to the Water-Works Company of Indianapolis, was laying water mains throughout the city. Even more important, 71 miles of sewers had been installed. Most houses still had backyard "privies," but more and more homes were installing the new "water closets," often tucking them under stairwells or in larger closets. Pumps were still a front or backyard fixture, but these, too, were moving indoors and the more expensive homes installed the new faucets.

Hoosiers are joiners and almost everyone in Indianapolis belonged to a club. Among the best-known were the fashionable Indianapolis Literary Club, the Fortnightly Club, Over the Tea Cup, the Matinee Musicale, Contemporary Club, the Indianapolis Women's Club, the Indianapolis Council of Women and the Art Association of Indianapolis headed by Mrs. May Wright Sewall (which gave an annual exhibition in the Propylaeum), and the Dramatic Club, Inc., which gave one-act plays written by its members, including one from the pen of Newton Booth Tarkington. On "lodge nights" men went to meetings of the Masons, Elks, Royal Arcanum, Ancient Order of Hibernians, Knights of Pythias, Red Men, Order of Chosen Friends. Union men attended meetings of the Knights of Labor, the American Order of Workingmen or locals of a craft union.

Babies were born at home, but after 1894 expectant mothers could be confined to Dr. Louis Burckhardt's Indianapolis Lying-In Hospital. Five private hospitals, called "sanitoriums," catered to the nervous diseases of women. Dr. O. S. Runnel's private hospital condemned the "starvation diets of most hospitals" and promised good food and lots of it to "build up" its patients.

Women wore shirtwaists, long, sweeping ankle-length skirts, black stockings and high-button shoes, and they copied the hourglass look with its wasp waist, leg-of-mutton sleeves and gored skirts, or the Gibson Girls with the attractive outdoor, athletic look.

Distinguished men such as Governor Albert G. Porter, a prominent Indianapolis attorney, wore Prince Albert coats, high silk hats and neatly trimmed beards. Other men wore stiff hats and derbies in pearl gray, black and brown, and grew mustaches and sideburns in a variety of styles. Most men chewed tobacco or smoked cigars purchased at Charlie Mayer's tobacco shop. Young sports puffed on the new tailor-made cigarettes—called "coffin nails"—which came packed with a picture postcard of a bare-limbed actress.

Older boys read the much-preached-against dime novels, which actually cost a nickel, their prices forced down by the candy interests. Under such banners as *Pluck and Luck* and *Work and Win*, they offered thrilling tales featuring Deadwood Dick, Buffalo Bill, King Brady, Nick Carter, Frank and Dick Merriwell—honest, simon-pure, square-jawed heroes who crushed dastardly villains, saved mortgages, solved complex mysteries and rescued beautiful heroines in distress.

Homes were cluttered and badly ventilated. Sofas were overstuffed and piled with pillows. Each chair had its antimacassar, each table a crocheted doily. Every home had a rubber plant, a patented rocker, a lounge, a bookcase with glass doors, a red plush photograph album, a loud-ticking clock on the marble-topped mantel and a grandfather's clock that "bonged" out the hour in the hall or deep within the house. In winter the home was heated by a base burner, an iron monster trimmed with shiny nickel standing stolid on flared feet with fire gleaming behind its double-mica eyes, an ash box in its base, a stove pipe jutting out from its back, curving up into the wall. Summer was a magic time when families sat on the front porch, drinking ice cold lemonade and listening to sentimental songs played on a mandolin.

The new safety bicycle, introduced in the 1890s, gave an extra fillip to spring and summer. Indianapolis, old-timers recalled, went "bicycle crazy." Bike clubs and riding clubs flourished; the Zig-Zag Club, distinctive in their brilliant uniforms, were famous for their "century" runs on Sunday. The Wheeling League of Broad Ripple bicycled between Broad Ripple and Thirtieth Street on the canal towpath. Bicycle stores and repair shops filled lower Pennsylvania Street. Three Indianapolis manufacturers did a million-dollar business with their trademarked Ben Hur, Outing and Bellis bicycles. Young men took their best girls riding on the new tandem bike, the bicycle built for two.

Sports began to occupy Indianapolis' time and interest. Butler's rugby team's annual Thanksgiving game at the fairgrounds was a local event. Golf debuted in the 1890s and Indiana's first bona-fide golf links, the Indianapolis Country Club, was built in 1897 on the site of the present Woodstock Country Club. Students home from college introduced the new game of tennis. Everybody played croquet, condemned by some ministers because young ladies often exposed their ankles. Down on the levee in smoke-filled back rooms, sporting men watched bare-knuckle prizefights.

But the city's consuming interest was baseball. Indianapolis had fielded the Military and Great Westerns in the late 1860s and the Blue Legs, its first professional ball team, in 1876, and in 1887 it entered the big leagues. John Brush, enterprising owner of the When Store, bought the St. Louis franchise of the National League and moved it to Indianapolis. The team played in the city for four seasons, but after the 1890 season Brush moved it to New York, where it became the Giants, now the San Francisco Giants. At the turn of the century Indianapolis became a charter member of the new American Association, and Brush and John H. Watkins, formerly of the Detroit team, fielded the Indianapolis Indians. The team played their games at a new park west of town on Gray Street, but later moved to Washington Park.

Behind their plumed fans, ladies whispered about Mrs. Fanny Osbourne, formerly of Indianapolis, christened Frances Matilda Vandegrift, who had parted her name in the middle to become Frances Van de Grift and later the wife of Samuel Osbourne. The marriage had many ups and downs, and in 1875 Fanny left her husband to study art in Paris, taking with her the Osbournes' seventeen-year-old daughter and two sons. At Grez she met and fell in love with a man a dozen years younger, the tall long-haired writer Robert Louis Stevenson.

Back in the States and three years later, Fanny wrote Stevenson asking him to join her in California. The youthful writer dropped everything and after a rough ocean crossing and an 11-day cross-country train ride he arrived feverish and ill in San Francisco. Under Fanny's tender care the author regained his health, and in May of 1880, after the Osbourne divorce became final, Stevenson married Fanny.

Two spectacular and tragic fires brought grief and shock to the city and, in their wake, produced more stringent fire laws and an inspection system. The first, at the Bowen-Merrill Company, occurred on Monday, March 17, 1890. The four-story building on Washington Street became a raging inferno and ten city firemen were carried to their death under tons of falling debris when the roof and floors collapsed. The fire raged for two days before it was extinguished, and not until Friday were the bodies of all the firemen recovered. The city immediately rallied to aid the dead and injured firemen's families with a large relief fund.

The second tragic fire occurred in the freezing cold of January 21, 1892. Shortly after midnight fire was discovered in a group of old buildings on the corner of Illinois and Georgia Streets occupied by the Surgical Institute and filled with crippled men, women and children undergoing treatment. Arriving firemen and spectators found the buildings "wrapped in flames" and most of the inmates trapped within their walls, their cries and screams filling the night air. When the "night of horror" was over and the fire extinguished, rescuers carried out 19 charred bodies, mostly of children, to be laid out in silent rows on the burned and trampled lawn.

Gas fever swept the state and the city in the mid-1880s following the discovery of a 3,500-mile-square gas field at Eaton, near Muncie. Everybody immediately became a wildcatter, and hundreds of grandiose schemes were hatched in clubs, bars and city halls. Muncie, Anderson, Kokomo and Noblesville offered free fuel to industry and became boom-towns. By 1890 nearly 500 wells had been sunk, and production was estimated at two million cubic feet per day.

In Indianapolis four natural gas companies were formed to tap the field, whose southwest rim came within five miles of the city. As the companies hit gas, they funneled it into upright pipes on East Market and Washington Streets, lit it and provided the city with giant and spectacular flambeaux. By 1889 the four companies had invested $2,500,000 in their ventures, laid 50 mains and counted 11,000 customers. The city's 40 coal dealers dwindled to five or six.

Spurred by the success of other nearby towns, the Manufacturers' Natural Gas Company was formed to provide free fuel. Its plan, first revealed in 1888, was imaginative and ambitious. It would lay a 16-inch main, 15 miles long, around the Belt Railway line, supply this with three or four smaller lines, and "allow factories located on the land, the owners of which have contributed to the line, to tap it and receive free gas." Once the line was in, the Board of Trade said with no little pride, "Indianapolis would have no rival in the world as a profitable location for manufacturing." But in 1891, to preserve gas, the legislature forbade the burning of flambeaux, and by the turn of the century the gas began to wane, finally giving out entirely in 1905. The great gas boom was over.

Electric lights and the telephone heralded a new age. Indianapolis residents saw Mr. Alexander Graham Bell's new wonder at the state fair in 1877, and the following year the state's first telephone exchange was established in Indianapolis. The telephone caught on quickly and the square wooden box, with its bells, hand crank, and curved neck and mouthpiece, became a familiar sight in homes and business houses. By 1895 the Central Union Telephone Company, the outgrowth of a consolidation of Bell and Edison Telephone, had over 2,000 subscribers. Long distance was introduced in 1893 by connecting lines with the Long Distance Telephone System and allied lines.

All was not so smooth sailing for the new Indianapolis Light and Power Company formed in 1881 with David Marvin as president and former mayor John Caven as vice-president. Their application for a franchise encountered stiff opposition from the city council, who expressed little confidence in the idea of electric lights. After some months of pressure and prodding, the council grudgingly issued a franchise for what they skeptically termed "the so-called electric lights," but turned down an offer to light the city streets with electricity.

The new company built a central station on South Pennsylvania, reputed to be among the first in the nation. Conduits were laid and the Union Depot was wired for electricity. On January 12, 1882, the first electric lights clicked on in the depot and families for miles around turned out to watch the new-fangled bulbs glow. Four years later the company renewed its offer to light the city and, on being turned down again, planned a demonstration. It erected five towers equipped with Brush arc lights on the Circle, one overlooking each of the four avenues and a giant 153-foot tower in the center. In 1892 the city fathers capitulated and gave the power company a ten-year contract for street lighting. Five years later over 800 electric lights glowed on Indianapolis streets, marking the end of the gaslight era. Many residents basking in the glow of the new lights could recall its inventor, Thomas A. Edison. He had been a telegrapher at the Western Union office in Indianapolis in 1864, and even then, people said, his mind had been full of ideas for wonderful new marvels.

Another of Mr. Edison's little marvels was also delighting Indianapolis families, the hand-cranked, spring-wound table-model phonograph. It played little cylinders for records and reproduced its tinny, high-pitched sounds through a flared horn that was available in a deluxe model with floral decorations. Near the turn of the century the cylinders were replaced by thick lightweight disks, and the phonograph was ensconced in shiny cabinet models with built-in horns.

Most of the big hits on the new records were penned by Indiana songwriters, including the hardworking, hustling and sentimental Harry and Albert Von Tilzer, the professional names of the Gumbinsky brothers from the south side of Indianapolis. The prolific Von Tilzers turned out over 3,000 pop tunes which they wrote together or in collaboration with others.

Albert collaborated with Jack Norworth, famed as the partner of Nora Bayes, to write "Take Me Out to the Ball Game" and Harry joined with Harry Sterling to turn out "Wait 'Til the Sun Shines, Nellie." Both songs are listed by the American Society of Composers, Authors and Publishers as among its 100 all-time song hits. The Von Tilzer boys also had fun turning out such outrageous songs as "Will the Spearmint Lose Its Flavor on the Bedpost Overnight?"

The 1890s brought the new electric streetcars, called trolleys, and by 1898, 350 cars clanged and banged over 100 miles of single track, their poles and "plows" crackling and sparking as they glided along overhead electric wires. The changeover from mule cars to electrics in 1895 had precipitated a small crisis, the mule drivers threatening to quit rather than pilot the new cars with their "bottled lightning," but John P. Frenzel, a banker and president of the reorganized Indianapolis Street Railway Company, smoothed things over. Cars no longer stopped in midblock or waited for passengers. Schedules were rigid and were disrupted only when pole and plow slipped off the wires, sometimes the work of small boys who also delighted in placing dynamite caps on the tracks and listening for them to go off in a row of loud explosions.

Summer streetcars were special favorites, open on both sides, their 12 rows of wood or straw seats placed crossways and pewlike, equipped with reversible backs so that the seats and not the cars were turned around at the end of the line. To boost passenger volume, the streetcar company bought 200 acres of wooded hills and ravines overlooking the White River and Canal and turned it into Fairview Park with a restaurant, bowling alley, refreshment stands, merry-go-round and picnic areas. Band concerts were given regularly on Sunday and a number of outdoor plays were staged on the west bank of the canal, the seats arranged in tiers on the opposite shore.

Among the new marvels was the horseless carriage. Indianapolis got its first look at one when Charles Black, a carriage manufacturer, imported a Benz from Germany. He had driven the contraption around the downtown area and before he learned to control it, smashed up a buggy and demolished two store windows. Fascinated by the car, Black built one of his own, around 1891. Black's automobile, like most of the early cars, consisted of a one-cylinder gasoline engine mounted under the rear seat of one of his fancier carriages. The model proved to be a success in its short trial runs, but Black made no attempt at manufacturing it.

Three years later in nearby Kokomo, Elwood Haynes, a native of Portland, successfully tested another horseless carriage, on the Pumpkinville Pike, three miles southeast of the city. The car, built to Haynes' specifications by Elmer and Edgar Apperson of Kokomo, was driven for about a mile and a half into the country at a speed of some seven miles an hour, turned around and driven back. Haynes and Apperson incorporated in 1898 to manufacture the Haynes-Apperson Car, but later dissolved the corporation and Haynes and the Appersons formed separate Kokomo corporations to make cars under their own names, the brothers calling their new car the Apperson Jack Rabbit machine. A year later, Black started production of his first automobiles and Indiana's new industry, the automobile, much of it to be centered in Indianapolis, was born.

Ministers and newspapers exhorted against the city's levee, an area reaching out from the Union Depot, along Illinois Street, across Washington, trickling off into Market and Ohio. The levee was a noisy, gaudy, bawdy place of dives, bright lights, clicking dice and clinking glasses, loud pianos and singing waiters, thronged after dark by men in hard hats, flashy vests and equally flashy diamonds. Bars, gambling dens and houses of ill-repute were everywhere. The 1890 census takers reported that Indianapolis had almost as many brothels as New York City. Queen Mab's was the most elegant parlor house in town and champagne was served with the traditional call of "company, girls!"

Reformers and newspapers campaigned against corrupt politics and urged the adoption of the Australian, or secret, ballot. Reform tickets were regularly defeated, both major parties voting blocks of "floaters," buying votes at the going rate of ten dollars and stuffing ballot boxes. Democrats or Republicans, depending upon who won the most votes, automatically set up cries of fraud, theft and collusion the day after an election. Fights, an occasional riot and arrests were common features of election day. The most serious riot occurred the year Negroes were first permitted to vote in a city election. A fight broke out between whites and Negroes (which, it was charged, was caused by the police), and before the melee was brought under control, one man was dead and dozens were injured.

Of the five Indianapolis mayors from 1881 to 1901 three were Republicans, four were attorneys, and two were both Democrats and Irishmen, marking the crossover of the city's Irish to the Democratic party, where they would remain a force for years. The three Republicans were Daniel W. Grubbs, John B. McMasters, and Caleb S. Denny, who served two terms, 1886-1890, 1893-1896. The city's sixteenth mayor, Thomas L. Sullivan, was the first mayor to be born in the city. Sullivan and Denny had sons who would embrace their fathers' politics and serve as mayors in the 1930s.

Most colorful of the mayors and one who would leave an indelible impression on his city, state and party was Thomas (Tom) Taggart, a shrewd, amiable Irishman with a born gift for politics and the manipulation of men. The undisputed political boss of Indiana, Taggart had risen to power after the national election in 1880, when he was personally credited with carrying Marion County for Grover Cleveland against Benjamin Harrison. In the 1890s, Tom Taggart's soft-spoken word was law and he was on his way to national political fame.

Born in County Monaghan, Taggart amassed a fortune and built the mammoth French Lick Springs Hotel at French Lick (which the Sheraton chain would buy from his bankrupt estate in 1929). The big hotel, with its luxury suites and mineral baths, catered to tired millionaires who came to French Lick in private railroad cars, and was also the gathering place of the great and powerful figures of the national Democratic party, who came to the "Tammany of the Middle West" for advice and counsel.

As mayor of Indianapolis, Taggart fought for a park system, got the necessary funds from the city council and bought 900 acres in the northwestern part of the city along the White River. Other purchases followed, laying the foundation for the Indianapolis city park system. All this was not accomplished without some grumbling from a city that in 1868 had turned down 30 acres for a park offered by the heirs of Calvin Fletcher.

Taggart was the party's national chairman from 1900 to 1908 and a delegate to every Democratic national convention from 1900 to 1924. In 1912 Taggart, supporting Thomas R. Marshall of Indiana for President, threw his weight behind Woodrow Wilson on the twenty-eighth ballot and won the nomination of Marshall for Vice-President. In 1924 Taggart entered U. S. Senator Samuel Ralston as a favorite son and on the ninety-second ballot of that strife-torn convention ran Ralston's vote up to 196¾, behind Alfred E. Smith and William Gibbs McAdoo but ahead of John W. Davis, who won the nomination.

Chapter 17

A PRESIDENT AND
A MONUMENT

EARLY IN THE AFTERNOON of June 25, 1888, the telegraph carried the news that the Republican national convention at Chicago had nominated fifty-five-year-old Benjamin Harrison of Indianapolis for the Presidency.

Harrison received the news at his law office in the Wright Building on East Market Street. When enthusiastic crowds gathered on the street outside, Harrison came downstairs, acknowledged their plaudits, called for his carriage and was driven through cheering streets to his big, fashionable house on North Delaware Street, where his family awaited him. That night thousands of people gathered outside the Harrison home, jammed the street, trampled the Harrison lawns, broke down part of the white picket fence and paraded up and down Delaware Street with bands, torchlights and costumed marchers.

Harrison, a resident of Indianapolis for 24 years, had been born on his grandfather's farm at North Bend, Ohio, the son of a Congressman, and named for his great-grandfather, one of the signers of the Declaration of Independence. During the Civil War he had commanded the Seventieth Regiment of Indiana Volunteers, taken part in the Kentucky and Tennessee campaigns, and been with Sherman at Atlanta and on his march to the sea.

A graduate of Miami University in Oxford, Ohio, in 1852, he was admitted to the bar the following year and married Caroline "Carrie" Scott. In 1854 the Harrisons came to Indianapolis, where the twenty-one-year-old Benjamin set up a law practice. His law firm prospered, mostly as the result of handling railroad litigation, and Harrison was elected city attorney in 1857, secretary of the Republican State Central Committee and reporter for the State Supreme Court. A deeply religious man, he taught Sunday school and became an elder in the Presbyterian Church in 1861. Upon his return from the war, Harrison again turned to law and politics, making an unsuccessful bid for the governorship and serving one term as a U. S. Senator.

Perhaps the only thing dignified about the campaign of 1888 was its two candidates. While party leaders and party hacks wheeled and dealed, Harrison and the Democratic candidate, the rotund incumbent President Grover Cleveland, remained aloof. Cleveland regarded it as undignified for a President to campaign actively and remained in the White House. Harrison's campaign managers also regarded it as undignified for their man to beat the bushes for votes, and when they suggested a "front porch" campaign, Harrison, the soul of dignity himself, quickly concurred. In deference, however, to his wife and complaining neighbors, a reviewing stand was set up in University Square, and there the sobersided Harrison greeted the thousands who came to Indianapolis by rail and wagon to confer, meet with or merely get a glimpse of the brown-bearded man who might be President.

To greet the visiting dignitaries, a group of Harrison's friends, Benjamin Walcott, Charles Martindale, Henry Fraser and James Wright, formed the Harrison Marching Society, a group of about 150 young men who dressed in pearl-gray derbies, blue flannel coats and trousers, and white vests, and carried gold-headed canes. They met visitors at the station and escorted them about the city, arranged hotel reservations, arranged conferences with Harrison and marched in torchlight parades. In August the group became a permanent organization and founded the Columbia Club, a name suggested by Harry New. The first officers were Edward Daniels, president; Henry S. Fraser, secretary; Otto Gresham, treasurer, and Colonel Oran S. Perry, marshal. The club's first home, purchased in 1889, was the old William Morrison residence on the Circle, the first house in the city to be lighted with the new incandescent lights.

Indianapolis was tumultuous throughout the summer and fall as excursion trains brought Harrison supporters to meet the candidate, marchers paraded through the streets and Harrison men sang "Grandfather's Hat Fits Ben." One of the largest crowds in the city's history turned out to hear James G. Blaine, "The Plumed Knight," who came to Indianapolis to speak for Harrison at Tomlinson's Hall.

Republicans with a well-filled war chest spent money lavishly and recklessly, a good share of it appropriated for the purchase of votes. Indiana was a pivotal state and nominally a Republican stronghold, but it had elected four Democratic governors since 1872 and only one Republican. In many cities (Indianapolis was an outstanding example) the party won elections or made good showings by voting Negroes, floaters or dead men—a practice not confined to the Republicans. A flagrant example of vote buying came to light a few days before the election of 1888 and erupted into a national scandal.

It started with a circular letter directed to Indiana county chairmen written by William W. Dudley of Richmond, treasurer of the national Republican party. A copy of the letter was stolen from the mail by a Democratic postal clerk and turned over to the Indianapolis *Sentinel*, which spread its brazen details across the front page. Dudley's instructions were explicit: "Divide the floaters into blocks of five and put a trusted man with the necessary funds in charge of these five, and make him responsible that none get away and that all vote your ticket. . . . Make a personal appeal to your businessmen to pledge themselves to the entire day." With publication of the letter, Dudley charged that somebody was robbing the United States mail and demanded an immediate investigation. But the damage was done, the story was on the wires, and voters and editors were shouting "Corruption!"

Cheering crowds gathered at the Harrison home on election night to serenade the man elected the nation's twenty-third President, and there were parades and bonfires and celebrations all over the city. But Harrison's victory had a hollow ring. He was a minority President, losing to Cleveland by 90,000 popular votes and winning only because the Electoral College gave him 232 votes to Cleveland's 168. His margin of victory in his own state was slim—fewer than 2,400 votes—and he had even failed to carry his own Marion County.

In the wake of the Harrison election there was a nationwide cry for reform. Across the nation, in city after city, grand juries listened to charges of bribery and fraud at the polls by both parties. The following year, nine states, including Indiana, adopted the Australian, or secret, ballot and passed other legislation strengthening the voting system.

On March 4, 1889, while members of the Harrison Marching Society looked on and thousands of other Hoosiers stood in the Washington rain, Harrison took the oath of office, Cleveland graciously holding an umbrella to shield him from the drizzle. Harrison proved to be a good but ineffectual President who presided over a nation in a transitional period. Honest, earnest and brusque, he was called, with some unfairness, the "White House ice chest." The administration was marked by much legislation that was negated or proved ineffective, raids on the public treasury by Civil War veterans, and passage of the nation's first billion-dollar budget. Hoosiers were prominent in the administration and Harrison appointed Indianapolis' Samuel Merrill, the bookseller, as consul-general to Calcutta and former Governor Porter as minister to Italy. Mrs. Harrison, although in failing health, worked hard at her duties as First Lady and became the first president-general of the Daughters of the American Revolution when it was organized in 1890.

Renominated by the Republicans on the first ballot at the 1892 convention, Harrison was again pitted against Grover Cleveland, but this time Cleveland turned the tables, rolling up a plurality of 372,736 votes, carrying Indiana by 37,125 votes and winning 277 electoral votes to Harrison's 145. The election was also marked by a personal tragedy for Harrison: two weeks before the election Mrs. Harrison died, and Indianapolis and a nation mourned her passing.

When his term was over, Harrison returned to Indianapolis and the practice of law. In 1896, at the age of sixty-three, he married Mrs. Mary Dimmick, an attractive widow of thirty-eight, a niece of Mrs. Harrison and her secretary for many years. The following year a child was born, Elizabeth, who would help brighten the remaining years of an ex-President's life.

While Republicans and Democrats were charging each other with fraud and alternately winning elections, Indianapolis was a center for a great deal of less orthodox political activity—much of it reflecting the growing discontent of farmers and workingmen who believed they had been "sold out" by the two major parties.

The Greenback party, now the Greenback-Labor party, staged its 1884 national convention in the city, voted to support Benjamin Butler, the candidate on the Anti-Monopoly ticket, and again proved it had more passion than votes. The late 1880s brought the newly formed Farmers' Alliance and the Farmers' Mutual Benefit Association to town for meetings—two of many groups born of 20 years of depression on Indiana farms. In September 1890 the alliance gathered in Indianapolis for a state convention. Delegates came from the Greenbackers, the Union Labor party and the Grange, and before the session ended they voted to form a new People's party, with a hammer and a plow as their emblem, symbolizing the solidarity of farmer and wage earner. Their platform denounced high taxes and the rising public debt and condemned child labor and the use of public money to build railroads and factories.

The new People's party polled fewer than 17,000 votes in the 1891 election, but the defeat only stiffened their determination. It continued to meet and reports grew of a rising and powerful third-party movement, independent of the two major parties. In November 1891 the Farmers' Alliance was joined by the Farmers' Mutual Benefit Association. Thousands of delegates from all over the West poured into the city for a convention, and it was decided to form a third national political party.

In May 1892, the year of the second Harrison-Cleveland election, the People's party (their name shortened to the Populists) met in convention at Indianapolis, nominated a state ticket and named a slate of delegates to the national convention of the party at Omaha, Nebraska. Judge Walter G. Gresham, a convert to Populism and one of the candidates defeated by Harrison in the G.O.P. convention of 1888, was announced as the party's Presidential nominee, but Gresham demanded he be nominated unanimously, a condition the party couldn't guarantee, and he withdrew. In his place the party named General James B. Weaver of Iowa, a former Greenbacker.

The Populists sang "Good-Bye, Party Bosses" at their rallies and parades in Indianapolis, but the song apparently made little impression on Indiana voters. In the November balloting the Democrats swept the election, the Populists polling less than four percent of the total. Nationally the Populists won over a million votes and became one of the few third parties to win electoral votes.

Laboring men were showing their discontent and frustration by joining unions, 55 of them in Indianapolis in the 1890s, including the Union for Working Girls. The unions campaigned for improved wage rates, sick benefits and workmen's compensation. A gentle, passionate man from Terre Haute and a familiar figure around the Indianapolis legislative halls and railroad yards was making headlines and labor history. Eugene V. Debs was leading the first industry-wide union, the American Railway Union, challenging the powerful Railroad Managers' Association and the Pullman Company, winning occasionally but losing on bloody picket lines and in the courts and eventually serving a jail term, his union in shambles. Indianapolis unions formed the Central Labor Council in 1880 and five years later the state's 77 unions came together under the aegis of the Indiana Federation of Trade and Labor Unions. The rising power of the unions was beginning to be felt in the legislative halls and virtually every session of the Indiana General Assembly after 1885 had to deal with labor bills.

The Panic of 1893, seventeenth in American history and destined to last four years, added to the political, social and economic ferment. Indianapolis newspapers daily recited the unhappy litany of banks and businesses closing, factory doors shut, payrolls and wages slashed, workingmen's meetings, city appropriations and work relief programs. The Commercial Club set up the Relief Committee, headed by Colonel Eli Lilly, to find jobs for the unemployed men, and its Finance Committee, with John H. Holliday as chairman, sought funds for the needy. The Panic raised the old question of "hard" versus "soft" money and the growing importance of silver versus gold—subjects that men in Indianapolis argued heatedly and endlessly.

As the depression worsened, farmers, laborers, Populists and other debtor groups turned more and more to free silver as a panacea. Populists and free-silver men controlled the 1896 Democratic convention, which nominated William Jennings Bryan. The silver-tongued Bryan had set the convention on fire with his thundering "Cross of Gold" speech, which displeased and angered a great many Democrats, including John P. Frenzel, an Indianapolis banker, party leader and delegate. Returning home, Frenzel, who believed that Bryan was a dangerous man and his theories just as dangerous, set about organizing a rump "Gold Bug" convention that met in Indianapolis, repudiated the party's silver plank and nominated its own national ticket—not with any expectation of winning, but in the hope of stopping Bryan.

Republicans flooded Indianapolis with anti-silver pamphlets and leaflets, praising the sturdy qualities of their candidate, William McKinley, an advocate of the "Full Dinner Pail." McKinley sat on the front porch of his home in Canton, Ohio, but Bryan swept across the nation in the first modern "whistle-stop" campaign. He came to Indianapolis in October to hold a vast audience spellbound at Tomlinson's Hall. Among those who listened to the passionate, strong, mellow voice of Bryan was a high school youth who immediately decided upon a political career— Claude C. Bowers.

The Republicans swept Indiana and the nation in the fall. During the first year of McKinley's term, prosperity began to return, slowly at first, then with a rush. By 1900, when McKinley again defeated Bryan, Populism had run its course and silver was a dead issue—replaced by the rising spirit of imperialism resulting from a 113-day demonstration of U. S. power, the Spanish-American War, in 1898.

Jingoists and the Eastern mass-circulation "yellow press" had been agitating for a war with Spain since the badly misgoverned Cuban peoples had revolted against their Spanish oppressors in 1895. To add fuel to the propaganda a mysterious and still unexplained explosion occurred on the U. S. battleship *Maine* "on a friendly visit" to Havana Harbor, with a loss of 260 officers and men, among them a twenty-two-year-old sailor, Harry S. Keys, son of Mrs. J. J. Turner of Indianapolis.

Amid cries of "Remember the *Maine*," President McKinley reluctantly declared war on Spain on April 25, 1898, marking the end of 33 years of peace since the Civil War. Indiana's quota was four regiments of 1,000 men and two batteries. Governor James A. Mount ordered the Indiana National Guard to report at the fairgrounds in Indianapolis and by the following evening he could report that his state was the first to fill its quota.

Troops were organized into the 157th to 160th Regiments and the Twenty-seventh and Twenty-eighth Light Batteries, Indiana Volunteers. In May, McKinley called for more troops, the state's quota this time being one regiment of white and two companies of Negro volunteers and a signal corps, the Fourteenth.

Departing soldiers left Indianapolis "in the spirit of boys off on a picnic" and reported to training camps in Virginia and Tennessee, where, except for the Twenty-seventh Battery and two other units, they remained. The Twenty-seventh was sent to Puerto Rico and was on the firing line ready for action when word arrived that Spain had sued for peace.

Among those who did get to Cuba and were wounded at Santiago was William E. English, a former congressman who served as an unpaid aide-de-camp to sixty-two-year-old Joe Wheeler, an ex-Confederate general. English, the son of William H. English of political, hotel and theater fame, returned to Indianapolis to become president of the Board of Park Commissioners and national commander of the United Spanish War Veterans. At the battle of El Caney in the Philippines in 1899, the commander of the American forces, Indiana's Major General Henry W. Lawton, a Civil War veteran and campaigner against the Plains Indians, was killed by enemy bullets. A bronze statue of Lawton was erected to his memory in Indianapolis' Garfield Park, today one of the few reminders of a conflict that John Hay called "that splendid little war."

During much of the 1890s the Circle was enclosed by a high wooden fence splashed with 24-sheet theatrical and circus posters. Behind the fence the oft-proposed and long-discussed Soldiers' and Sailors' Monument, Indianapolis' most famous landmark, was rising to its full majesty of 284 feet—the first monument ever erected to the common soldier.

A Civil War monument had been first proposed in an 1862 *Journal* story that suggested each county pay for a block "with the names inscribed on it of the veterans from each county." At least twice after the Civil War the legislature failed to act on proposals to erect a monument in Crown Hill Cemetery. Plans of a veterans' group to raise funds came to a dead end.

In 1884 the Grand Army of the Republic took up the cause and adopted resolutions at their annual encampment calling for a Civil War monument in Indianapolis. Under the leadership of Department Commander General James A. Carnahan, the G.A.R. raised $23,380 by 1887. Under G.A.R. prodding, the 1886 Republican and Democratic conventions endorsed the project. In 1887 the General Assembly passed a bill establishing a monument commission and appropriated $200,000 to build the monument "on the ground commonly known as Circle Park."

The original commission consisted of George J. Langsdale, editor of the *Greencastle Banner* and first president, Samuel B. Voyles of Salem, D. C. McCollum of LaPorte, and Daniel M. Ransdell and George J. Johnson of Indianapolis. James G. Gookins, an Indianapolis artist, was chosen secretary. (Ransdell resigned in 1889 and was replaced by General Thomas W. Bennett of Richmond. When Bennett died four years later, his place was filled by William H. English.)

The commission invited ten of America's leading architects to submit sketches and placed advertisements in newspapers of leading cities in the U. S. and abroad announcing the competition. Seventy designs were submitted and in January 1888 the commission unanimously selected the design, "Symbol of Indiana," by Bruno Schmitz of Berlin, Prussia. Schmitz, a friend of Gookins, Herman Lieber, Julius Lemcke and Theodore Stempfel of Indianapolis, came to Indianapolis in February to receive his appointment as supervising architect. Frederick Bauman of Chicago, famed for his "floating pier foundation" theory, was named deputy architect.

Work on the monument began in 1889 and the cornerstone was laid in August, with President Harrison and Governor Alvin P. Hovey among the principal dedicatory speakers. The name "Circle Park" was changed to "Monument Place." The fountains on the east and west sides of the monument were found to be too small and were torn out and replaced.

The legislature abolished the commissioners in 1895, appointing a three-man board of regents with General Fred Knefler of Indianapolis as president and General Lew Wallace of Crawfordsville and Major Gustavus V. Menzies of Mount Vernon as the other members. Wallace resigned after the first meeting and was replaced by General Jasper Packard of New Albany.

William H. English suggested the addition of statues of Indiana men representative of Indiana's participation in four wars. As the statue of Oliver P. Morton was already available (standing in the Circle, dominant even in still life and seemingly overseeing the work), three other pieces of statuary were ordered: George Rogers Clark, representing the Revolution; William Henry Harrison, the War of 1812; and Governor James Whitcomb, the War with Mexico. The dramatic pieces were executed by an Indianapolis sculptor, John J. Mahoney. Colored sketches of the monument were sold and James Whitcomb Riley wrote "Monument for the Soldiers," urging in its final lines:

> *And see that you build it stately,*
> *In pillar and niche and gate,*
> *And high in pose as the souls of those*
> *It would commemorate!*

The enterprising John Edwards of Indianapolis erected a high board fence around the construction site and sold the space for advertising.

The 30-foot high figure of "Victory," which would crown the monument, arrived in its enormous crate—a lady of 13,900 pounds designed by George W. Brewster. "Miss Indiana," as Hoosiers called her, was modestly attired even for statuary in those times: a Grecian-style, loose, nonrevealing gown fell from neck to toe, with elbow-length sleeves. The handsome bronze lady wore an eagle on her brow and held a torch high in her left hand. In her right hand was a sword pointed downward and resting upon a globe eight feet in diameter, upon which the lady's slippered feet were firmly placed. The board explained that the sword represented the army, "to which victory was always due"; the torch was emblematic of the "light of civilization," and the eagle "typical of the freedom resulting from the triumph of light." There was a report on the day that "Victory" was placed atop the monument that a finger was broken off and taken home by one of the workmen, who cut it up into rings and sold them at handsome prices as souvenirs. Indianapolis got its first formal look at "Victory" during the twenty-seventh annual G.A.R. encampment in 1893. Through the offices of Colonel Eli Lilly, chairman of the Citizens' Executive Committee (which arranged for the comfort of the 75,000 visitors who swamped the city), the giant lady was uncrated and formally introduced in all her 30 feet of glory.

The Soldiers' and Sailors' Monument—tribute "to Indiana's Silent Victors," the phrase credited to Fred Fertig—was formally dedicated on May 15, 1902. Built of gray oolitic limestone from the quarries of Owen County, Indiana, it had taken 12 years to complete at a cost just under $600,000 and was said to be the second highest monument in America. Dedication day was a day to remember. The ceremonies started with a mammoth street parade in which survivors of the Mexican, Civil and Spanish-American Wars marched under their colors to blaring bands through flag- and bunting-draped streets lined with thousands of people. Formal ceremonies began at ten o'clock, with General Lew Wallace as master of ceremonies. The principal address was given by General John W. Foster, the U. S. minister to China, a former Secretary of State under Harrison and grandfather of John Foster Dulles. James Whitcomb Riley read a poem, "The Soldier," a chorus of 200 raised their voices in song and the band played a march composed for the occasion, "Messiah of the Nations" by John Philip Sousa (whose own band appeared frequently in concert at Tomlinson's Hall).

In the afternoon there was another parade, vesper services at the monument and a program by the Christ Church choir; and at night special patriotic programs in Tomlinson's Hall and English's Opera House were followed by a spectacular fireworks display. It was near midnight when an exhausted Indianapolis climbed into bed.

Chapter 18

THE GOLDEN AGE
OF LITERATURE

FOR FIFTY YEARS, from 1871 to 1921, Indiana writers and poets dominated America's popular literature. Their books were on all best-seller lists, their plays among the longest running in New York, and their novels among the first to be bought and adapted for the new motion pictures. It was Indiana's Golden Age of Literature and for most of those years Indianapolis shared honors only with New York as an important literary capital and a major publishing center.

The Golden Age began in 1871 with the publication of Edward Eggleston's *The Hoosier Schoolmaster*. Besides Eggleston and his brother George from Vevay, there were Charles Major, Shelbyville; Maurice Thompson, Crawfordsville; William Vaughn Moody, Spencer and New Albany; Evaleen Stein, Lafayette; Caroline Virginia Krout, Crawfordsville; George Ade, Kentland; George Barr McCutcheon, Lafayette; Gene Stratton Porter, Geneva; the maverick of the Golden Age, Theodore Dreiser, Terre Haute; and Lew Wallace, whom Crawfordsville shared with Indianapolis. As for the capital city, it boasted James Whitcomb Riley, Kin Hubbard, Mary Hartwell Catherwood, Meredith Nicholson and Booth Tarkington.

George Ade, humorist and author of *Fables in Slang*, plays and musical comedies, had a favorite story about the Golden Age. As he told it, an Eastern lecturer came to Indianapolis and, after a few opening remarks in which he paid tribute to Indiana's literary reputation, invited any authors in the audience to come forward and share the platform with him. Whereupon, Ade related, the entire audience, with the exception of one man in the rear of the hall, made a rush for the platform. "What about him?" asked the lecturer. "Oh," was the reply, "he writes too. It's just that he's deef and didn't hear what you said."

Except for the work of Dreiser, Tarkington and Moody, the novels and poetry of Indiana writers were rustic, sentimental, nostalgic and romantic—in tune with an age when sentiment and romance were fashionable. Part of their success also lay in a changing America. Thousands of families were moving from farm to towns and from towns to cities. Life was becoming more complex, and to those who had recently exchanged the farm and small town for the busier life of the city, Hoosier writers offered a remembrance of things past or an escape from a world they never made. As for realism, it was acceptable in popular novels if it stayed within the well-defined bounds of early twentieth-century middle-class morality and did not offend the new capitalism. Booth Tarkington's realism could be published in the pages of the staid and conservative *Saturday Evening Post*, but Dreiser's books were damned and banned for dealing realistically with social problems and sex.

The dramatic and still dashing fifty-three-year-old Lew Wallace, who spent his summers in Crawfordsville and his winters in Indianapolis and whose life had been bound up with so much of the city's early history, became a national figure in 1880 with the publication of *Ben Hur: A Tale of the Christ*. A million copies were sold before 1911 and it became one of America's most popular and longest lived novels.

As Wallace told the story, he had fallen in with Colonel Robert G. Ingersoll, the famed agnostic, aboard a train to Indianapolis, both on their way to speak at a soldiers' reunion. Wallace had written some 16 chapters of *Ben Hur*, and as he listened to Ingersoll's views on God and religion, he determined to refute the eloquent disbeliever and promptly revised and enlarged his story line and interwove it with the life of Jesus. Wallace, who was not a member of an organized religion, declared the writing of the book converted him to a belief in God and in the divinity of Christ.

Theatrical producers saw the book's strongly contrasted central characters, stirring episodes and thrilling chariot race as pure theater and they came knocking at Wallace's door. For years Wallace turned them down, but he finally negotiated a contract with Klaw and Erlanger with the understanding that the book's language would be retained and Christ would not be shown. Erlanger got around the latter problem by depicting Christ as a shaft of light.

The spectacularly mounted *Ben Hur*, in six acts and 13 scenes complete with four treadmills, live horses and chariots, opened at the Broadway Theater in New York in November 1889 with Edward Morgan in the title part, and William S. Hart as Messala, a role later played by another great silent-film star, William Farnum. In the 21 ensuing years *Ben Hur* was produced over 6,000 times, vying with *Uncle Tom's Cabin* as America's longest running and most performed play. In 1926 *Ben Hur* became a silent movie hit with Ramon Navarro as Ben Hur, Francis X. Bushman as Messala and Carmel Myers as Iras. The film was successfully revived in 1931 with the addition of a sound track. In 1959 it was remade for wide screen, Technicolor and stereophonic sound and won the Academy Award as the best picture of the year.

Ben Hur made Lew Wallace a wealthy man, but his last book, *The Prince of India, or Why Constantinople Fell*, published in 1893, was less successful. Wallace invested the book's profits in the building of Indianapolis' first apartment house. He died in Crawfordsville in 1905, ending a long career as lawyer, soldier, diplomat, governor of the New Mexico Territory and writer. His statue was erected in the Hall of Fame in Washington, D. C., five years later.

In the same year that *Ben Hur* was rolling off the presses, Dickson's Opera House in Indianapolis was the scene of an evening of "character and dialect poems by James W. Riley," a local poet whose work appeared regularly in the *Journal*. It was Riley's first public appearance in the city and he drew a good house. His verse was popular and he was a superb actor, with a born talent for moving an audience to laughter or tears.

James Whitcomb Riley, born in nearby Greenfield in a big house on the National Road, was the third of six children. He studied law in his father's office, gave it up, tried his hand as a sign painter, and joined a medicine show, where he developed a talent for acting as well as writing verses and song lyrics. He drifted back to Greenfield in 1873, served briefly as editor of the *Greenfield Commercial*, and under the name of "Jay Whit." contributed verses to its columns as well as to the *Saturday Mirror*, a literary paper published in Indianapolis. In 1877 he joined the staff of the *Anderson Democrat* and later that of the Indianapolis *Journal*.

For the *Journal* Riley covered routine assignments and began to contribute verses signed by "Benj. F. Johnson, of Boone" which became a regular feature of the paper. Riley put the pieces together in a book and, when no publisher would take them, joined in 1883 with George C. Hitt, the business manager of the *Journal*, and published them in a paperback under the title *The Old Swimmin' Hole and 'Leven More Poems*, the " 'leven more" including the imperishable "When the Frost Is on the Punkin." Hitt and Riley printed 1,000 copies of the book, which were speedily sold over the counter of the *Journal* office.

Among those who picked up a copy of Riley's little paperback was

William C. Bobbs of the Bowen-Merrill Company. Bobbs sought out the then thirty-year-old Riley and offered to print and distribute a second edition. The poet agreed and the men shook hands—the handshake serving as their only contract during the more than 25 years in which Bowen-Merrill and its successor, The Bobbs-Merrill Company, published more than two score of Riley's books.

Riley's success and fame grew as book after book rolled off the Bobbs-Merrill presses: *Afterwhiles, Old Fashioned Roses, Rhymes of Childhood, Home Folks, Out to Old Aunt Mary's, The Lockerbie Book, Green Fields and Running Brooks, Riley Songs O' Cheer, The Hoosier Book, The Days Gone By and Other Poems, While the Heart Beats Young, Songs of Friendship.* Everyone read James Whitcomb Riley. His verses were favorites for home, church and school entertainments. Ministers, orators, politicians, lecturers quoted them in sermons and speeches. People framed his poems in their parlors, halls and bedrooms.

The great body of Riley's work was sentimental, nostalgic, bucolic, homespun; full of faith, optimism, good cheer—written by a sensitive craftsman with an ear for speech and an ability to express the feelings common to ordinary people. Some of his work was authentic folk poetry, and some of it—"Little Orphant Annie," "When the Frost Is on the Punkin," "The Raggedy Man," "The Old Man and Jim," "The Old Swimmin' Hole," "Out to Old Aunt Mary's" and "The Object Lesson" —had a built-in immortality. None of his poetry tackled great social or political themes or dealt with great emotional crises. Nearly all of it was a valentine to a past that may or may not have existed, but described exactly as most people wanted to remember it, as in the lines:

> O the days gone by! O the days gone by!
> The apples in the orchard, and the pathway through the rye;
> The chirrup of the robin, and the whistle of the quail
> As he piped across the meadows sweet as any nightingale;
> When the bloom was on the clover, and the blue was in the sky,
> And my happy heart brimmed over, in the days gone by.

Most of his work was written in dialect designed to give flavor and character to his good-humored lines. Critics divided on the authenticity of the dialect, but few ever quarreled with Riley's portrait of children. They were real children; barefoot boys and girls with smudged cheeks and scraped knees who were selfish, elfish, impudent, naïve, alternately mischievous and sorry. Riley, who genuinely loved children, captured their spirit, their lively chatter, their breathlessness, their excitement, their eagerness, even the fun of being wide-eyed and scared as in "Little Orphant Annie":

> Little Orphant Annie's come to our house to stay,
> An' wash the cups an' saucers up, and bresh the crumbs away,

An' shoo the chickens off the porch, and dust the hearth, an' sweep,
An' make the fire, an' bake the bread, and earn her board-an'-keep;
An' all us other childern, when the supper-things is done,
We set around the kitchen fire an' has the mostest fun
A-list'nin' to the witch-tales 'at Annie tells about,
An' the Gobble-uns 'at gits you
　　Ef you
　　　Don't
　　　　Watch
　　　　　Out!

As he became famous, Riley moved from a small rented room to the elegant Denison Hotel and later to a two-and-a-half-story Victorian house on Lockerbie Street, today a memorial open daily to visitors. Indianapolis still remembers him as a puckish, dapper man, immaculately dressed, wearing a white waistcoat and a huge gold watch chain, a flower in his buttonhole, pince-nez eyeglasses, walking leisurely along the street. At the Bobbs-Merrill retail store a table was reserved for him on the balcony near the railing, and customers could look up and find the great man writing or checking his royalty accounts. A confirmed bachelor and bon vivant, Riley was also a familiar figure in the city's best restaurants and bars. He had an affection for the bottle and he liked nothing better than to spend an evening drinking with old and close friends such as Eugene Debs or the local newspapermen. Many an older Indianapolis resident recalls meeting "Sunny Jim" in the wee hours of the morning weaving his uncertain way home.

New York and Indianapolis schools celebrated Riley's birthday with special exercises on October 11, 1911. In Indianapolis he rode through streets lined with schoolchildren—much like a conquering hero. The following year his birthday was celebrated all over America.

When Riley died on July 22, 1916, a nation mourned the sixty-six-year-old poet who had become so much a part of their lives. His obituary filled pages in the country's press. Over 35,000 men, women and children filed past his body as it lay in state under the dome of the state capitol. A contest developed between Greenfield and Indianapolis over his burial, and after angry words had been exchanged, the poet was buried in Crown Hill Cemetery.

Paralleling the success of James Whitcomb Riley was that of his publisher, Bowen-Merrill, which in 1903 became The Bobbs-Merrill Company. The firm, as Arthur W. Shumaker has pointed out, was an important factor in the rise of Indiana literature. That a local firm could publish local materials and market them nationally was a great stimulus to writers.

The new firm had tasted success with Riley's *Old Swimmin' Hole* and they began to look for other manuscripts. Will C. Bobbs called on Meredith Nicholson, a reporter on the *News* whose verse was attracting attention. Nicholson, a native of Crawfordsville, had lived in Indianapolis since he was six years old. A high school dropout, he had been a drugstore clerk, printer's devil, court reporter, and since 1884 a member of the *News* staff. Bobbs and Nicholson met nightly over a jug of cold milk and went through Nicholson's portfolio, selecting and discarding until they finally collected enough poems for a slender volume, *Short Flights*, published in 1891.

John Curtis, now recognized as a pioneer in the new techniques of book promotion, had an idea, revolutionary in a day when book advertising was confined to single-column listings. "Let's find a manuscript with popular appeal," Curtis suggested to Bobbs and Charles W. Merrill, "and take big display space in newspapers all across the country and get people to go into bookstores and ask for it." The search for such a manuscript ended one afternoon in 1896 when a Shelbyville lawyer, Charles Major, came in with the manuscript of a romantic novel, *Charles Brandon, Duke of Suffolk*. Curtis retitled the book *When Knighthood Was in Flower* (borrowing the line from a Leigh Hunt poem, "The Gentle Armour") and launched it with the first national advertising campaign for a single book.

Supported by newspaper advertising and enthusiastic reviews, *Knighthood* was a sudden and overwhelming success. During much of 1899 it was one of the nation's three best-selling novels and it went on to sell a million copies and to become a Hearst-Cosmopolitan production starring Marion Davies. The book and its promotion established Bowen-Merrill as a book publisher, changed the entire concept of book promotion and opened new vistas for novel writing and publishing.

Curtis' promotional talents gave a big boost to Meredith Nicholson's first novel, *The Main Chance*. Now promoted to vice-president in charge of the firm's New York office, he plastered the city with billboards reading "Wait for the Main Chance," probably the first teaser campaign in book history. It became a best seller and in 1905 Nicholson again hit the best-seller lists with a romantic thriller, *The House of a Thousand Candles*, which became a long-run stage hit and a successful motion picture.

The new firm also planned a novel. At an editorial conference one day it was agreed that a good novel on George Rogers Clark and the Vincennes campaign offered tremendous sales possibilities. The firm talked to Maurice Thompson of Crawfordsville, a native of Fairfield, Indiana, who had a reputation for works on archery and nature sketches, and Thompson agreed to write the book. The result was *Alice of Old Vincennes*, published in 1900, which was an instantaneous success and a minor classic. It still thrills thousands of readers in the 1970s. *Lazarre* by Mary Hartwell Catherwood of Indianapolis was also suggested and written under the firm's direction. A historical romance based on the lost Dauphin of France, it was a success as a book and as a stage play with Otis Skinner.

The national advertising and publicity of the Indianapolis firm brought manuscripts and authors knocking at its door. It published Mary Roberts Rinehart's best-selling mystery *The Circular Staircase*, after other publishers had turned it down. Its authors were household names: Harold McGrath, Louis Joseph Vance, David Graham Phillips, Emerson Hough, Gelett Burgess, Zona Gale, Talbot Mundy, Hallie Erminie Rives, Earl Derr Biggers, Ring Lardner, Irving Bacheller, Howard Chandler Christy, Marion Harland, Anna Katharine Green and George Randolph Chester. It published Benjamin Harrison's *Views of an Ex-President*, Senator William E. Borah's *The League of Nations*, John T. McCutcheon's *In Africa*, Warren G. Harding's *Our Common Country*, Albert J. Beveridge's *The Meaning of the Times*. It developed a textbook department and published some of the first histories of Indiana offered in public schools. Its Child Classic Readers sold three million copies. In 1910 The Bobbs-Merrill Company moved from its Washington Street location to a new five-story brick and marble office building on the north side of University Square.

One Indiana writer, however, successfully published many of his own works, although his later books bore the Bobbs-Merrill imprint. He was the self-taught writer-artist Frank McKinney Hubbard, known as Kin Hubbard, creator of the famed *Abe Martin of Brown County*, one of Indiana's and the nation's most beloved fictional characters. Hubbard was among the best, if not the best, of the crackerbarrel philosophers.

Hubbard, born in 1868 in Bellefontaine, Ohio, the son of a newspaper publisher, attended Bellefontaine schools, toured the south as a silhouette artist, got involved with amateur theatricals, and worked around newspapers and theaters in Detroit. He was hired by the *News* as the city's first full-time cartoonist, fired three years later, and rehired in 1901.

Hubbard's new job was to turn out political caricatures and sketches. While touring during the 1904 campaign he sketched a number of rural characters that amused him and back in the office he fashioned a composite character into a one-column panel cartoon and wrote a caption for it. The editor liked it and on December 31, 1904, Abe Martin was born, an almost formless, scarecrow-looking farmer with baggy pants, ragged coat, shapeless hat, button eyes and chin whiskers. For a backdrop he used country stores, county fairs, and town halls, and he created a group of rustic characters whom Abe Martin quoted but who never appeared in the panel. Among them were Lafe Budd, the village dandy; Newt Plum, the town constable; Miss Fawn Lippincut, the village belle; Mr. and Mrs. Tilford Moots, always at sword's point; Miss Tawney Apple, daring in her manner and dress.

Like Riley, Hubbard cast his sentences in the idiom of the rustic, blessing his Abe Martin with trenchant wit and native shrewdness. Some of his sharpest wit was reserved for politics and politicians, as demonstrated in these barbs from *Abe Martin's Almanac for 1907*:

I don't see what some o' the spring candidates expect to gain by having their pictures printed.

Now and then an innocent man gets sent to the legislature.

Ther's some folks standin' behind the President that ought t' git around in front where he kin watch 'em.

I wish somebuddy would make a new Republican speech.

Uncle Ez Pash has voted the Dimmycratic ticket free of charge all his life.

Farmers, faced with the endless chores in running a farm, could appreciate such lines as "Al Johnson talks o' selling his farm and movin' t' town where there's some place to loaf" or "It must be nice t' live in the city an' understand lawn mower jokes and pick your milk off the window sill." A thigh slapper was his comment, "You allus find a retired farmer hangin' around a bank." And there was warmth in his comment, "Of all home remedies a good wife is the best."

Hoosiers loved *Abe Martin*, which was syndicated in over 300 newspapers and quoted everywhere. Vice-President Marshall's famous quip, "What this country needs is a good five-cent cigar," was right out of *Abe Martin*. In addition to the daily *Abe Martin* panel, Hubbard also turned out a Saturday feature, *Short Furrows*, for the *News* and published his works under the signature of the Abe Martin Publishing Company. Among the two dozen he published were *Abe Martin's Almanac*, *Abe Martin's Scrapbook*, *Abe Martin of Brown County, Indiana*.

Hubbard died in December 1930 (his wife in 1970), but *Abe Martin* continued to live through the years, durable as Indiana limestone. He continues as a daily feature of the Indianapolis *News* and a syndicate still furnishes *Abe Martin* panels to many newspapers. In the heart of Brown County State Park stands the Abe Martin Lodge and some 20 guest cabins named for some of Hubbard's best-known characters.

Dean of Indiana letters in the Golden Age was Booth Tarkington, born Newton Booth Tarkington, of Indianapolis. Epitome of "The Gentleman from Indiana," he was a novelist, playwright, short-story writer, artist, art collector, and occasional politician. He was twice winner of the Pulitzer prize, for his novels *The Magnificent Ambersons* (1919) and *Alice Adams* (1922), and a member of the American Academy of Arts and Letters.

The great body of his work mirrored the upper middle class of the Middle West and he probably made more use of Hoosier settings, particularly Indianapolis, where he was a lifelong resident, than any other Indiana author. A conservative and a traditionalist, his work ranged from the romantic *Monsieur Beaucaire* (1900) to the humorous *Penrod* series (begun in 1914) and the realism of *Alice Adams*. As Alexander Woollcott once wrote: "The fabric of life as Tarkington saw it contained the hum of lawn mowers, the swish of garden hose playing at sundown on the phlox and petunia and heliotrope; the sound of neighbor calling neighbor; the fragrance of new-made bread sifting from summer kitchens."

Tarkington was born July 29, 1869, at 520 North Meridian Street, then the best residential area of the city, into an environment that he would write about so often. Fun-loving and imaginative, Tarkington played hooky so often from Shortridge high school that his family packed him off to Phillips Exeter Academy. From there he went on to Purdue, where he wrote a newspaper column and had uproarious weekends at Sigma Chi fraternity with George Ade and John T. McCutcheon. Transferred to Princeton, he turned his student days into a prolonged frolic. He had a good time and didn't graduate.

Back home in Indianapolis, Tarkington gained a reputation as a gay blade, a two-fisted drinker and, in the opinion of head-shaking neighbors, a "ne'er-do-well." Few knew that Tarkington was also spending long hours at a drawing board in his home trying to be an illustrator. He mailed out sketch after sketch, accumulating a bushel basket of rejection slips, chalking up a single sale, for $21, to *Life* (which, with *Judge,* was then the leading humor magazine).

Sustained by a legacy from his rich Uncle Newton of California, for whom he had been named, Tarkington switched from illustrating to writing, which, for a long time, proved as frustrating and unrewarding. His first novel, *Monsieur Beaucaire*, found little interest at McClure's, where his sister, Hauté (once courted by James Whitcomb Riley and now Mrs. Ovid Butler Jameson), had personally taken it. McClure, however, expressed interest in *The Gentleman from Indiana*, and Mrs. Butler telegraphed Tarkington to rush the manuscript to New York. After anxious weeks a letter of acceptance arrived signed by Hamlin Garland, whose closing lines read: "You are a novelist."

To confirm Garland's judgment, *The Gentleman from Indiana*, published in 1899, climbed to the top of the 1900 best-seller list and has since never been out of print. *Monsieur Beaucaire*, published the same year, was an immediate success, and in 1902—the same year Tarkington's old friend McCutcheon published his best selling *Graustark*—it opened for a long run on the Broadway stage with Richard Mansfield in the title role.

The hardworking, hard-playing Tarkington, famous at thirty, wrote the unsuccessful *Cherry* and the best-selling *The Two Vanrevels*, in 1902 married Louisa Fletcher, the daughter of Stoughton Fletcher of the banking family, and was elected on the Republican ticket to one term in the Indiana legislature.

More novels and plays followed—*The Man from Home* (with Harry Leon Wilson), *The Beautiful Lady*, *The Guest of Quesnay*, *The Conquest of Canaan*, and *In the Arena, Stories of Political Life*, which dramatized the corruption of politics and was, logically enough, based on his experience in running for office and serving in the legislature.

Tarkington dressed elegantly and moved in fashionable circles but remained a practical joker and the life of the party. But his gay life and his increasing use of alcohol, a weakness of many Indiana writers, eventually put a strain on his marriage. On November 13, 1911, his wife was granted a divorce and the custody of their daughter, Laurel. A year later he remarried, bringing his new bride, Susanah Robinson of Dayton, to live in the big, comfortable Tarkington home at 100 Pennsylvania Street. The marriage turned out to be a happy one. The new Mrs. Tarkington combined forces with the family doctor and got him to stop drinking. Tarkington's productivity soared. From his typewriter came *The Flirt*, *The Magnificent Ambersons*, *Penrod*, *Penrod and Sam* and the other *Penrod* books, *The Turmoil*, *Alice Adams*, *The Midlanders*, *Seventeen*, *The Plutocrat*, *Claire Ambler*, *Kate Fennigate*, one-act and full-length plays, and the *Little Orvie* series for the *Saturday Evening Post*.

He built a new house at 4270 North Meridian Street, a mansion of nine bedrooms and a ballroom, where, except for part of the year he spent at Kennebunkport, Maine, he lived until his death at age seventy-six on May 19, 1946. Nearly blind in his later years, he dictated his novels, refusing to permit the handicap to interfere with his production. He resisted change and opposed Franklin D. Roosevelt, the New Deal and Paul V. McNutt. Voting a straight Republican ticket, he wrote: "To my old-fashioned mind, the liberty we lose when the government plans our future security is worth more than the benefit this security could possibly give us. Hardship, it seems to me, is a part of life, a test and builder of character."

Chapter 19

WHEELS FOR A
NATION

On JANUARY 1, 1900, nearly a dozen Indianapolis families bundled up against the chill, piled into "horseless carriages" and chugged off in smoke and noise to pay their traditional New Year's Day calls on friends and relatives. In downtown Indianapolis, a Greenwood and Franklin Electric Railway car came to a stop after a 12-mile run from the Greenwood shops south of the city. The families in their new cars and the Greenwood Railway car ushered in the city's age of wheels, nearly four decades in which Indianapolis would become one of America's leading manufacturers of fine motorcars and the interurban capital of the world.

Hoosiers took to the automobile as they had to the bicycle. It was love at first sight. Within a few years after C. H. Black and Elwood Haynes had assembled their first cars, 50 Indiana cities were assembling and manufacturing 256 makes of cars and trucks. Indianapolis, as usual, was the leader and, for a time, the first capital of the early auto industry. Its carriage makers, millwrights, bicycle makers and others became auto manufacturers, their plants turning out over 60 different makes of cars—among them some of the most famous names in American motorcar history: Marmon, Stutz, Duesenberg, Empire, Premier, Waverly, National, Overland, Cole, Chevrolet, Parry, Pathfinder, Lafayette.

The cars of 1900 were beginning to look a little less like horseless buggies, but they still operated with a lever and their engines were in the rear under the seat. Within a decade steering wheels were introduced (in 1903, on the right side, in the manner of European cars); engines went up front, a seat over the radiator enjoying a brief moment of glory; pneumatic tires replaced solid tires, and designers stressed "classy and racy lines." Front fenders that flared to keep off the mud were redesigned front and back to conform with wheels, running boards were introduced, and hand cranking was replaced with a self-starter and 80-hour batteries. The touring or open car remained the basic automobile, but it now had a top, the body was enclosed, and doors were introduced. From one cylinder, motors went to four, six, eight and twelve.

Indianapolis-built cars were propelled by gasoline, fuel oil or electricity and often had but one thing in common: they were expensive. Most cars made in the city were custom-made marvels of industrial craftsmanship and were priced accordingly. Indianapolis ranked fourth in auto production in 1907, second in 1913, but by 1920 failed to place in the top ten although its dollar volume equaled that of the burgeoning Detroit, the Hoosier city's most important rival. It was a clue that assembly-line, low-cost mass production was taking over, but local auto makers ignored it. Competition, high business mortality, the Great Depression and, as John Bartlow Martin put it, the city's industrial "hardening of the arteries" eventually brought an end to auto making in the city.

The automobile brought a demand for better roads. The State Board of Health began listing auto accidents as a cause of death, recording three in 1906, 100 in 1915, over 1,000 in 1928. To combat automobile thieves, the 1921 legislature authorized a 16-man department of motor-vehicle police and gave them traffic powers three years later. The first license plates were issued by the state in 1911. The first state highway department was created in 1917, attacked in the courts and confirmed in 1919, providing for a highway system connecting county seats and cities of over 3,500 population. The first gasoline tax was imposed in 1923. Over 2,500 Hoosiers were arrested in 1925 for exceeding the speed limit of 35 miles per hour.

Sporting young men and engineers raced cars on back roads and farmers complained of the noise and the smoke. The Indianapolis Automobile Racing Association was formed, made up of industry representatives and sportsmen. In November 1905 it staged a 100-mile "open race" at the state-fair grounds, and W. F. (Jap) Clemens set a world record with an average speed of 52.93 miles per hour. The fairgrounds were also the site of a record-breaking 24-hour grind. The drivers were Clemens and Charley Merz, and they started out in late afternoon on November 16, driving at night with the help of Prest-O-Lite lamps installed around the track. Heavy frost made goggles useless and each driver could only manage 30 minutes at the wheel before his eyes became swollen shut by the merciless winter wind. They finished the 24 hours with 1,094 miles to their credit.

At 161 South Street, the Waverly Company, a former carriage and bicycle manufacturer, made the Silent Waverly Electric, "the car ladies preferred." The firm turned out its first car in 1898, a runabout, but by 1912 it was offering a five-passenger limousine with three windows on each side and entered from a center door. Other Waverly models included a Brougham Coupe, Victoria Phaeton, Roadster and Stanhope. The National Motor Vehicle Company at 2100 East 22nd Street also manufactured electrics, offering ten models.

The Chevrolet brothers, auto racers and mechanics, came to Indianapolis and made the Chevrolet Frontenac. David Parry's enormous wagon and carriage factory became the Parry Motor Car Company in 1911 and a part of the General Motors empire in 1930. Today it is the Chevrolet truck body plant. Out on Oliver Avenue the Marion rolled off assembly lines, with nickel-plated trimmings, ventilated front windshield and electric lights. The Herff-Brooks Company made the Marathon as well as a car under their own name.

Pathfinder, made by the Motor Manufacturing Company, boasted it was the "King of Twelves." Its advertising was peopled with polo players, uniformed chauffeurs, and fashionably dressed men and women, with copy directed to "those fortunate ones of the earth's elect." A Pathfinder seven-passenger touring car, with accompanying status, cost $2,750, and for a model with "special enclosed body," $4,800. For contrast there was the Empire, a one-seater with gas tank behind, four cylinders, promising to "look as classy and perform as well as the most costly cars you can buy," for only $850. Among the most widely advertised of Indianapolis-made cars was the American Underslung, made by American Motors, which operated with "a noise so faint that one could scarce distinguish it from silence." The Empire Automobile Company promoted its "Little Aristocrat," a five-passenger touring car, for $950. The Henderson delivered a wire-wheeled five-passenger touring car for $1,585. The 1909 Overland, made by Willys, which later moved to Toledo, Ohio, promised "only pedals to push" while claiming to be the "quietest, most reliable and cheapest roadster on the market."

Three of the most famous and celebrated luxury cars in America were made in Indianapolis: Stutz, Marmon and Duesenberg. The Stutz firm, founded in 1912 by Harry C. Stutz, an early auto racer, was launched with an advertising campaign that exploited the new car's participation in the first Indianapolis "500." The Stutz Bearcat was as much of a symbol of the Roaring Twenties as F. Scott Fitzgerald and John Held, Jr., who frequently used the car as a symbol of "flaming youth," filling a Stutz with flask-toting, raccoon-coated collegians and short-skirted flappers. The made-like-a-fine-watch Duesenberg was the product of German-born Fred and Augie Duesenberg. Fred had taken up bicycle racing in 1898 and discovered he had a flair for the mechanical. With his

INDIANAPOLIS-BUILT MOTORCARS, 1898-1937

This listing of Indianapolis-built automobiles is from the *Indiana History Bulletin*, February 1967, based on research by Wallace S. Huffman, automobile historian. Of the more than 250 makes of cars built in Indiana, Indianapolis was the leader with 64 different makes.

MAKE	MANUFACTURER	DATES
Allen Steamer	Allen Steamer Co.	———
American	American Motor Car Co.	1905-1920
Atlas Knight	Atlas Engine Works	1912-1913
Best	Best Motor Car Co.	1910
Bicar	Cyclecar Engineering Co.	1914
Black	C. H. Black Mfg. Co.	1899
Black Hawk	Stutz Motor Car Co.	1929-1930
Brock	———	1920
Brock	Spacke Machine & Tool Co.	1920-1921
Coats (Steamer)	George A. Coats	1922-1924
Cole	Cole Motor Car Co.	1909-1925
Colonial	Colonial Auto Co.	1917-1921
Comet	Economy Cycle Car Co.	1914
Craig Hunt	Craig Hunt Motor Car Co.	1920-1923
Cross	Harry Cross	1924
Cyclop	L. Porter Smith & Bros.	1910
Duesenberg	Duesenberg Motor Co.	1920-1937
Economycar	Economycar Co.	1914
Elgin	Elgin Motors, Inc.	1916-1924
Elco	Bimil Buggy Co.	1915-1916
Empire	Empire Motor Car Co.	1898-1919
Ford	Ford Motor Co.	1914-1932
Frontenac	Chevrolet Brothers	1922
Gibson Girl	Cecile E. Gibson (cycle)	1903
Hassler	Hassler Motor Co.	1917
H. C. S.	H. C. S.	1920-1926
Henderson	Henderson Motor Car Co.	1912-1915
Herff-Brooks	Herff-Brooks Company	1914
Hoosier Scout	Warren Electric & Machine Co.	1914
Ideal	Ideal Motor Car Co.	1912
Indianapolis	———	———
Lafayette	Lafayette Motor Co.	1920-1924

MAKE	MANUFACTURER	DATES
Lindsay	Lindsay Russell Co.	1903
Lindsley	J. B. Lindsley & Co.	1908-1909
Lyons Atlas	Atlas Engine Co.	1914
Lyons Knight	Atlas Engine Co.	1914-1916
Mais	Mais Motor Truck Co.	1910-1914
Marathon	Herff-Brooks Company	1912
Marion	Marion Motor Car Co.	1905-1915
Marmon	Nordyke & Marmon Co.	1905-1933
Marmon-Herrington	———	1931
Merz	Merz Cyclecar Co.	1914
Mohawk	Mohawk Auto & Cycle Co.	1903-1904
Monroe	William Small Co.	1914-1924
Moore	———	1907
National	National Motor Vehicle Co.	1903-1924
National Electric	National Auto & Electric Co.	1900
Overland	Standard Wheel Co.	1906
	Overland Auto Co.	1907-1913
	Willys-Overland Co.	1911
Parry	Parry Motor Car Co.	1910-1913
Pathfinder	Motor Car Manufacturing Co.	1911-1918
Pope Waverly Electric	Pope Motor Car Co.	1903-1904
Premier	Premier Motor Mfg. Co.	1903-1904
Rex	Rex Motor Car Co.	1908
Roosevelt	Nordyke & Marmon	1929-1930
Schebler	———	1907
Spacke Deluxe	Spacke Machine & Tool Co.	1915
Standard	———	1902
Standard Truck	———	1918
Stratton Premier	Stratton Motor Corp.	1923
Stutz	Ideal Motor Car Co.	1912-1935
	Stutz Motor Car Co.	1912-1936
Vaughn Runabout	Marion E. Vaughn	1912
Waverly Electric	Waverly Co.	1898-1916
White	White Steam Wagon	1903
Wizard	Wizard Motor Co. (cycle car)	1904-1919

brother, he turned out some of the world's finest automobiles and racing cars. The 1929 roadster, chassis only, priced at $8,500 was designed "to outclass, outrun and outlast any car on the road." The luxurious Marmon was made by a former flour-milling manufacturer, the Nordyke & Marmon Company. Its famed "Yellow Jacket" racers, streamlined, painted in black and yellow with long pointed tail, helped give their passenger cars extra sales impetus. During World War I the Marmon was purchased in quantity by the French government for its army staff and Marmon advertised "this signal honor" as a "tribute to the judgment of every Marmon owner."

Stutz and Duesenberg outlasted all of the city's car manufacturers, Stutz closing its doors in 1935, Duesenberg in 1937. The last of all Indiana car manufacturers, Studebaker of South Bend, closed in 1963. Today, except for the custom-made Avanti made in the former Studebaker plant, there are no passenger cars made in Indiana. An attempt by a newly formed Indianapolis company to build a new Duesenberg failed in the 1960s.

The city's passion for wheels was not confined to the automobile. Indianapolis and Indiana conducted a long-standing love affair with interurbans—the new electric cars that carried passengers and freight between towns and cities in a logical extension of street railway service.

Charles L. Henry, who owned the Anderson Mule Car line, coined the name and E. D. Durand, a director of the Census Bureau, defined it: a railway having less than half its trackage within the limits of a municipality. The Indianapolis, Greenwood and Franklin line, which inaugurated regular service ten days after its initial run on January 1, 1900, fitted the description and formally became the first Indianapolis interurban. A second line opened a few months later, from Greenfield to Indianapolis, and dozens of others quickly followed.

Probably in no other state did interurbans strike the popular fancy as they did in Indiana. By the end of 1900 over 678 miles of electrics were operating, and eight years later the "windsplitters" were humming over 2,300 miles of track in 72 of the state's 92 counties. It was a replay of the early days of the railroads, and nearly all the interurban companies made the same mistakes.

The first lines were plagued with trouble. Equipment was untried and hauls were short. Some tried to operate on batteries and found them impractical. Electric current was both DC and AC. Contact poles had to be redesigned to stay on the overhead wires at high speeds and for long runs. Steam railroads objected to the electrics crossing their tracks and went to court, most of the cases being decided in favor of the interurban companies. Eventually equipment improved, current was standardized, and the short lines expanded and merged. A few cities resisted the inter-urbans. At nearby Crawfordsville the city fathers declared they didn't want the "windsplitters" running down their Main Street. Construction crews defied them, fought a pitched battle with police and firemen equipped with firehoses, and the tracks went in.

Indianapolis had a special problem. Ten lines radiated out from the city, bringing 100 electric cars every day into the downtown area. The loading and unloading of passengers and baggage on city streets pre-sented a traffic hazard—blocking the way of horses and buggies, the new automobiles, and the three high-seated, wire-caged mail delivery trucks the Indianapolis post office was testing in 1903.

The problem was solved with the construction of a giant million-dollar traction terminal on West Market, the largest in the world, which was formally opened on September 12, 1904. Just as the Union Depot combined all the steam lines, the new terminal combined all the electrics under one roof. Arrivals, departures and transfers were handled more comfortably, and it provided space for offices, ticket counters and bag-gage. The city also pioneered a joint ticket office opened in 1905, the Indianapolis Freight Terminal, capacity 100 cars, and the Industrial Ter-minal. Popular with riders was the "2,000 Penny Coupon" which of-fered $20 in rides for $17.50 and was good on all member lines of the Central Electric Railway Association.

By 1910 over 400 electric interurbans arrived and departed the trac-tion terminal every 24 hours, bearing names like the Muncie Meteor, the Kokomo Traveler, the Marion Flyer, the Wabash Valley Flyer, the Honeybee. They brought over five million passengers in and out of the city annually, most of them central Indiana farmers and their families come to savor the sights and sounds of the city. The early cars were heavy and cumbersome, but these were soon replaced by sleek, light-weight steel models. Some offered all-chair parlor cars, others dining and smoking sections. Although most electric lines ran single cars, two- and three-car trains were not uncommon. Interurban sleeper service was inaugurated in 1903 when a Holland Palace Car, operating over four lines, connected Indianapolis with Columbus, Ohio.

Interurban excursions were popular. Lines ran theater trains to Indian-apolis, with a special late car that departed after the final curtain. Trips were offered to Niagara Falls, part of the ride on connecting steam lines. Special shopping trains ran on designated days. The Indianapolis Cham-ber of Commerce chartered an interurban to take the city's wholesalers to visit their retail customers in the small towns.

There were accidents, wrecks, collisions. The worst disaster was a head-on collision north of Kingsland in 1910 which claimed 42 lives. In Indianapolis 20 persons were killed and scores injured after a Honeybee

(Indianapolis, New Castle and Eastern) crashed into a truck and trailer at Twenty-first and Emerson Streets. Perhaps the only holdup of an interurban took place at Maywood, southwest of Indianapolis. Two men flagged down a Terre Haute, Indianapolis and Eastern car bound for Martinsville, climbed aboard, and forced the terrified crew and passengers to line up outside on the roadbed, where they robbed them of over $1,000 in cash and valuables.

For a good share of their corporate lives, most of the interurban lines were in financial trouble. Failures began in the days following World War I, coincident with the introduction of low-cost, mass-produced automobiles, buses and trucks. Receiverships, mergers, sales, reorganizations became common. The prosperity of the 1920s brought some financial stability, but it was destroyed by the cruel depression of the 1930s. A wave of bankruptcies followed. In 1930 the larger interurban lines consolidated and became a part of the Midland United Company, Samuel Insull's giant railroad and utility holding company. The new organization, the Indiana Railroad, became the largest interurban in the world, in 1931 operating 956 miles of tracks. But in 1932 the Insull empire crashed, and three years later the Securities and Exchange Commission, under the Public Utility Act, ordered the separation of electric railways and utilities. A crippling six-week strike in 1937 provided an added blow. In 1941 the last of the interurbans, the Indianapolis and Seymour line, successor to the interurban that had been first in the city in 1900, ended in fire and smoke. In September the line's two remaining electric cars smashed head-on between the two cities. The interurban era was over.

Chapter 20

A SOUND OF ENGINES

O N DECORATION DAY of 1911 a black and yellow Marmon "Wasp" racing car roared into the straightaway of the new Indianapolis Motor Speedway, its flat nose and pointed tail end almost obscured by the exhaust from its six cylinders.

A checkered flag jerked and swished into the wind, and Ray Harroun became the first man to win America's greatest automobile-racing classic —the Indianapolis 500-Mile Race. His time was six hours and 42 minutes—average speed, 74.9 miles per hour—and he collected $14,000 for piloting his car 200 times around the two-and-a-half-mile track.

The big racing oval and the 500-mile race represented the efforts of four Indianapolis businessmen who had pooled their resources to provide a testing ground for automobiles and thrills for a growing body of race fans. Three of the men were prudent businessmen, James A. Allison, Arthur C. Newby and Frank H. Wheeler. The fourth was the flamboyant Carl G. Fisher, who, perhaps more than any other man in Indiana, was tuned to the new century.

Fisher was a restless, energetic, shrewd businessman and a born promotor. He loved anything that moved—bicycles, motorcars, boats, balloons, the new aeroplanes. Born in Greensburg, Indiana, in 1874, he had quit school at the age of twelve shortly after his family moved to Indianapolis. He sold candy on trains and at seventeen, when the bicycle craze hit, put his meager savings into a modest bicycle-repair shop. Within a year he had talked a manufacturer into giving him a line of credit, opened a retail store and started building and racing bicycles.

When automobiles came in, he was among the first to own one. He became a pioneer auto dealer and a good enough auto racer to team up for half-mile dirt-track exhibitions with Barney Oldfield, Louis Chevrolet, Tom Cooper, Earl Kizer and Walter Winchester. In the summer of 1901 he earned nearly $20,000 at county fairs by pitting a one-cylinder Winton against the fastest horses in the area, letting the horse take the lead until the last few feet, then nosing him out in a whirlwind finish.

He gloried in stunts. To advertise his car agency (which carried so many different makes it resembled an auto show), he persuaded a pioneer balloonist, Captain G. L. Bumbaugh, to help him introduce the 1908 Stoddard-Dayton by flying one over the city. The balloon, with the glistening white car attached to steel cables, Fisher at the wheel, Bumbaugh in the back seat, floated 2,000 feet in the air over downtown Indianapolis at the peak of the rush hour. Thousands stopped to gape, other thousands jumped into cars and on bicycles and followed the balloon. Bumbaugh touched down at Southport, seven miles outside the city, to admiring crowds.

In 1904 an inventor, P. C. Avery, asked Fisher's help in financing a new lighting system to replace the unsatisfactory kerosene auto lamps. Avery's system consisted of a cylinder filled with compressed carbide gas that, pumped through copper tubes to perforated forked ends and lighted with a match, gave off a brilliant light. Fisher approached Jim Allison, the manufacturer of the Perfection Fountain Pen, and together they formed the Prest-O-Lite Company. The light was an immediate success, but there were problems. The carbide gas was tricky to handle. Their first plant, a frame shed in back of a corner lot at the intersection of Pennsylvania and Twenty-eighth Streets, burned down, and explosions and fires forced them to seek new plant sites regularly. The Indianapolis city council, plagued with complaints, banned the charging of Prest-O-Lite tanks within the city limits. Fisher and Allison then built a charging plant on the banks of the White River southwest of the city, and later another in the vicinity of Speedway. The business grew and expanded. In 1917, 13 years after they had invested their original $2,000 in Prest-O-Lite, Allison and Fisher sold the company to Union Carbide and Carbon Corporation for a reported nine million dollars.

Success in business enabled Fisher to indulge himself, but race tracks and fast cars remained his first love. One night in 1908, so the story goes, he was returning from a business trip with Lem Trotter, his real estate adviser, and their car broke down several times. Fisher helped Trotter get out and get under and complained volubly that there ought to be a race track where car manufacturers could test their cars before foisting them off on the public. "Put them in competition with each other on a track," he suggested, "and they would damn well have to improve them." Trotter asked Fisher why he didn't build one and Fisher said he didn't know of a good site.

Trotter found one—the old Pressley farm owned by Kevi Munter and the Chenoweth family, some 15 minutes from downtown Indianapolis. Fisher instructed Trotter to take options and invited Arthur C. Newby of the National Motor Vehicle Company, Frank H. Wheeler of the Wheeler Schebler Carburetor Company, Jim Allison, and Stoughton Fletcher, the banker, to come in with him. Newby, like Fisher, had been a bicycle enthusiast who had forsaken two wheels for four. A native of Monrovia, Indiana, he had spent his boyhood in California and come to Indianapolis in 1882. In 1890 he organized the successful Indianapolis Stamping Company to make bicycle parts and four years later he sold it, the firm becoming the Diamond Chain Division of the American Bicycle Company. Newby invested his profits in the Hay and Willits Company, makers of Outing Bicycles, organized the Zig-Zag Cycling Club and the Outing Bicycle Team. In the spring of 1898 he built the Newby Bicycle Racing Oval at what is now the intersection of Central Avenue and Thirtieth Street. The quarter-mile board track had a football gridiron in the infield and a 15,000-seat grandstand. In July the League of American Wheelmen held their national championships at the oval and drew capacity crowds. Interest in the track waned with the coming of the automobile and Newby closed the oval and joined the National Motor Vehicle Company.

Banker Fletcher withdrew after the second meeting of the group on the grounds that his bank might not approve of his participation, and Fisher, Allison, Newby and Wheeler formed The Indianapolis Motor Speedway Company, capitalized at $250,000 with Fisher, president, Newby, first vice-president, Wheeler, second vice-president and Allison, secretary-treasurer. The Pressley farm was purchased for $72,000, and plans went ahead for the 1909 program which the new partners agreed would open with the national balloon races on June 5, motorcycle and auto races the Fourth of July weekend, the motorcycle championships in August and more auto races on Labor Day weekend.

That year everything went wrong. The Fourth of July auto races were postponed and of the 12 balloons entered in the June championships, only five got off the ground, among them Fisher's *Indiana*, with Captain Bumbaugh as co-pilot. The day was marked by a tremendous traffic jam, which kept thousands away from the turnstiles. Paid admissions totaled 3,500 but 40,000 watched the balloon race free outside the grounds. The motorcycle races were a fiasco. The crushed stone and tar track proved hazardous and many cyclists withdrew. The 25-mile race was called off for lack of entries and only three riders entered the ten-mile race, won by E. G. (Cannonball) Baker of Indianapolis.

Tragedy and a series of accidents marred the auto races. Under the pounding of speeding cars, the track broke up into a nightmare of ruts and chuckholes. On the opening day a driver and his riding mechanic (mechanics were mandatory in the early races) were killed. During the running of the 300-mile Wheeler Schebler Race, Charley Merz's car spun out of control and plunged into a crowd of spectators, killing Merz's mechanic and two of the spectators. The race was called off with 26 laps to go. Officials of the American Automobile Association indicated it would sanction no further races at Indianapolis, but Fisher hastened to assure them he would immediately rebuild the track.

Fisher replaced the old track with 3,200,000 paving bricks grouted in cement. James J. Jeffries, former heavyweight champion of the world, in town for appearances, was the first to ride around the newly completed brick oval. Auto sprint races were held in December, but near-zero weather produced only a limited number of entries and small crowds.

A series of moderately successful but accident-free auto races, 42 events ranging from 5- to 200-mile races, were held in the spring. Crowds were estimated at 60,000. In June the Speedway's "Aviation Week" featured Wilbur and Orville Wright, both of whom had once been boys in Richmond, Wilbur having been born in Millville. Walter Brookins made national headlines by taking a Wright biplane to a new world's altitude record, 4,384 feet. The auto racing over Labor Day drew crowds of 15,000 each on Saturday and Sunday and produced a modest profit. The National Balloon Races were held at the Speedway in mid-September, but most of the contestants, including Fisher and Captain Bumbaugh in the *Indiana II*, were forced down by heavy rains in Pittsburgh.

Meeting after the 1910 programs, the partners agreed something had to be done. They had sunk well over $700,000 into the Speedway and it was still unsuccessful. Talk turned to eliminating the number of races and perhaps concentrating on one big event—a 1,000-miler or a 24-hour run. Before the year was out the partners agreed upon an annual 500-mile race on Decoration Day.

The 1911 race drew 40 entries and 80,000 spectators. Some of the racing greats were in the lineup—Art Chevrolet, Howdy Wilcox, Charley Merz, Spencer Wishart, Ralph DePalma, Bob Burman. The list of cars included such names as Mercedes, Simplex, National, Stutz, Mercer, Velie, Benz, Fiat, Cole, Pope-Hartford, Buick and Amplex. The race was marred by seven crashes, one bringing death to a riding mechanic and another serious injuries to a driver and his mechanic. Eleven cars finished behind the winner, Ray Harroun, who had driven the race without benefit of a riding mechanic. Harroun had rigged up the automobile industry's first rearview mirror—the first of many new automotive products to be tried and tested on the Indianapolis Speedway.

Spurred by the success of the 1911 race, Speedway officials upped the 1912 purse to $50,000, for a race that drew 90,000 spectators and was won by Joe Dawson of Indianapolis at the wheel of an Indianapolis-built National. The race was a heartbreaker for Ralph DePalma. He was leading the race by three laps when his Mercedes quit one mile from the finish line. DePalma and his riding mechanic got out and began pushing the car, moving it slowly along the inside of the track. As he crossed the finish line, the crowd came to its feet and roared its acclaim for a man who knew how to lose.

New speed records were set each year. When the track was closed in 1917 by World War I, drivers had pushed the mark up to 89 mph, the record set by Ralph DePalma, who had come back to win in 1915. It remained the top speed until Jimmy Murphy was clocked at 94.48 in 1922. Three years later Peter DePaolo, driving a Duesenberg, became the first to drive the 500 miles with an average speed of 101.12 mph, a record that stood until 1932, when Fred Frame came in the winner with 104.14 mph. From then on speeds of over 100 mph became commonplace, the over-125 mark set in 1951, the over-150-mph mark set in 1965. Spectators and drivers also went home earlier. It had taken Ray Harroun over six and a half hours to complete the first race, but A. J. Foyt consumed only three hours and 18 minutes in winning the 1967 classic.

Chapter 21

NEW CENTURY,
NEW VOICES

INDIANAPOLIS IN THE EARLY YEARS of the new century was growing, an "open-shop town" where labor was cheap and plentiful and invested capital was easily doubled and trebled. The New York Central Railroad built "the world's largest locomotive hospital" in Beech Grove at a cost of five million dollars. Jim Allison and Carl Fisher built the city of Speedway and sold it to a Detroit syndicate. The Panic of 1907 interrupted the boom, its effect more harsh on labor than on capital, and it gave birth to the Federal Reserve System.

The movement from farm to city, accelerated in the new century, swelled the city's population. A state 65 percent rural in 1900 was on its way to becoming 55 percent urban in just three decades. Census figures disclosed that 72 Indiana counties, mostly rural, lost 29 percent of their population before 1930. Of the counties showing gains, six accounted for 88 percent of the state's intercounty migration, with Marion and Lake Counties the leaders. The population in Indianapolis rose from 169,164 in 1900 to 233,650 in 1920. Ten years later it was 314,194.

The city's first skyscraper, the 17-story Merchants Bank Building, went up in 1912 just north of the bank's newly built four-story building on South Meridian Street. For 50 years, until the City-County Building opened in 1962, it was Indianapolis' tallest building. The new post-office building, covering the entire block between Pennsylvania and Meridian, Ohio and New York, opened in 1905.

A new newspaper, the Indianapolis *Star*, made its debut on June 6, 1903, its owner, George F. McCulloch of Muncie, its city editor, Merle Sidener of Indianapolis. A year later the *Star* absorbed the eighty-one-year-old Indianapolis *Journal* and in 1906 the *Sentinel*. It moved to its present location at 307 North Pennsylvania Street in 1907.

It was a good time for starting new enterprises, for enlarging established ones. Nineteen-year-old John Hook opened Hook's Economy Drug Store, offering brand names at cut prices. Before he was forty he owned 20 stores, and in 1970 the chain expanded to 123 stores under the presidency of his son, August F. (Bud) Hook. A tribute to John Hook, a restored nineteenth-century drugstore and museum was built by Bud Hook on the Indiana State Fair grounds in 1966. As a publishing center the city boasted dozens of good printers and typographers: Carlton and Hollenbeck, Pierson's, Burford's, and the new shop of George Cornelius, destined to become one of the largest in the Midwest. L. S. Ayres purchased the Hubbard block for its new home in 1904. The William H. Block Company, founded in 1896 by an immigrant schoolteacher from Austria-Hungary, moved from its one-story department store on Washington Street to new and larger quarters at Market and Illinois Streets. Wasson's, once the Beehive Store, dating back to 1870, added another building to its Washington Street store. L. Strauss & Company, formerly the Eagle Clothing Store, moved to larger quarters on Washington Street. Mrs. C. J. Walker, born in a slave cabin in Louisiana, opened the C. J. Walker Manufacturing Company to make a hair-dressing formula. It made her the first Negro woman millionaire in America.

The Pembroke Arcade, patterned after buildings at the 1893 World's Fair, connected Washington with Virginia Avenue, and the Virginia Avenue viaduct, opened in 1892, joined the north and south sides of the city. White-bearded "Pop" June held forth at his Shell Oyster Bay on South Illinois Street, and a noon lunch at Stegemeier's consisting of soup, two choices of meat, three vegetables, dessert and a drink cost 25 cents. The Flat Tire Club, founded in 1902 to assist stranded motorists, became the Hoosier Motor Club in 1911. Streets were becoming hazardous for pedestrians and drivers alike. Traffic was a mad mix of horses and wagons, automobiles, bicycles, trolleys and interurbans.

Among the city's showplaces were the Fisher, Allison and Parry estates, big, sprawling mansions on vast acreages of grass broken up by enormous flower beds and winding, graveled roads, with garages, greenhouses, and studied wildernesses filled with game and birds. Allison's estate on Cold Spring Road, on a bluff overlooking five artificial lakes, cost over two million dollars and took 30 servants to run. The house featured a chandelier of silver and bronze in the main lobby, a built-in pipe organ, giant fireplaces, an aviary of Italian marble, mahogany woodwork and inlaid floors, and custom furniture. The estate also boasted a swimming pool, perhaps the first in the city.

David M. Parry's estate in Golden Hills consisted of 100 acres, with a spacious mansion to match. With two children by his first wife and seven by his second, he needed a big house. The colorful Fisher, who at thirty-five had married an Indianapolis girl, Jane Watts, 11 years his junior, built his showplace in northwest Indianapolis near Riverside. It was a vast place, the living room being 60 feet long, with billiard tables, Oriental rugs, pianos, enormous fireplaces that burned all day, gardens, greenhouses, and garages, and a tennis court enclosed in glass for year-round use with a platform on the sidelines so that James Whitcomb Riley, a frequent visitor, could watch the play.

On Sixteenth Street, between Talbot and Pennsylvania, the new John Herron Art Institute opened on November 20, 1906, through a bequest in the will of John Herron to the Art Association of Indianapolis. Gifts came in from Mr. and Mrs. James V. Sweetser, Daniel P. Erwin, Julius Pratt, and Henry Schnull, the wholesale grocer and banker. The James E. Roberts and Mary Milliken Funds were established.

The city also had a new liberal arts coeducational college, Indiana Central, opened in 1905 on a 60-acre campus in the University Heights area and sponsored by the Evangelical United Brethren Church (which in 1968 joined with the Methodists to become the new United Methodist Church).

Indianapolis' first college, Butler University, moved for its second and last time, to Fairview Park on the rapidly growing north side. Arthur Jordan, an Indianapolis philanthropist, gave one million dollars to construct its main building, Jordan Hall. Young men at Butler were playing a new game, basketball, invented by James Naismith of Ontario, and it was catching on with players and spectators.

Basketball became a particular favorite of high schools and in 1911 the Boosters Club of Indiana University staged the first statewide high school tourney, marking the beginning of a madness that sweeps the state each year as lean, long-limbed Hoosier high-schoolers vie for the state title. The Indiana High School Athletic Association, founded in 1903, sanctioned the tourney starting in 1912. Not until 1955 did an Indianapolis school, Crispus Attucks, win the state championship, under the coaching of Ray Crowe. The school made it two in a row and came back in 1959 to win again.

A 65-bed unit of Methodist Hospital was completed in 1908, the result of a campaign by a group of Methodist Young People. Supported by prominent citizens such as Booth Tarkington, an Indianapolis council of Girl Scouts was started in 1919. Six years later the council opened

Camp Dellwood on a 141-acre estate, the gift of Dorothy Dell Moffett. The Indiana Federation of Business and Professional Women was organized in 1913, with Miss Nell Armstrong of Indianapolis as first president. An Indianapolis branch was formed one year later.

Theater, traveling shows and the circus dominated entertainment. Then moving pictures arrived. The first were peep shows for a penny, the pictures on a continuous reel of film that moved as the viewer turned a crank. Its inventor, Thomas A. Edison, pleased with a flood of pennies, was opposed to further development of his "kinetoscope." But he was forced to change his mind. In 1896 he sanctioned the projection of his tiny images on the rudimentary equivalent of today's theater screen. Nickelodeons took over vacant stores in almost every downtown block and the *News'* Abe Martin commented that "folks that used t' go home when they couldn't go nowheres else now go t' th' five-cent the-aters." At the Grand, the city's principal vaudeville house, the new films were used as "chasers," a device to clear the house before the next show. Then movies began to grow up. *The Great Train Robbery* was the first film with a story line and well-edited frames. By the 1920s a standard movie program consisted of a feature, a two-reel comedy, a cliff-hanging serial and a newsreel. Skilled piano players added realism to the silent films and accompanied the "community sing" which opened the early movie shows. First to show the new full-length movies was the Orpheum on East Washington Street and the Alhambra on West Washington, east of Illinois. In 1916 the Circle Theater opened, the first deluxe motion-picture house west of Broadway, a giant and ornate cavern with deep pile rugs in the lobby, statuary in niches, paintings on the wall—one of the first examples of the lavish movie palaces of the century, in 1970 the last of them to fall before a wrecker's ball.

New state laws affected the city. The State Bureau of Labor was established to inspect factories and mines. A compulsory-education law required all children from six to fourteen to attend school. Reformers pushed through an anti-cigarette law which forbade the manufacture and sale of cigarettes within the state. The law proved unenforceable and in 1909 it was repealed and cigarette sales were forbidden only to minors.

J. Frank Hanley, governor from 1905 to 1909, conducted an investigation and found that state funds had been misappropriated. His office claimed that he had recovered nearly $190,000, and one state official was prosecuted for embezzlement. The result was the Public Depository Law aimed at safe and honest care of public funds. An anti-lynching bill was passed, directed at stamping out self-appointed vigilante groups called "whitecaps" who whipped and maltreated alleged offenders against society. The bill climaxed a "whitecap" raid on the Ripley

County jail in which a group of hooded men took five prisoners out and hanged them from nearby trees.

A disastrous flood in 1913 brought tragedy and suffering. The flood followed five days of torrential rains which raised the White River and Fall Creek five to eight inches. Smashing through the White River levee at Morris Street, the churning water swept away the West Washington Street bridge, made Washington Street a lake, isolated the west side, poured tons of water into some 10,000 homes and caused damages estimated at well over 25 million dollars. It was months before the battered city recovered.

Indianapolis men enjoyed a moment of glory on the national political scene. For a time at the turn of the century, the youthful and brilliant Albert J. Beveridge, apostle of the new imperialism, flashed like a meteor on the national scene.

Beveridge's maiden speech in the Senate—on a joint resolution declaring that the Philippines were a territory of the United States and should be retained as such—created a sensation. The Spanish-American War, in Beveridge's view, had confirmed America's role as a world power, and the events in Cuba, Puerto Rico and the Philippines were an opportunity to dominate world trade "forever." But most of all, he spoke in soaring rhetoric of the God-given mission of Anglo-Saxons to rule and improve the world of the brown and yellow peoples. It was a neat package of expansionism and racism.

Beveridge, who had been born in Ohio in 1862, came to Indianapolis as a fledgling lawyer. He tried to join the law firm of Benjamin Harrison and, as Beveridge would later recall, was snubbed. He then joined the firm of McDonald and Butler and the Meridian Street Methodist Church, then the Sunday gathering place of the "best" people and the leaders of the Republican party. He made speeches at every opportunity, and in 1889 he was elected U. S. Senator by the General Assembly after 11 ballots. He was reelected in 1905.

Beveridge's imperialism was controversial. His speech in the Senate and his "March of the Flag" speech given to packed houses across the country—including overflow crowds at Tomlinson's Hall—shocked even moderate expansionists and unsettled President McKinley, who probably remembered that it was spread-eagled oratory of this sort that had forced him to declare war on Spain in the first place.

Ex-President Harrison delivered a quiet rebuke on New Year's Eve, 1900 at the dedication of the Columbia Club's new building on the Circle. The aging Harrison, only three months away from death, was the guest of honor. Also on the program was the poised, articulate thirty-seven-year-old Beveridge, just back from the Philippines, full of the new imperialism. Standing under the electric lights that illuminated his newly unveiled portrait, his hair and beard now a silvery white, Harrison talked softly and quietly of the need to respect the autonomy of nations and challenged the concept of an imperialism that interfered with such a policy. "Hail to Columbia," he concluded in ringing tones, "the home of the free, from which only freedom can go out." The Columbians cheered.

Eventually Beveridge was chastised by his fellow Senators, his President, and his party, and he failed for reelection to a third Senate term in 1910. He joined with Roosevelt in the Bull Moose Progressives movement, lost, ran again as a Republican in 1922, and lost again. In the field of biography he was more successful. His *Life of John Marshall* won the Pulitzer prize in 1920 and two volumes of a projected work, *Abraham Lincoln*, were published before his death in Indianapolis in 1927.

Charles Warren Fairbanks, a successful Indianapolis railroad lawyer and U. S. Senator from 1897 to 1905, became the nation's twenty-sixth Vice-President, under Theodore Roosevelt, in 1905. Fairbanks was a formidable power in Indiana politics and was nationally famous as the chairman of the U. S. delegation to the Joint High Commission that settled difficulties with Canada in 1898. The fact that he also owned the powerful Indianapolis *News* was one of the best-kept secrets in town.

Fairbanks had rejected Mark Hanna's offer to become McKinley's running mate in 1900, but accepted the Vice-Presidency under Roosevelt in the hope of becoming the Presidential candidate in 1908. Roosevelt, however, threw his support to William Howard Taft, who received the nomination on the first ballot. In 1912 Fairbanks got revenge for Roosevelt's perfidy. He was one of the leaders of a successful drive to crush Roosevelt's bid for the G.O.P. nomination. Fairbanks ran again for the Vice-Presidency in 1916, on the ticket with Charles Evans Hughes, but was defeated by Woodrow Wilson and another Hoosier, Thomas R. Marshall.

Two Indiana men, above all others, were symbols of the conflict between new social and economic philosophies. One was David M. Parry, a small, neat bantam cock of a man; the other the gentle, blue-eyed Eugene Victor Debs, a labor leader and a convert to Socialism.

David M. Parry was president of the Parry Automobile Company. He was also a chairman of boards; involved with insurance companies and railroads; president of the Indianapolis Board of Trade and the Commercial Club; and in 1902 he became president of the National Association of Manufacturers. He represented the new capitalism, powerful, entrenched, organized, unyielding. Parry was its spokesman and perhaps the most outspoken foe of American labor in any century.

He believed "it is the business of every man to honestly get all he can" and the trade union movement was "a standing mob engaged in open rebellion against the government." He believed labor could only "achieve its goals by revolution" and charged that the country could not run on an eight-hour day. His fighting anti-labor talks brought standing ovations at the National Association of Manufacturers national convention in Indianapolis and the Citizens' Industrial Association of America meeting at the Claypool Hotel. He wrote an anti-labor book, *The Scarlet Empire*, and established the N.A.M.'s first bureau of information to influence political parties and public officials.

Parry's posture was unwittingly driving men into the new labor unions, the new Socialist party and other political movements. To many workingmen he symbolized what the muckrakers like Upton Sinclair, Frank Norris and Ida Tarbell were writing and talking about: unbridled, irresponsible capitalism that fattened on child labor and created slums and poverty.

Much of the new American union movement was centered in Mr. Parry's backyard. Indianapolis' central location attracted many early labor unions, and they set up headquarters in the city. One of the giants of the labor movement, bushy-browed, cigar-smoking, Shakespeare-quoting John L. Lewis, set up his United Mine Workers office on the eleventh floor of the Merchants Bank Building. Serving with him was the man with whom he would be locked in battle in the 1930s, William Green, later the president of the American Federation of Labor. The Indiana Federation of Labor was founded October 8, 1903, a consolidation of the state's burgeoning unions.

Parry's antithesis was Eugene V. Debs, a soft-spoken Alsatian born in Terre Haute in 1855 who had left school to go to work in the railroad yards for 50 cents a day scraping paint off the cars. He became a locomotive fireman, quit because his mother worried, went back to railroading and founded the American Railway Union. His union was smashed by the railroads, the politicians and the courts, and while serving a jail term he studied, read, talked and meditated, and out of his disillusionment, his resentment, his common cause with the poor and the downtrodden, he became a Socialist. He stumped for Bryan in 1896 because the Populists endorsed him, but after Bryan lost, he joined with Victor Berger to form the Social-Democratic party, which in 1900 became the Socialist Party of America.

Indianapolis was the site of the party's first conventions. On March 6, 1900, the Socialists nominated Debs for the Presidency, against Bryan and McKinley—the same year Bryan came to Indianapolis formally to accept the Democratic nomination on a platform outside the statehouse. It was the first of five times Debs' party would nominate him.

He joined with Bill Haywood to found, at Chicago, the International

Workers of the World, an industrial union as opposed to the American Federation of Labor, which was organized according to craft. He became involved with the case of the McNamara brothers, John and James, charged with the dynamiting of the Los Angeles *Times* Building in which 21 persons died. William J. Burns, a detective, tracked John McNamara to his Monument Circle office in 1911, where he was arrested. Unions shouted "Frame-up!" and charged that Burns was a "kidnapper"; Burns charged that Debs had hired a hundred men to assassinate him. When James McNamara confessed, the A.F.L. repudiated the McNamaras, but Debs defended them. "If you want to judge John McNamara," he declared, "you must first serve a month as a structural-iron worker on a skyscraper, risking your life every minute to feed your wife and babies, then be discharged and blacklisted for joining a union."

Nominated for the fourth time in Indianapolis, in 1912, Debs doubled his vote. In 1916 he declined to run and during World War I was jailed under the Espionage Act. Nominated while in jail, he polled over 900,000 votes in the 1920 election, a clue to America's growing discontent.

Chapter 22

OF WAR AND PEACE

W HEN WAR ERUPTED in Europe in 1914, it seemed remote and none of our business, but three years later, as spike-helmeted Germans marched across Europe and wolf packs of German U-Boats attacked Atlantic shipping, Americans took sides.

Indianapolis, in the heart of the nation, mirrored feelings common to the country. Sentiment ranged from immediate intervention to open sympathy for Germany. In the middle were the peace groups of the city—the Indiana Peace Society, the Women's Peace Party, and the World Peace Foundation with Charles W. Fairbanks as president—and people like novelist Booth Tarkington, who abhorred war but urged preparedness.

As war came closer, Republican Governor James P. Goodrich called a conference of farmers, grain dealers, canners and county agriculture agents to mobilize the state's food production. In March Tomlinson's Hall could not contain the enormous crowds that turned out for a pro-Ally meeting. Railroads mobilized; the Chamber of Commerce set up a war-contracts division; the Y.M.C.A. made plans for entertaining soldiers stationed in the city. Indianapolis was patriotic and prepared.

When war was declared on April 6, 1917, recruiting stations reported enlisting more men in Indiana than in any other state. Richard Lieber was appointed military secretary to the governor to rally German support. Will H. Hays, chairman of the state G.O.P. committee, and Tom Taggart, a former Indianapolis mayor and national Democratic chairman, were named to head the State Council of Defense. When Hays was called to Washington, Michael Foley, an Indianapolis attorney, was named to take his place.

City boys and farm boys put on itchy, high-collared brown uniforms. The First Indiana Regiment of Field Artillery, made up of recruits and National Guard units from Indianapolis, Fort Wayne and Lafayette, assembled at Fort Benjamin Harrison, with Colonel Robert H. Tyndall of Indianapolis commanding. The First Indiana became the 150th Field Artillery of the famed Forty-second Rainbow Division commanded by General Douglas MacArthur and part of the first detachment of American troops to land in France. A group of Indianapolis physicians, Drs. John Oliver, David Ross, Frank Morrison and O. G. Pfaff, formed the 500-bed Eli Lilly Base Hospital, later Base Hospital 32. The unit was stationed at Contrexeville in the Vosges Mountains about 350 miles from Paris. While Congress debated a draft bill, Governor Goodrich set up the nation's first conscription program and put it into operation. Evans Woollen, the banker, was named the federal fuel administrator and Dr. Harry E. Barnard the federal food administrator. County councils for defense were formed, with "Liberty Guards" to seek out slackers and traitors, keep order and ferret out subversion. Labor leaders and organizers protested Ordinance 35 passed by the Indianapolis City Council, making it unlawful to speak out or write against the United States government or "to incite, urge or advise strikes or disturbances in war-related plants."

Anti-German feeling ran high after America's entry into the war. There were rock throwings, roughing-up of German citizens, reprisals against German-Americans who failed to buy bonds or display the flag. The board of education banned teaching the German language in city schools. The Deutsche Haus became the Athenaeum; the Turnverein, the Indianapolis Athletic Club; the Maennerchor, the Academy of Music.

Indianapolis put four Liberty Loan drives over the top. There were parades and block parties, and distinguished visitors such as Grandpère Joffre, Marshal of France, and movie stars such as Douglas Fairbanks, Charlie Chaplin and Mary Pickford. A huge war chest was erected on the circle. Prices and wages went up, the wages never quite meeting the rising prices. Families hung service flags in their windows, a blue star for each man in uniform, a gold star for a loved one who had given his life in the "war to end war" and "to make the world safe for democracy." Daylight Saving Time was introduced. There were wheatless Mondays, meatless Tuesday, heatless days, lightless days, Sundays without gasoline. Families planted Victory Gardens. Prest-O-Lite turned out munitions. Allison's revised and rebuilt Liberty airplane engines and designed a 24-cylinder engine, largest of its time, for a giant biplane which was never used. The Indianapolis Speedway became an aviation repair depot and landing field for planes plying between Dayton, Ohio, and Rantoul, Illinois.

On November 7, 1918, a United Press bulletin announced the signing of the Armistice and Indianapolis went dancing in the streets. The celebration was at its peak when the telegraph wires clicked off denials and corrections.

The premature armistice bulletin, which would go down as one of the most amazing contretemps in journalistic history, was the work of an ex-Indianapolis newspaperman, Roy Howard, directing head of United Press who three years later would be business director of the powerful Scripps-Howard chain.

Four days after Howard's first bulletin, November 11, 1918, the Allies announced the signing of the Armistice and the end of the war. This time it was for sure and the city became a bedlam. Cheering, shouting, wild-with-joy masses of people packed the downtown streets and the Circle. Church bells, fire bells, factory whistles, sirens, streetcar bells, automobile horns sounded.

In May 1919 the city cheered itself hoarse again as soldiers of the 150th Field Artillery and the doctors, nurses and enlisted men of Eli Lilly Base Hospital 32, back from the war, marched under a great victory arch spanning North Meridian Street. As they marched around the Circle with their flags and bands—with the first motor apparatus of the Indianapolis Fire Department as part of the procession—a living red cross was formed on the steps of the monument.

In all, some 130,000 Indiana young men and women had marched away to World War I and death had claimed 3,354 men and 15 nurses in camp and on foreign battlefields. Among those returning were innumerable victims of poison gas and other new weapons of the first of the modern and impersonal wars.

Returning doughboys joined the new American Legion and the Veterans of Foreign Wars, just as Civil War veterans had joined the Grand Army of the Republic, to keep old friendships and war memories alive and to lobby for benefits. The American Legion, founded in 1919, selected Indianapolis as the site of its national headquarters at its convention in Minneapolis the same year. In 1920 a special session of the General Assembly authorized construction of the War Memorial Plaza in downtown Indianapolis, including a national headquarters for the American Legion. Marcus Sonntag of Evansville was named chairman of a 15-member committee to carry out plans.

To make way for the new five-block memorial between Meridian and Pennsylvania Streets, old landmarks were razed—but not without protest, petitions, court suits.

Construction of the memorial occupied most of the 1920s. Marshal Foch came on November 4, 1921, bringing with him a stone from the time of Caesar, a part of a bridge destroyed at historic Chateau Thierry in 1918, engraved with "an acknowledgment of France's friendship for a valiant ally." On July 4, 1927, General Pershing, commander of the A.E.F. in World War I, came to lay the cornerstone of Memorial Hall.

The completed memorial, its buildings executed in Indiana limestone and marble, is one of the most impressive and beautiful of the nation's permanent tributes to the men of World War I. The three-story main memorial building has a shrine room and a 500-seat auditorium, and the walls of its grand staircase and corridors incorporate panels displaying the names of over 130,000 Hoosiers who served in the various services. The two other buildings contain the national headquarters and the Indiana department of the American Legion and its auxiliary, the National Forty and Eight, and a number of other patriotic groups and auxiliaries. On a granite base in the center of the south staircase of the memorial building facing University Park is the largest sculptural bronze casting ever produced in America, *Pro Patria* by Henry Hering.

Indianapolis ushered in the Roaring Twenties by celebrating its one-hundredth birthday in June 1920, and after the pomp and the pageantry were over—six days of music, speeches, church services, three pageants and a downtown parade with 122 floats—the swinging part of the population began to create one of the giddiest, gaudiest, most tasteless, happiest and saddest eras in history.

It was a decade in which two men based in Indianapolis exercised, at different times, great power in the state: the Reverend Seitz Shumaker, superintendent of the Anti-Saloon League, and D. C. Stephenson of the Ku Klux Klan. Shumaker dominated the early years, virtually controlling the Indiana General Assembly, and Stephenson, the later years. Their organizations also became allies in upholding old-time religion, bone-dry prohibition and a twisted brand of 100 percent Americanism.

The Reverend Shumaker, a Methodist clergyman, built his organization in and around evangelical pulpits and called his Anti-Saloon League "the church in action." Unlike the Klan, the League sought donors instead of members and it built up a sizable war chest. In 1917 Shumaker pushed through a statewide prohibition act. Challenged and upheld in the courts, the act became effective April 2, 1918—a year before the War Prohibition Act. In 1919 Shumaker again "cracked the ecclesiastical whip" and the state legislature ratified the Eighteenth (Prohibition) Amendment.

Bootlegging became a major business. The city was a transportation center, a convention city, a thirsty city. Illicit whiskey poured into town from stills in Kentucky, from Terre Haute (a crossroads for gangsters), from Chicago, from the East. Roadhouses sprang up toward Ravenswood north of Broad Ripple. Speakeasies were everywhere. Newspapers and ministers decried the lack of enforcement, but no one paid them much heed.

There were scandals, some connected with prohibition, some not. There were charges that city councilmen and police were being bought, that policemen were getting payoffs from bootleggers, the speakeasies, the roadhouses. Governor Warren McCray got into financial difficulties and resigned April 29, 1924. He was sentenced to a ten-year prison term for using the mails to defraud. Some saw events as part of the moral breakdown brought on by prohibition, restless men home from the war, the new philosophy of "get everything you can."

Indianapolis' Carl Fisher, his Speedway and other Indianapolis ventures booming, was one of a trio of promoters riding the peak of the nation's greatest land boom, the Miami-madness of the 1920s.

Fisher's interest in Miami went back to 1913, when he bailed out John S. Collins, a successful New Jersey horticulturist, who had run out of money building a bridge from Miami to the beach. Fisher invested $50,000 and, when the bridge was finished, decided Florida was the place. After World War I he built hotels and launched a high-pressure razzle-dazzle advertising campaign; he created the Miami Beach bathing beauty and staged bathing-beauty contests. Reputedly worth 30 million dollars, most of it in speculative profits, Fisher put ten million into the Montauk (Long Island) Beach Development Company, divorced his first wife, remarried, and built a fabulous estate in Miami Beach. Then his luck changed.

In 1926 Florida real estate prices began to decline, a signal that the boom was over. In September a hurricane flattened the Miami area, the ocean inundating Miami Beach. Fisher was nearly wiped out. His Montauk Beach Development Company went into receivership in 1932. When Fisher died in 1939, he was reputedly worth less than a million dollars, most of it tied up, his only landholding in Indianapolis being a lot in Crown Hill Cemetery, where he was interred after a spectacular funeral at Miami Beach.

A skinny, music-struck kid from Emmerich Manual High School and a new brassy and blue sound came together in Indianapolis. The kid was Hoagy Carmichael, born in Bloomington in 1899, and the music was jazz, born in New Orleans.

In the 1920s jazz was moving north, brought by the black men who had created it. Indianapolis, home of 35,000 Negroes, 11 percent of the total population, one of the highest ratios of any Northern city, became a jazz capital to rival Chicago. The new music, which started in the city's black and tan joints, sporting houses, cheap vaudeville houses, speakeasies and roadhouses, quickly found its way uptown to big ballrooms and country clubs. Indianapolis was a town of jazz enthusiasts and the crossroads stopover of all the early great jazzmen, Don Redman, McKinney's Cotton Pickers, Jean Goldkette. It gave one of America's most famous jazz bands its start, the Wolverines, which included jazz's golden boy Bix Beiderbecke, who carried his cornet under his arm in a brown paper bag. The Wolverines drew crowds to the now long-gone Casino Gardens west of the White River between Sixteenth and Twenty-second Streets. In nearby Richmond was a tiny phonograph recording studio tucked away in a corner of the Starr Piano Company, the home of Gennett Records. Here King Oliver's Creole Jazz Band made the first recording of a jazz session, and eventually all the greats of the new sound came to make records on the Gennett gold label, now valuable collector's items.

As a boy and a young man Hoagy Carmichael lived alternately in Bloomington and in Indianapolis as his father changed jobs. His mother helped the family fortunes by playing piano in movie houses. Hoagy held an odd assortment of jobs and spent long hours with a black friend, Leslie Duval, learning the magic of the seventh and flatted third of 88 piano keys. He got a job playing piano in a Greek restaurant, moved to cheap joints, then to a red plush sporting house on North Illinois Street, gave it all up and went back to high school, graduated, and enrolled as a law student at Indiana University. He studied hard and got his law degree, but they were music-haunted years in which he played with bands and formed Carmichael's Collegians, which appeared regularly in Indianapolis. He wrote the jazz classic "Riverboat Shuffle," recorded by the Wolverines on a Gennett label, and Mills Music bought it. On a lush night on the Indiana University campus he hummed the opening bars of "Stardust," hurried to the Book Nook and found part of it on the piano, finishing it one night in Indianapolis. A schoolmate, Stuart Gorrell, gave it a name, Gennett recorded it, Mitchell Parish wrote the lyrics and after a modest beginning it became a hit.

When Paul Whiteman's band played at the Indiana Theater in Indianapolis, Hoagy and Frank Hostetter hurried up from Bloomington to meet their old friend Bix Beiderbecke. "Pops" Whiteman, a mountain of a man with a small mustache, invited Carmichael to join the band and to record "Washboard Blues." Carmichael's acceptance set him on the road to a career as a singer, composer, star of motion pictures, radio and television, a man whose works were among the best of the popular music for nearly four decades.

There were others who went to the big time from Indianapolis: Slide Hampton, J. J. Johnson and Wes Montgomery, legendary figures in the field of jazz; Clifton Webb and Robert Paige of stage and screen, Elden Blackledge, the magician. Dick Powell, one of the city's most popular singers, went to Hollywood and fame in the early musicals, later switching to tough-guy parts and becoming one of the town's first big TV tycoons. Indianapolis-born Noble Sissle, whose father was minister of the city's largest Negro congregation, became a professional musician, toured the Midwest Chautauqua circuit, enrolled at Butler where he wrote the school's cheer song, "Butler Will Shine Tonight," and formed a band. After serving overseas in World War I he formed a vaudeville act and teamed up with Eubie Blake to write and produce two successful Broadway musicals, *Shuffle Along* and *Chocolate Dandies*, in the mid-1920s.

It was a dancing era and a time of big bands and sweet, mellow music. There were tea dances, country club dances, dances at Riverside Park, the Athenaeum, the Indiana Roof, the Lyric Theater Ballroom, the Casino Gardens—the dance halls were places of soft, flickering lights and romance. Most popular of the dances were the fox-trot, the slow fox-trot, the waltz, the Lindy Hop, the 400 and, for the more athletic, the Charleston. Later came the dance marathons at Riverside Park, with tired partners fighting to stay awake and morbid crowds to cheer the straggling couples on.

Indianapolis had a new and popular poet, William Herschell of the *News*, already famous for his wartime hit, "Long Boy," who wrote homely, sentimental, rustic poetry in alleged Hoosier dialect. Following closely in Riley's footsteps, he chose appealing and heartwarming themes. He became a much beloved character and was probably the best of many poets who tried their hand at Riley's successful formula. Much of his work, however, was synthetic, and little of it proved durable. In Indiana he is remembered for his "Ain't God Good to Indiana?" first published in the *News* on May 31, 1919.

Chain stores proliferated, the Indianapolis-based Hook chain counting 40 stores, the Haag Drug chain 19. The expanding city-based Standard Grocery store fought a new state chain-store tax in the courts. Woolworth's sold only items that cost five and ten cents. Most families lived on $25 a week or less. Henry Ford's proposal to pay his workers five dollars a day shocked the local auto community, notorious for its low wages.

New industries came to Indianapolis—in 1929 the P. R. Mallory Company and the Westinghouse Lamp Works. Forerunner of the giant RCA complex was a Radio Corporation of America plant on East Michigan Street. Industry, after a slight halt for postwar adjustment, was generally booming through most of the 1920s.

The first of the state highways and improved roads reached out from the city, financed by federal aid and the state gasoline tax. On weekends roads were clogged with "flivvers" or "tin lizzies," the Model T Fords, butt of a thousand current jokes but making the automobile available even to low-income Indianapolis families. Many were heading for the new parks, whose principal architect was Richard Lieber, a German immigrant. His efforts would spur construction of half a dozen by 1933. Traffic accidents were increasing in the city, 43,393 in 1929, 99 resulting in death. Police reported the intersection at Washington and Illinois the most dangerous in town.

It was the golden age of sports. Paul D. (Tony) Hinkle's Butler University basketball team won the world's championship in 1929. Donnie Bush of Indianapolis, former manager of the Pittsburgh Pirates, took over the Chicago White Sox in 1929, to revamp a team in disrepute since the "Black Sox" scandal in 1919. Crowds filled Tomlinson's Hall weekly for the American Legion boxing shows where fight managers hoped to develop another Kid McCoy or Jack Dillon, Indianapolis fighters who had gone on to fame earlier in the century. Washington Park was jammed on Sunday for minor baseball and exhibitions.

The Indianapolis Motor Speedway changed hands in 1927, price $700,000. The new owner was Captain Eddie V. Rickenbacker, a pioneer auto racer and World War I flying ace of aces. Captain "Eddie" resurfaced the track with Kentucky rock asphalt and built an 18-hole golf course for added revenue. Busy with other projects, including his Eastern Airlines, Rickenbacker, after the first year, left the operations to T. E. "Pop" Myers, general manager since the first race in 1911.

Indianapolis saw more airplanes in the skies over the city. Plane services offered rides for $5 and $10. Sometimes there were daring wing walkers and stunt men to watch and more often than not Bob Shank of Indianapolis, a pioneer aviator, was at the controls. Planes were also being used to carry the mail. One of the early flights was from Frankfort to Indianapolis, the pilot landing in midwinter in a Ryan monoplane to find no one on hand to receive the mail pouch. Indianapolis became a stop on the nation's airmail routes in December 1928, and veteran pilots would later tell stories of mailing bricks to each other to profit from government air subsidies.

In August 1927 the city gave a tumultuous welcome to a flying hero, twenty-six-year-old Charles A. Lindbergh, the first man to solo across the Atlantic, New York to Paris, flying a single-engine airplane, *The*

Spirit of St. Louis. He sat atop an open car driven around the Circle past wildly cheering crowds, out Meridian to Thirty-eighth Street to the fairgrounds for formal ceremonies. He returned to the city some months later to set up the TAT-Maddux Transcontinental Airline, the first to offer coast-to-coast service, New York to Los Angeles, by plane and train in 48 hours, the airline passengers landing at Mars Airport at Indianapolis and taking a train at Union Depot. E. I. Lewis of Indianapolis, a member of the Interstate Commerce Commission, was the first to make the transcontinental hop. Tickets on sale at a Monument Circle office in 1929 cost $159.92 one way and the time was 36 hours. In December 1929 the line experienced one of its first crashes, the Ford Tri-Motor *City of Indianapolis* hitting a stump on landing, killing one and injuring two.

Well-dressed men and affluent actors wore fur-trimmed coats, derby hats, spats and fawn-colored gloves and carried a cane. Trousers had bell bottoms, coats were tight-fitting. For summer dances men wore white flannels, dark coats, white shoes. Golfers wore knickers. Flappers bobbed their hair and wore long, dangling necklaces and short skirts with tassels just over the knee. Legs were in fashion, bosoms were out. Most women and matrons lifted skirts to just below the knee and stayed with classic and revised styles, but by the end of the decade flapper and conventional styles reached sensible compromises.

Women won the vote with the Nineteenth Amendment in 1919. The Women's Franchise League, which had grown out of the Women's School League, founded in 1910 to elect a woman, Miss Mary Nicholson, to the all-male Indianapolis School Board, became the League of Women Voters. Headquarters of the Indiana League were moved to Indianapolis from Elkhart the following year, during the presidency of Mrs. Walter S. Greenough.

The Indianapolis *Sun* became the Indianapolis *Daily Times* as the result of its purchase by the Scripps-Howard chain. Roy Howard, who headed the chain, became president of the *Times.*

The movies learned to talk and by the end of the decade 13 theaters equipped with sound forced English's Opera House to advertise that its plays featured "real flesh and blood actors." Downtown theaters such as the Indiana—where Charlie Davis and his band were a big attraction—continued to present vaudeville, variety units and "stage presentations," but the days of vaudeville and combined film and live presentations were numbered.

Much of the 1920s was marked by a building boom, especially in low-cost "cottages," expensive residences and new club, office and hotel buildings. The Columbia Club, which had outgrown its old quarters, dedicated a new ten-story building in October 1925 and the next year

entertained Queen Marie of Romania, who was visiting America with
Princess Olena and Prince Nicholas. Businessman George Marott erected
the luxurious one-million-dollar Marott apartment hotel on Meridian
Street.

Radio crept in on a little cat's whisker, a vital part of the new crystal
sets, accompanied by the crackle of static, squeals and howls. By the
decade's end radio had passed from the batteries-on-the-floor to the all-
electric stage, from table models to consoles. Indianapolis' first radio
station, 9ZJ, built and owned by Purdue graduate Francis Hamilton in
his garage on North Alabama Street, took to the air on New Year's
Eve 1921. Mayor Samuel Lewis (Lew) Shank, after making his way
through a labyrinth of wires, recorded local radio's first blooper: standing before a live microphone, he asked Hamilton, "Do you mean to
tell me that people can actually hear me over this damn dingus?" As the
city boasted only a handful of sets, few heard him or his speech, the
program of popular tunes played by Mr. and Mrs. Noble Hilgenberg,
or the midnight vaudeville show from the B. F. Keith's theater broadcast by the way of an ordinary telephone receiver which Hamilton
had rigged up on stage.

Shortly after the first of the year the Indianapolis *News* and the L. S.
Ayres Department Store (which had just opened a new Radio Room)
became partners of Hamilton, and the station moved to the tenth floor
of the *News* building. Spring hatched another station, WOH, owned
by Hatfield Electric Company, radio dealers, who were joined in the
operation by the Indianapolis *Star*, then separately owned and a rival
of the *News*. Through a friendly cost-cutting arrangement stations took
to the air on alternate nights, but operating costs and lack of revenues
forced both off the air in 1923.

The city's airwaves were silent until election eve of 1924, when
WFBM, the city's first radio station destined for permanency, went on
the air from studios on the fourth floor of the Indianapolis Athletic
Club. The station was the collective brainchild of Clem Portman, John
Tribby, Hobart Ashlock and Frank Sharp, who sold the idea to the
Merchants Heat & Light Company, predecessors of the Indianapolis
Power & Light Company.

Interest in the 1924 election ran high. The Indianapolis *News* and
Times had arranged to project the results on screens opposite their
buildings. The Indianapolis *Star* rented the Cadle Tabernacle, set up
a screen in the choir area and hired the Indianapolis Concert Band to
provide music between voting returns. Not to be outdone, WFBM set
up screens around the utility building and poked loudspeakers out the
second-floor windows of the Athletic Club. The station went on the
air at 6:00 P.M. and, before it signed off at midnight, reported a Repub-

lican sweep of both state and nation. Republican Ed Jackson, openly supported by the Ku Klux Klan, became governor, and Calvin Coolidge, who was silent on the Klan as on other issues, became President.

In the spring of 1925, Noble Watson, a city radio pioneer, set up WBBZ at his Iowa Street home, but it survived only a few months. Undaunted, he teamed up with his brother, Carl, and in November 1926 came back on the air with WKBF from a Ford showroom on Washington Street. The station was a success and became the highly rated WIRE.

Watson's station and the competing WFBM filled the air with amateur hours, local musical groups, talks, religious programs, and Gus Edwards and his orchestra from the Athletic Club dining room. The *Times* sponsored the final 15 games of the 1925 State High School Basketball Tourney from the fairgrounds' Coliseum. The *News* and Prest-O-Lite jointly sponsored the 500-Mile Race. In 1927 WFBM launched the Wheeler Rescue Mission, which became the city's oldest continuous radio program. Popular with late Friday night listeners was an all-request program of organ music from the Circle Theater, with Dessa Byrd at the console and Ace Berry, the theater manager, at the microphone. In 1928 WFBM became a CBS affiliate (today an NBC outlet) and five years later WKNF joined NBC (now a CBS affiliate).

The networks ushered in radio's golden age, but both WFBM and WKBF continued to develop local programs with enormous followings. WFBM introduced such innovations as the first regularly scheduled newscasts, with Ken Ellington and the first local disc jockey, Don Hasting, who woke up 7:00 A.M. audiences with his *Pep Unlimited* show. (He was succeeded by Bill Kiley, later to become WFBM general manager.) Merle Sidener's *Christian Men Builders* on Sundays from the Third Christian Church was a popular religious hour and a radio fixture for 25 years. William H. Block sponsored the top-rated *Children's Hour.* Durward Kirby, who married a singer at the station, Mary Paxton Young, staged the *Early Birds,* popular with teen-agers. Gilbert Forbes of WFBM became "Mr. Radio News" and the only local radio newsman to serve as a war correspondent in World War II.

Radio was enlisted in the fight against crime, the Indianapolis police department being the third in the nation to install a radio system. Its station, WMDZ, began operations on Christmas Eve, 1929. Detective Jerry E. Kinney was credited with receiving the initial broadcast in his radio-equipped police car—a Stutz Bearcat. The local system was set up by Robert L. Batts, a Purdue engineering graduate, who established the first police radio system for the Detroit police in their fight against the notorious "Purple Gang." During his 22 years with the Indianapolis department, Batts established many important firsts, including the first two-way communications system between station and patrol cars, the first radio-directed motorcycles and pushbutton control of the entire police network from individual cars—an important factor in high-speed chases.

But radio and the rising crime rate, jazz and flappers, Florida real estate, fast autos and liquor were not all that occupied Indianapolis in the 1920s. Men were singing "The Fiery Cross on High" and donning whitepointed hoods and robes to write an unhappy and infamous chapter in the history of city and nation.

Chapter 23

THE MAN WHO WAS
THE LAW

FIERY CROSSES BURNED on America's hillsides in the 1920s, and the apostles of hate and bigotry dressed in white sheets and peaked hoods marched in its streets to the sound of muffled drums. The Knights of the Ku Klux Klan was reborn in the backlash of a world war.

The "Invisible Empire" of the new Klan was estimated at six million members at its peak and it exerted a tremendous influence on the political, religious and economic life of the nation. In three states, Oregon, Oklahoma and Indiana, it took over the government.

The Klan in Indiana was a one-man power structure named David Curtis Stephenson, a squat, powerfully built master salesman who exuded charm and good fellowship, but could be as dangerous as a timber rattlesnake. He was Grand Dragon of the Ku Klux Klan, and for a few short years he could proclaim without fear of challenge: "I am the law in Indiana."

At thirty-three he was wealthy as well as powerful. In his first 18 months as Grand Dragon of the Indiana "realm" his share of the "take" from Klan memberships and the sale of robes and hoods netted him a million and a half dollars. Some of his rich harvest he had invested in other enterprises, including a profitable coal and gravel business. The dollars and the growing membership of the Klan, estimated in Indiana at over a half-million, were translated into political and economic power. Stephenson could virtually dictate who stayed in business and he could elect governors, legislators, mayors and city councils and dispense choice statehouse jobs to Klan friends. He could get bills passed in the legislature and arrange for the building of new schools and roads. Genial Ed Jackson, a Republican, who as secretary of state had issued the Klan's charter, was governor and owed his election to Stephenson and his hooded empire.

The Grand Dragon lived like a kingmaker. His home in suburban Irvington was a showplace, and he maintained an expensive suite at the Washington Hotel, a fleet of Cadillacs and a yacht on Lake Michigan. He entertained lavishly, and in sharp contrast to the repressive puritanism of the Klan, he was a ladies' man, *bon vivant* and a frequently heavy drinker. Directing the affairs of the Klan from a handsomely furnished eight-room suite of offices on the third floor of the Kresge building in downtown Indianapolis, he kept a bust of Napoleon on his desk, called himself "the Old Man," and was always accompanied by armed bodyguards.

Stephenson's, and the Klan's, phenomenal rise to power is the story of human enterprise at its most sinister and cynical. It exploited the weak, the venal, the ignorant and naïve—the whole litany of the intellectually blind and the halt—and it unleashed all the repressions and tyranny of sex-haunted, guilt-ridden puritanism and Southern Fundamentalism on people whose only sin had been an accident of birth.

Both Stephenson and the Klan had inauspicious and uncertain beginnings. Born in Texas, Stephenson had received a grade-school education, worked in printing shops and on newspapers in Texas, Oklahoma and Iowa, became an active member of the Socialist party and in 1915 married and divorced the first of three wives. He volunteered for the Iowa National Guard and graduated from Officers' Training School at Fort Snelling as a second lieutenant. Stephenson later claimed he had gone overseas during World War I, but records indicate he spent the war at Camp Devens, Massachusetts.

Following his honorable discharge, Stephenson turned up in Evansville, Indiana, organizing veterans of the Thirty-sixth Infantry Division and selling coal-mining securities. He registered as a Democrat, entered the 1921 Congressional primary and was overwhelmingly defeated. Then Hiram Wesley Evans, a Dallas dentist and the new Imperial Wizard of the Ku Klux Klan, gave Stephenson the job of organizing the Klan in Indiana. Evans had just taken over the Klan after staging a *coup d'état* which unseated the founder of the revived Klan—"Colonel" William Henry Simmons.

Simmons, a preacher, promoter and Lanier College history instructor, had established the new Klan at Stone Mountain near Atlanta, Georgia, on Thanksgiving Night of 1915. The original Klan of Reconstruction Days, disbanded in 1896, had concentrated on white supremacy, but

Simmons' new version encompassed all the prejudices of the post-World War I world. Catholics, Jews and foreigners as well as Negroes now appeared on the Klan hate list, to provide a kind of bigot's delight.

The new Klan was also a super-patriotic organization. It was 100 percent American, isolationist, and opposed to all foreign influences which, as the Klan viewed it, placed the Constitution in dire peril. Ministers could find in the new Klan an outpost of Protestant Evangelicalism. It stood foursquare for the Bible, old-time religion, protection of American womanhood, punishment of transgressors and bone-dry prohibition.

Politically the Klan's ideology was more conservative than the generally conservative politics of the day and it divided sharply along geographical lines: it was Democratic in the South and generally Republican in the North. Reflecting its Southern origin, it also strongly advocated state's rights.

In short, the new Klan of the 1920s offered something for everyone, provided they were prejudiced, white, native-born, Christian and liked secret organizations with a ritual of gibberish words and phrases.

Despite the built-in success formula, Imperial Wizard Simmons' Klan wasn't very successful until 1920, when a pair of high-powered publicity agents and professional fund raisers came along, recognized the Klan's tremendous profit potential and proceeded to take over.

One of the pair, Edward Young Clark, was made Grand Kleagle, second in command, and Mrs. Elizabeth Tyler, the other half of the team, was made his assistant. They divided the country into eight "domains," each headed by a Grand Goblin, and subdivided these into "realms," or states, each in charge of a Grand Dragon. Membership was fixed at ten dollars, with four dollars going to the salesman, one dollar to the state sales manager, 50 cents to the Grand Goblin and the biggest share, $4.50, to the Atlanta headquarters. A highly profitable deal was also negotiated for the manufacture and sale of uniforms and the Searchlight Publishing Company was formed to turn out Klan newspapers, magazines and other printed material. Within 18 months after Clark and Tyler took over, the Klan could count 100,000 heads in pointed hoods carrying out a program of quiet terror across the nation. And the Klan's treasury grew.

The new Klan began to attract attention and enemies. A Congressional investigating committee looked into stories of Klan murders, floggings, kidnapping, threats, branding and mutilation, tarring and feathering. There was strong circumstantial evidence, but nothing to take to a court of law. Then the New York *World*, which had sparked the Congressional investigation, turned up a piece of evidence that split the Klan hierarchy wide open. Two years before, the newspaper reported, Clark and Mrs. Tyler had been arrested "at midnight in their sleeping garments in a notorious underworld resort . . . run by Mrs. Tyler." The couple had been charged with disorderly conduct and possession of liquor. The story led to the resignation of Clark, denunciations by Mrs. Tyler, charges and countercharges, and the growth of an insurgent group which was lovingly nurtured by the ambitious Dr. Evans, the Klan Kligrapp, or national secretary. In November 1922 the Dallas dentist took over as Imperial Wizard.

Evans' appointment of Stephenson marked the real beginning of the Klan in Indiana. The state was fertile ground for the expanding Klan, and Stephenson, now a registered Republican, proved to be a brilliant sales manager. He imported high-powered salesmen—many of them fresh from triumphs in Florida real estate—and fanned them out over the state, covering the byways as well as the highways. Money and memberships rolled in, and Evans, impressed with his protégé, added some 20 states to Stephenson's territory.

Stephenson, however, was more than a super-salesman. He was a genius at organization and administration, staging meetings, parades and conventions. He formed an active and powerful woman's auxiliary and the Kiddie Klan. He mobilized the money and power of the "Invisible Empire" behind political candidates, usually Republican, who were "100 percent American" and followed the Klan line. Merchants found the Klan could exert strong economic pressure; they not only joined but frequently paid tribute. Klan-approved stores carried red, white and blue signs with the letters "TWK" (Trade with the Klan). Bootleggers who took out Klan "licenses" found they could operate without fear of police or Klan raids.

Among Stephenson's achievements was the revival of the Horse Thief Association of 1852, which had been formed in lawless days to combat widespread horse thievery. The law permitted members to arrest individuals and punish them without benefit of formal trials. The association became the storm troopers of the Indiana Klan and they carried out their appointed tasks with pathological zeal. They descended upon lovers' lanes, raided stills, burned barns, tarred and feathered drunks, entered homes without warning or search warrants, flogged errant wives and husbands, law violators and alleged prostitutes. They also collected protection money.

As headquarters of the Indiana Klan, Indianapolis was a city in the grip of quiet terror. The Klan dominated the city hall, the school board, the police department. John Duvall's election as mayor was preceded by a mammoth Klan rally in his behalf at Cadle Tabernacle. Hooded men marched slowly past Catholic churches, temples and synagogues in silent warning. Acts of vandalism carried the sign of the KKK. Crosses were burned on the lawns of the unfriendly, and there were anonymous letters filled with hate, warning telephone calls in the small hours, and threats chalked on doorways and sidewalks. To further the segregation of the city's schools, a new Negro high school, Crispus Attucks, was built on the near north side. Parades of massed Klansmen were organized to impress and awe the populace. One parade on Washington Street, consisting of row after row of masked Klansmen marching slowly to the beat of muffled drums, took a whole hour to pass. Ministers who preached tolerance or defied the Klan were forced to resign. The Klan-dominated congregation of the Reverend Clay Trusty, Sr., burned a cross in his honor before demanding his resignation. In contrast, friendly ministers were often visited by hooded Klansman during Sunday services with an offering of greenbacks, a favorite device of the Klan for rewarding its faithful who worked in the vineyards.

Not everyone knuckled under to the Klan. In the vanguard of the fight against the invisible empire was the Indianapolis *Times* and its editor, Bob Gurley. Despite the loss of thousands of subscribers and untold thousands in advertising revenue, the *Times* exposed and attacked the Klan in its news and editorial pages. For its efforts the *Times* later won the coveted Pulitzer prize. The American Legion, in danger of being infiltrated by the Klan, defied the men in white by electing Frank McHale, a Catholic, as its state commander. There were other overt acts of defiance and thousands that went unnoticed and unheralded. Even passive resistance was an act of courage in the framework of the times.

Meanwhile, the Klan was sowing the seeds of its own destruction. Stephenson challenged Evans for control of the Klan organization and the bitter fight flared into the open. Stephenson had gained control of the Klan newspaper, *The Fiery Cross,* and he used its columns to glorify himself and to vilify his former mentor. Among other things, he charged Evans was plotting to use the Klan's power for the protection of organized crime. Evans retaliated by hitting Stephenson where he was most vulnerable. He circulated stories about the Grand Dragon's drinking and wenching, and in January 1924 the Evansville Klavern, meeting in secret conclave, considered a number of charges of immorality involving Stephenson and read him out of the national Klan. Stephenson reacted by seceding from the national Klan and forming his own organization.

Thus matters stood in January 1925, when Stephenson attended Governor Ed Jackson's inaugural banquet at the Indianapolis Athletic Club and was introduced to Madge Oberholtzer, a pretty, buxom young woman of twenty-eight and the daughter of Mr. and Mrs. George Oberholtzer of University Avenue. Stephenson and Miss Oberholtzer, an employee of the office of the Superintendent of Public Instruction, danced and chatted. Later they had a few dates.

Less than three months later, on April 2, 1925, the Grand Dragon of the Ku Klux Kan in Indiana was formally arrested and charged with sadistic assault upon Miss Oberholtzer. Twelve days later Miss Oberholtzer was dead and the charge was changed to murder. Klansmen as well as men of good will read the news with mingled feelings of shock and disbelief.

The evidence, however, was damning. On her deathbed Miss Oberholtzer, in the presence of reputable and respected witnesses, had dictated a statement covering several typewritten and notarized pages. It told of the woman's three-day ordeal at the hands of Stephenson. On Sunday night, March 15, according to the statement, she had been "forced" to board a train with Stephenson and en route she had been viciously assaulted and "mutilated." The Stephenson party, which included two of his bodyguards, got off the train at Hammond, apparently to escape the Mann Act, and registered at a hotel. There the distraught and wounded girl contemplated suicide "in order to save my mother from disgrace." Later in the morning she escaped her captors long enough to get to a drugstore and purchase 18 bichloride of mercury tablets. She took only six of the tablets "because they burnt so," and became deathly ill. Refused medical aid, she was driven back to Indianapolis in "great pain and agony" and held in a loft over Stephenson's garage until she was taken home by one of Stephenson's men at noon on Tuesday. Her family summoned doctors, but it was too late.

The trial of Indiana's Grand Dragon was venued from Indianapolis to Noblesville and proved a national sensation. A jury of ten farmers, a businessman and a truck driver listened for over a month to testimony that later occupied nearly 2,500 typewritten pages and brought in a verdict of second-degree murder. Judge Will H. Sparks of Rush County sentenced Stephenson to life imprisonment. His bodyguards, Earl Klenck and Earl Gentry, were acquitted.

Stephenson, who did not take the stand in his own defense, went to prison asserting he had been "framed" by the Evans' crowd and confident that Governor Ed Jackson would pardon him. But Governor Jackson didn't. The Klan, as well as Stephenson, had been on trial at Noblesville, and some of the unsavory political machinations of the Klan were now spread on the record. Public opinion was running strongly against the Klan and there was disillusionment within its own ranks. It was obvious the days of the invisible empire were numbered in Indiana, and politicians from the governor on down were busy disassociating themselves from Stephenson and the men in white sheets.

There were ugly footnotes to the Klan story. From his prison cell an embittered and abandoned Stephenson swore vengeance and produced for the Indianapolis *Times* and a Marion County grand jury several "black boxes" containing his records. Among other public officials, Indianapolis' mayor, John Duvall, was indicted by a Marion County grand jury. Duvall resigned his office, was found guilty of a misdemeanor and fined $1,000 and sentenced to 30 days in jail. Six councilmen who had accompanied Duvall into office also resigned and were fined. Friends of the mayor paid his fine and he started serving his sentence on February 4, 1931. Duvall's conviction signaled the end of Republican control of city hall for the next 16 years.

Although the power of the Klan diminished after Stephenson's conviction and the resulting scandals, the Klan remained a factor in Indianapolis and Indiana, as well as in America, until the early 1930s, when the Klaverns finally broke up. Unhappily, there remained those with minds still wrapped in white sheets who found new banners and new voices of hate and bigotry to follow.

Chapter 24

CRISIS AND
UPHEAVAL

INDIANAPOLIS NEWSPAPERS on October 29, 1929, carried the story of the collapse of the bull market, the historic "Black Tuesday" on the New York Stock Exchange that heralded the Great Depression.

As the city entered 1930, Indianapolis bankers and business leaders were generally optimistic. Their year-end forecasts saw the first few months of the new year as "a period of lowered activity," but trends were "favorable for a recovery in the late months of the year."

The city's new mayor, fifty-three-year-old Reginald H. Sullivan, who took office in January, echoed the confidence of the city's business leaders. Mayor Sullivan, a Democrat, came from a family with roots deep in the city's history. He was sworn into office by his father, Thomas L. Sullivan, who had been mayor of the city from 1890 to 1893, the first son of a former mayor to become the city's chief executive. Mayor Sullivan, a former state and county Democratic chairman, was also a great-grandson of Jeremiah Sullivan, the legislator who had coined the city's name back in 1821 when Indianapolis had been only a dream.

But expressions of confidence were not enough. Business and economic machinery continued to break down with baffling regularity. Although there were enclaves of prosperity, Indianapolis business ground to a halt. Some banks failed, factories closed or operated part time, jobs became scarce, wages fell to new lows. There were bankruptcies, foreclosures, downtown store windows boarded up. Property tax delinquencies doubled. University Square was filled with unemployed men. The Indiana State Fair permitted farmers to exchange sacks of grain for tickets. State, county and local welfare agencies were overwhelmed with demands for help. Indianapolis found itself torn between its log-cabin individualism and a new proposition that the welfare of its people in a depression was a responsibility of government.

There were some bright spots. The Indiana State Library and Historical Building was completed and opened. The Medical Center of Indiana University was expanded. The federal government built the Naval Reserve Armory. The city's first slum-clearance project, Lockefield Gardens, was started—designed to provide apartment homes for Negro families. Marian College opened in September 1937 on the former James A. Allison estate. Controlled by the Sisters of the Third Order of St. Francis of Oldenburg, it was coeducational and offered a four-year liberal arts course.

The Indianapolis Symphony Orchestra, an outgrowth of the Indianapolis Orchestra under Alexander Ernestinoff and Ferdinand Shaefer, was formed in 1930, with the dramatic Fabien Sevitsky, formerly of the Leopold Stokowski Philadelphia Orchestra, as conductor. Sevitsky was a showman as well as a musician, conducting without a score and sometimes stopping a concert to upbraid latecomers or to lecture matinee commuters rushing off to catch a train or trolley.

At the Indianapolis Motor Speedway, Rickenbacker was determined to keep the "big one" going, although the depression had closed every major auto racing track in the country. He hired a press agent, Steve Hannegan, a former Indianapolis newspaperman, reduced the prize money, increased time trials to ten laps to bring in extra revenue, and introduced a modified stock-car formula to attract entries from auto manufacturers.

When drivers arrived for the 1933 race, they were displeased with the turn of events, especially the reduced prize and dwindling fund subscriptions. When one of the drivers, Howard (Howdy) Wilcox of Indianapolis, was disqualified for a diabetic condition, the drivers served formal notice on the morning of the race they would not take part in the race unless Wilcox was permitted to drive. A grim Rickenbacker faced the drivers, including Wilcox and his substitute, Mauri Rose, both dressed and ready to drive. Rickenbacker's speech was short. He sympathized with the drivers' position, but declared he could not permit Wilcox to endanger his life or that of the other drivers. Then he delivered an ultimatum: either the drivers got back in their cars and were ready to drive in five minutes or he would announce to the world they had refused, call off the race, refund every dollar taken in and close the Speedway.

The 15-minute warning bomb went off. Rickenbacker gave the traditional order for the drivers to start their engines. For a moment no one moved. Then a few drivers shifted their feet; others began to look uneasy. A few moved toward their cars. Motors roared. The threatened drivers' strike was over and the big race was on.

William B. Stokely came to town and acquired the Van Camp Packing Company, famous for its pork and beans but in financial straits and on the verge of closing. Van Camp became a Stokely subsidiary, and later the companies merged to become Stokely-Van Camp, with headquarters in Indianapolis. Erwin Wetzel and George Stark, sausage makers, enlarged their business and Stark, Wetzel & Company, Inc., was on its way. The depression had an effect on another packing operation, an experiment in "industrial democracy," the employee-operated canning company, Columbia Conserve, out on Churchman Avenue near the Belt Railroad tracks.

The Columbia experiment was the brainchild of William Hapgood, one of three sons of a successful Chicago plow manufacturer. After graduating from Harvard, Hapgood worked for a Chicago wholesale grocery firm, then applied for a job at Armour. When he was turned down by the meat packer because he was a "radical," his father bought him a small canning plant in Indianapolis on South Meridian Street which Hapgood turned into a modest success.

In 1917, after the death of his father, Hapgood, who believed that "political democracy is meaningless without industrial democracy," converted the plant into what he later described in hundreds of after-dinner speeches as "a laboratory to test relations of workers with owners and technicians."

Under the Hapgood plan, a committee of ten employees was elected by the workers to run the business. Work hours were cut from 55 to 50 a week, time clocks were abolished, pension, sick and accident plans were instituted, and in-plant classes started, including classes to train workers for white-collar jobs. Most radical of all was the introduction of an annual wage in an industry that was highly seasonal. Workmen's pay was based on need, and in 1930 unmarried workers were receiving $22 a week and married men $33 plus $2 for each child—well above local pay scales. In 1925 a stock-sharing plan was inaugurated which provided that all net profits after dividends were to be turned over to employees and used for the purchase of the company's common stock. Five years later Columbia employees, through trustees, owned the controlling interest in the company (61 percent).

Hapgood's experiment brought denunciations from fellow Indianapolis businessmen. They called him a "Socialist," a "sentimentalist," and charged his plan was "destructive to the moral fiber of workingmen." Hapgood ignored the critics. He was proud of his experiment and as proof he pointed to the continuing profits of Columbia Conserve, in 1929 over $120,000.

In 1930 Hapgood's only son, Powers, a brilliant and militant union leader, came to work at Columbia, bringing with him John Brophy and Dan Donovan, equally militant unionists, and a labor friend, Leo Tearney. For a young man of thirty-one, Powers had led a full life. He had quit Harvard to work in the coal and iron mines, become an organizer for the United Mine Workers and acquired a long record of arrests, not unusual for labor organizers in the years when labor was fighting for recognition. He became a Socialist, broke with U.M.W. President John L. Lewis and, preceding the 1927 convention in Tomlinson's Hall, Indianapolis, had the audacity to support John Brophy for the Presidency.

Powers Hapgood arrived at Columbia as the depression closed in. The company was losing money but policy precluded the firing of workers. It did cut wages and by July 1933 employees were working for half their 1930 wages. Things came to a head with the announcement of plans for a national advertising campaign to bolster sagging sales. Powers and his group led a fight to jettison the program and to use the money to restore wage cuts. Workers and management divided on the issue. Brophy, Donovan and Tearney denounced William Hapgood as "autocratic" and, worst of all to them, a "capitalist." Powers, who had taken time out to run for governor on the Socialist ticket, returned and threw his support to his father. With the issue deadlocked, production ground to a halt. William Hapgood, for the first time beginning "to doubt the wisdom of letting workers decide issues by a majority," fired the three labor men and established a board of directors to work with the Plant Council. Powers Hapgood walked out with his labor friends, although he continued to live with his father on their 600-acre farm.

The finale of the Columbia Conserve story was ironic. Hapgood was working on a new guaranteed annual wage plan in 1942 when the Columbia workers, to the glee of the business community, went out on strike. The strikers were back to work a week later, but Hapgood refused to pay back wages and the workers filed suit against the trustees who held their common stock. A Marion County Superior Court judge ordered the trust dissolved and the stock distributed individually to all who had worked at Columbia since January 1, 1925. Columbia Conserve had come full circle: it was again an orthodox capitalistic enterprise. It also signed a contract with the C.I.O.

In the 1932 elections President Hoover, who had been elected in a landslide, was swept out in another. Franklin D. Roosevelt, champion of "the forgotten man," carried all but six Republican states and a nation sang "Happy Days Are Here Again."

In Indiana the voters gave Roosevelt an overwhelming victory and elected the first Democratic governor in 16 years, Paul V. McNutt, who attracted national attention by running ahead of Roosevelt in the balloting.

McNutt was the first of Indiana's modern governors, a symbol of the new political strength of the nonpolitical American Legion, the second and last of the state's strong governors. McNutt also presided over one of the most momentous administrations in Indiana history. He gave the nation a preview of the New Deal and he reigned as undisputed boss of the capital city. Critics labeled him "tyrant" and "dictator," a "Hoosier Hitler."

Paul Vories McNutt, a handsome man looking not unlike a matinee idol, was born in Franklin and lived in Indianapolis, Martinsville and Bloomington. As a boy he was brilliant, brash and ambitious, early nurturing a dream that one day he would be President of the United States.

At Indiana University he was the "Big Man on the Campus," a rival of Wendell Willkie of Elwood. He obtained his law degree at Harvard and in 1925, at the age of thirty-four, became dean of the Indiana University Law School, the youngest dean of an accredited law school in the nation. He joined the Bloomington post of the American Legion, became local and state Legion commander, in 1928 the Legion's national commander, and in 1932, a young man in his early forties, governor of Indiana. All of this was not bad for a young man who, as Republican Gaylord Martin put it during the campaign, was "a lawyer who had never tried a case or a soldier who never fired a gun" (the latter a reference to the fact that McNutt had not seen overseas duty).

McNutt came to the governorship at a time when the state was deep in the depression, citizens were clamoring for action, and the state government was broke and facing a deficit of over three million dollars. Favored with near-record Democratic majorities in both Senate and House, McNutt forces whipped through a state government reorganization act and a fiscal program that provided for the state's first gross income and intangibles tax, auto license, liquor and other taxes, and the pooling of the state's resources in the general fund. The speed and efficiency with which the bills were passed led to charges that the legislature was a "rubber stamp."

Most controversial of the McNutt measures was the reorganization bill, which reduced the state's clumsy 169 agencies to eight functional departments, executive, commerce and industry, audit and control, education, public works, state, law, and treasury. Administrative control and responsibility were centralized in the governor, and, except for the private secretaries of elective officials, McNutt had authority to appoint the staffs of all departments as well as to abolish agencies at will. The act brought cries of "dictatorship" from the opposition and strained relations between McNutt and some Democratic leaders jealous of their powers. To critics McNutt replied that the plan modernized Indiana's government so it could run like a big corporation and cited savings of two million dollars annually.

To avert a school crisis, the McNutt administration diverted tax receipts into the school system, with payments per teaching unit reaching $500 in 1936-37. It was a radical move for Indiana but a common practice in 27 other states. McNutt kept Indiana ahead or in stride with the New Deal, the state often being first to cooperate with federal agencies in establishing new projects. The year the Social Security program was outlined, McNutt called a special session to provide conforming legislation. Pledged to consider only Social Security problems in its 14 days, the special session passed bills providing for unemployment compensation, and for pensions for the blind, aged and dependent. Model laws were enacted governing banks, building and loan associations, credit sales and insurance companies. The 1933 banking law, improved in 1935 after operating tests, was considered one of the best in the nation.

There were reactions against the new taxes and the volume of new laws. Among the early targets was a bill providing for the skipping of municipal elections, designed to save $300,000 as a budget-balancing measure. Republicans charged that the McNutt administration was afraid to face the electorate with its record. Small retailers protested the gross income tax, which they claimed doomed their business since they were forced to pay the tax even if they failed to show a profit. The new gross income tax and intangibles tax were, on the other hand, praised by the state's farm groups. During the 1933 General Assembly 10,000 farmers had massed on the Circle in Indianapolis (at the call of the Indiana Farm Bureau) and marched on the statehouse to present petitions asking for the new taxes. Passage of the new laws by the rural-dominated legislature moved the *Hoosier Farmer* to declare, "Not since 1851 has an Indiana General Assembly accomplished as much for the 'forgotten man.' "

Charges flew that the new Liquor Control Act, passed in 1933 in anticipation of Repeal, created a "monopoly" for friends of McNutt. Under the law, out-of-state brewers were ordered to distribute their beer only through ten importers licensed by the state. To answer charges of monopoly, the law was amended to provide for no fewer than 100 importers to hold "port-of-entry" licenses. Republicans regarded it as significant that no more than a dozen port-of-entry permits were ever issued and those were held by deserving Democrats with close ties to McNutt.

There was also a young man named John Dillinger from Mooresville who was proving embarrassing to the administration as well as an expensive thorn in the side of bankers and insurance men.

The Dillinger story began with the escape of ten long-term convicts from the Michigan City Prison in July 1933. Several days later the police at Lima, Ohio, picked up Dillinger, a paroled Indiana convict, on information that he had engineered the break. Before Dillinger could be extradited, six of the Michigan City prisoners descended on the Lima jail, shot the sheriff and freed Dillinger. The consolidated gang returned to Indiana, and, almost as well armed and mobile as the inadequate state police, the gang embarked on an unprecedented wave of bank robberies in and out of the state, among them the State Bank of Massachusetts in Indianapolis, where the gang escaped with $20,000.

The Michigan City jailbreak and the state's failure to capture Dillinger brought political repercussions and charges concerning the operation of the state's penal institutions. There were investigations, firings and reorganizations, most of the fired officials being Republican holdovers.

Dillinger was captured at Tucson, Arizona, and returned to the Lake County Jail at Crown Point under armed guard. But no sooner had the administration drawn a sigh of relief that Dillinger was in jail than the news broke that he had escaped by holding his guards at bay with a wooden gun. This brought new denunciations of the state's penal system and demands for another investigation.

Dillinger became "Public Enemy No. 1," succeeding Al Capone on the FBI's wanted list. J. Edgar Hoover sent his agents to track him down. FBI men caught up with him in St. Paul, but he escaped. In July 1934 the Dillinger saga came to an end as FBI agents gunned him down in front of a Chicago theater.

Paul V. McNutt fabricated one of the most powerful political machines in the history of the state, a well-oiled and smoothly functioning machine that exercised tight and positive control over the Democratic party and wielded undisputed power over the state. It was a formidable machine, and it was not overlooked in Washington, where Roosevelt and James A. Farley, national chairman of the Democratic party, were looking toward the 1940 nominations. It was obvious that McNutt was planning to be the candidate for President.

Counterpart of Roosevelt's Farley was McNutt's Frank McHale, lawyer, banker, politician, as powerful a boss in Indiana as Kelly in Chicago and Boss Hague in New Jersey. McNutt, McHale and Pleas E. Greenlee, the governor's patronage secretary, had put the finishing touches on the Democratic machine after the 1932 elections. As a first step they had swept out all Republican officeholders, replaced them with loyal McNutt Democrats and instituted the now historic "Two Percent Club." Under the plan all state employees paid two percent of their earnings into the treasury of the Democratic party. Announcement of the club brought denunciations from Republicans, but McNutt replied it was more honest to take money from party workers than utilities or special-interest groups. (An issue in every campaign during the 1930s, the two-percent-club plan is now a permanent fixture of both the Democratic and Republican parties.) As a second step, the McNutt forces formed the Hoosier Democratic Club and announced that contributions to the club would not reach the state's party treasury. When Earl Peters, state party chairman, protested, he was appointed to a subcommittee loaded with McNutt men.

The McNutt forces demonstrated their power in the 1934 Senate race and the nomination for governor in 1936. Seven candidates were in the field for the U. S. Senate post, including Earl Peters, who had resigned as state chairman to make the race, and Reginald Sullivan, a former mayor of Indianapolis, supported by U. S. Senator Frederick Van Nuys of Indianapolis. Van Nuys was on the outs with McNutt and outspoken against patronage dispensed by Greenlee. On the eve of the convention, McNutt named Sherman Minton of New Albany, public counsel for the Public Utilities Commission, as his candidate. Minton was named on the fourth ballot, elected, and went on to become Senator and a Supreme Court justice.

In 1936 McNutt named Clifford M. Townsend as his candidate to succeed him. It was a three-way race, with Senator Van Nuys supporting E. Kirk McKinney, head of the Indiana Home Owners Loan Corporation, and Pleas Greenlee, who had been fired by McNutt for announcing his candidacy. McNutt controlled the convention. The Marion County delegation, pledged to McKinney, held up the convention half an hour, split its vote and sent the Townsend bandwagon on its way to a first-ballot victory. Townsend, with the McNutt-McHale machine behind him, won the governorship with the largest Democratic majority recorded up to that time.

McNutt was now outmaneuvered. Roosevelt, with a third term obviously in mind, exiled McNutt to the Philippines, where he served with distinction as high commissioner and later ambassador. Roosevelt brought him back to Washington in 1939, apparently so he could keep an eye on him. In 1940, when McNutt had planned to run for President, he watched instead his former college rival, Wendell Willkie, go down to defeat on the Republican ticket.

Chapter 25

WORLD WAR II—
AND AFTER

W HEN JAPANESE BOMBERS attacked Pearl Harbor on December 7, 1941, Indianapolis was among the best-prepared cities in the U. S. Two years before, while the city was torn between isolationism and sympathy for the Allies, the Chamber of Commerce had moved to convert the city's metalworking industries to national defense. As a part of the "Arsenal of Democracy," Indianapolis became "Toolmaker to the Nation," the city's factories running full blast, payrolls doubling, 9,000 new homes rising for the city's swollen population.

Thousands of Indianapolis sons and daughters were among the 388,000 men and women from Indiana who marched off to war, 10,000 of them to die in camps and on battlefields all over the world. Indianapolis worked hard, bought War Savings Bonds and made the best of shortages and rationing. Allison Division of General Motors made the V-1710 aircraft engine, 70,000 of them, that powered the famed P38's, P39's, P51's, P40's. At its peak in 1943 the plant employed 23,019 persons working three shifts seven days a week. In January 1945 the plant rolled out America's first jet engine, the J33, which would set a standard for 13 years. Hundreds of other plants turned out products for a war whose logistics were staggering.

The war had a tremendous impact on the city's economy. Industrial production soared from 140 million dollars in 1939 to 940 million dollars just 15 years later. Factory employment more than doubled, a rate of increase half again as rapid as that of the country as a whole. More than

30,000 were employed in producing transportation equipment, many times the number employed by the pioneer auto companies at the peak of their local production. It also marked the city's closer integration with the national economy. More national business firms—Bridgeport Brass, Ford, Chrysler, RCA, the Western Electric Company—found Indianapolis a good location. Many local firms were merged or sold to become divisions or subsidiaries of national corporations.

The movement from farm to city, halted by the depression, but given new stimulus during the war, was reflected in growing population figures: 386,972 in 1940; 427,173 in 1950, and 476,258 in 1960, the largest gains of any Indiana city. A state population two-thirds agricultural in 1860 was two-thirds urban by 1960, and one out of every four persons lived in Indianapolis.

Significantly, Indianapolis was no longer a headquarters for international unions. In the 1930s the unions had shifted their bases to such new power centers as Washington, D. C., as they had come to realize the importance of national legislation. Of the more than a dozen international unions once headquartered in Indianapolis only three remained, the Stonecutters, the Barbers and the Painters. The national merger of the A.F.L. and C.I.O. in 1958 brought a consolidation of the fifty-five-year-old Indiana Federation of Labor and the twenty-year-old C.I.O. into the Indiana State A.F.L.-C.I.O., their combined headquarters in Indianapolis.

Two other historic landmarks were also passing. The Indianapolis City Hall, built in 1909, and the Marion County Courthouse were being replaced with the 28-story City-County Building, a modern rectangle of steel, concrete and glass, started in 1959 and financed by a 32-million-dollar bond issue. Across from the state capitol a new state office building was erected in 1953.

For many residents the most symbolic of the postwar changes was the passing of English's Opera House and the adjoining English Hotel. The property vested in the English heirs since 1932 had been deeded to the William E. English Foundation and then sold to the Equitable Life Assurance Society. The announcement that the insurance company planned to erect a new department store building to be leased to the J. C. Penney chain brought a storm of protest, much of it from sentimental citizens. But the modern building, curving gently with the arc of the Circle, went up anyway, to give a new look to the city. The move brought about construction of yet another building bearing the English name. Will English had specified in his will that if the building was demolished, a new building was to be erected and used solely for charitable organizations. In keeping with the provisions of his will, the English Foundation Building was erected on North Alabama Street, the home of the Indianapolis United Fund and dozens of the city's social welfare organizations.

Before the war, in 1939, Indianapolis had a glimpse of a new marvel, television, demonstrated by Philco engineers at the Antlers Hotel and in the fall at the Indiana State Fair. In 1944 Gerald D. Smith and Marion E. Stevenson opened an experimental station at Smith's home on West Thirtieth Street. It was bought by the P. R. Mallory Company, its test patterns valuable in the development and improvement of the TV parts which the company was manufacturing. William H. Block Company started a station, but voluntarily surrendered its F.C.C. permit in favor of minding the store. Local television emerged from its experimental stage on May 30, 1949, as WFBM-TV took the air with a telecast of the 500-Mile Race. It also telecast the last encampment of the once numerous and martial G.A.R., their numbers reduced to a handful of aged but spry veterans riding in a parade in an open car. In October a second station went on the air, WTTV, Bloomington and Indianapolis, owned and operated by Sarkes Tarzian, a Bloomington-based electronics manufacturer. Five years later WISH-TV came on the air, followed by WLW-I in October of 1957.

Coincident with the introduction of television, WFMS began broadcasting a new radio sound in 1957—static-free FM. Two years later WFBM-FM went on the air. By the 1960s seven FM stations were broadcasting.

There was an important change in newspaper ownership. Eugene Collins Pulliam, publisher, financier, promoter, and then owner of WIRE radio, acquired the Indianapolis *Star* and four years later purchased the Indianapolis *News*, moving the *News* to the *Star* building at 307 North Pennsylvania Street. The newspapers continued to be published separately.

The new publisher was a native of a small town in Kansas, son of a Methodist home missionary. He attended DePauw University in Greencastle, Indiana, worked on the school newspaper, became a police reporter on the Kansas City *Star* and later published small dailies and weeklies in Kansas, Florida, Oklahoma and Indiana. He was one of the founders of Sigma Delta Chi, the national journalism society, and at eighty-one years of age (in 1970) the oldest living member of their Indiana Journalism Hall of Fame.

Death by heart attack claimed two Indianapolis mayors in succession. Mayor Robert Tyndall, a Republican, who had served so ably during World War II, died July 9, 1947. He had succeeded Mayor Sullivan in office, Sullivan having been reelected in 1939. (Between Sullivan administrations, John W. Kern, another Democrat, was mayor. He resigned to accept a federal judgeship, Wallace A. Boetcher serving out his unexpired term.) Mayor Tyndall, a native of the city, was a banker and professional soldier who had seen action and led troops in the Spanish-American War and World War I. His unexpired term was filled by City Controller George L. Denny, son of Caleb S. Denny, who had once served two terms as the city's chief executive.

Albert G. Feeney, a Democrat who came to office in 1948, died on his fifty-eighth birthday, November 12, 1950. Feeney had been active in the McNutt administration and was a former superintendent of the Indiana State Police, Marion County sheriff and a recognized safety expert. City Controller Phillip L. Bayt, Jr., an attorney, became mayor but resigned before his term was up to campaign for reelection, and City Council President Christian J. Emhardt filled out the few months of his unexpired term.

In the 1951 campaign Bayt, a conservative Democrat, was defeated by Alex M. Clark, a Republican lawyer and former municipal court judge. Bayt came back, however, to win in 1956, resigned to run for the nomination for U. S. Senate but lost and in 1962 was part of a game of musical chairs allegedly plotted by Senator Vance Hartke to bring harmony to the Democratic machine in Marion County.

The plot began with the unseating of Mayor Charles Boswell, who was also chairman of the Marion County Democratic Committee. Boswell and the party were at loggerheads, and with a postmastership coming up, the boys in the smoke-filled room put together a master plan: Boswell would resign as mayor to become postmaster (the new federal post precluding political activity and making his resignation as county chairman mandatory); Albert Losche would resign temporarily as city controller; Bayt would resign as city prosecutor to become city controller, and Judson Haggerty, Democratic candidate for prosecutor, would be named prosecutor to replace Bayt. It was a brazen plan, and when the newspapers disclosed it, there were howls of protest. The Indianapolis *Times* ran a coupon on the front page asking its readers to vote on the question: "Do you want Boswell for Mayor or Postmaster? Why?" Over 3,000 replies poured into the *Times* office, and Irving Leibowitz, managing editor of the *Times*, reported "almost unanimous condemnation of the plan."

But part of it did go through. Mayor Boswell resigned August 4, 1962, to become postmaster and seventy-year-old Albert J. Losche became mayor to fill out his unexpired term. But the game stopped there. The plotters had what they wanted: the chairmanship of the Marion County organization.

One of the powers in the Democratic party of the 1940s and 1950s was Frank E. McKinney, who became national party chairman in 1950-51, the choice of President Harry S Truman. McKinney's background was politics and banking. The son of an Indianapolis fireman (who years later became chief), he worked as a messenger for the Meyer-Kiser Bank while taking extension and home-study courses in accounting. Later he became an auditor and cashier at the Peoples State Bank.

Elected treasurer of Marion County in the 1930s—then a lucrative post by virtue of a system which permitted the treasurer to retain six percent of all delinquent taxes collected—he invested his salary in a large block of Fidelity Trust Company stock. In January 1935 McKinney became president of Fidelity, then the smallest bank in town. In 1960 he took over the pioneer American Fletcher National Bank and became chairman of the board. Today AFNB and Indiana National are the largest banks in town.

In 1945 race driver Wilbur Shaw, three-time winner of the Indianapolis 500-Mile Race and a wartime executive of the Firestone Tire and Rubber Company, tested a new synthetic tire at the Indianapolis Motor Speedway. Heartsick at the dilapidated condition of the track and grounds, he visited Rickenbacker at his Eastern Airlines office in New York and found him more interested in selling than rebuilding the Speedway. Rickenbacker suggested a price of $750,000.

Shaw found money available for the purchase, but most of it had strings attached. On the advice of Homer Cochrane, an Indianapolis investment broker, Shaw talked with Anton (Tony) Hulman, Jr., a former Yale athlete, sportsman and president of Hulman & Company of Terre Haute. Hulman was interested and Joe Cloutier, treasurer of Hulman & Company, was authorized to open negotiations with Rickenbacker and obtain the necessary mortgages. On November 14, 1945, the principals met at the Indianapolis Athletic Club, and Hulman became owner of the Speedway. Wilbur Shaw was named president and general manager and Hulman assumed the chairmanship of the board. Leonard Marshall was named secretary; Cloutier, treasurer; Joseph L. Quinn, Jr., safety director, and Al Bloemker, publicity director. "Pop" Myers was retained as vice-president. The track was opened for the 1946 race in which only seven cars finished.

In 1947 the track faced its second strike. The American Society of Professional Automobile Racing (ASPAR), with Ralph Hepburn as president, demanded a fixed percentage of the gate receipts and threatened to pull its drivers. With sports editor Bill Fox of the Indianapolis News as arbitrator, ASPAR capitulated after 48 hours of round-the-clock negotiations. The race itself was a close one, with only 28 seconds separating the winner, Mauri Rose, from second-place Bill Holland.

The 1950s brought many changes to the Speedway. A private-plane crash near Fort Wayne took the life of Wilbur Shaw and two companions on October 30, 1954, and Tony Hulman took over as president and general manager. Hulman instituted a new building program. Eight of the nine wooden grandstands were replaced with structures of steel and concrete. A racing museum and office building was erected at the main entrance. A new control tower, tower terrace, garages and pits were built in 1957, as well as a new tunnel under the backstretch.

Hulman exercised his leadership in other ways. In August 1955, when the American Automobile Association, without warning, abolished its contest board, the new Speedway owner brought drivers, car owners, mechanics, fans and promoters together in Indianapolis for a series of meetings. On September 16, 1955, the United States Auto Club was formed to act as the new sanctioning and certifying body for racing. In 1958 Thomas Binford of Indianapolis, president of D-A Lubricant, became the USAC president, a post he held for 11 years. Howard S. Wilcox was national vice-president and Henry Banks director of competition.

Something new was added in 1957—the city's "500 Festival," a month-long program of local festivities that includes a parade of Rose Bowl proportions, a governor's ball, selection of a queen, and one of the country's richest golf tournaments. The extravaganza grew out of the efforts of four men, Howard S. Wilcox, Shrine official J. Worth Baker, former Mayor Alex Clark and racing promoter Joseph L. Quinn, Jr. Samuel J. Freeman was the Festival's first president, Wilcox vice-president, W. H. Book of the Chamber of Commerce, treasurer. Mrs. Frank E. McKinney became the first woman president in 1962. The magic number of the festival is 33—the number of cars that start in the big race. The festival committee consists of 33 members and the parade floats and bands are also limited to 33.

Starting with the 1948 race, speed records were shattered one after another. Bill Holland, the 1949 winner, broke the 120-mph mark, Bill Vukovich hit 130 mph in 1954, and Rodger Ward of Indianapolis pushed it past 135 mph in 1959. In 1965 A. J. Foyt, driving a Lotus-Ford, roared to victory at an average speed of 151.207 mph. Under Hulman's management prize money has doubled and tripled. George Robson, the 1946 winner, took home $42,550, but the 1967 winner (again A. J. Foyt) received $171,527, nearly $350 a mile for 500 miles.

Perhaps nowhere in America were the social and economic reforms of the New Deal fought more bitterly than in Indianapolis and Indiana. The state's unreconstructed conservatives staged a continuing and relentless fight throughout the 1940s and the 1950s against the increasing role of the federal government and the postwar programs of the Truman and Eisenhower administrations. The clash took many forms, involving movements, people, and legislation, and it embraced the whole spectrum of conservatism from right to far right. There were also those who were unkind enough to say it represented the city's and state's refusal to enter the twentieth century.

Indianapolis, so often the birthplace of organizations of the radical left and right, gave birth to another extremist group—the ultraconservative, anticommunist John Birch Society. Meeting in the living room of Mrs. Marguerite Dice, 11 men from as many states drew up the society's first charter and on December 9, 1958, formally organized and elected Robert H. Welch, an ex-candy manufacturer from Boston, as their president. H. J. (Joe) Pierson was named coordinator for the Indiana chapters of the society.

The society was named for a U. S. soldier from Macon, Georgia, who had been killed in China under somewhat cloudy circumstances 11 days after the end of World War I. The name brought a protest from County Assessor David D. Finney, a boyhood friend of Birch, who expressed fear the Birch family was being exploited by extremists.

Other Indianapolis conservatives were not prepared to take the extreme position of the Birchers, but they were active in other right-wing organizations, Americans for Conservative Action, the For America Committee and the Indianapolis-based Citizens Committee for Research, "a clearing house for Communistic activities" which numbered among its executives H. J. Pierson of the Birchers and the late Donald C. Bruce, Republican Representative to Congress from the Eleventh District.

The most conservative influence in the city, however, was William Henry Book, the shrewd, hardworking executive vice-president of the Indianapolis Chamber of Commerce. Writers and editors are generally agreed that few men in the city's history—even Morton, McNutt, Taggart and Stephenson—ever wielded so much power and influence as Bill Book. He ran Indianapolis.

A native of Virginia, Book spent his formative years in Columbus, Indiana, and was educated for the ministry at Franklin College, Franklin, Indiana. He joined the staff of the *News*, worked his way up to assistant city editor, served nine months as business administrator for the Indianapolis public schools, and in 1926 became director of government research for the Chamber of Commerce.

During the depression he served as McNutt's administrator of relief and, convinced the New Deal was taking America "down the road to Socialism," left the Democratic party. He became a foe of "government handouts" and successfully fought the city's and state's use of federal funds. He denounced centralization of power in Washington and was a proponent of self-sufficiency, individualism, home rule, pay-as-you-go. His philosophy was "hold-the-line," his perennial question, "Do we really need that now?"

Book was a trustee or a member of the board of directors of dozens of Indianapolis organizations, among them the Foundation for Voluntary Welfare, the Red Cross, Weekday Religious Education, Flanner House, United Fund, Mayor's Commission on Human Rights, Indianapolis Symphony Orchestra Society, and others. He was a Mason, a Kiwanian, a member of the Southern Club and the American Legion, an elder of the Disciples of Christ Church.

Book's influence extended to city budgets, zoning laws, taxes, sports, property assessments, pensions for police, textbooks for the schools. He accomplished much that was good for the city, but he also blocked hundreds of other actions that might have been. His word could mean life or death to the plans and futures of politicians, businessmen, civic leaders, college presidents and editors.

The bitter resentment of Indiana Republicans against the changing world created by the Democrats was reflected in the actions of the Republican-controlled legislatures extending over two decades.

In 1941 the Republican-dominated General Assembly created a constitutional crisis, seeking to strip a Democratic governor, Henry F. Schricker, of his appointive powers by means of a series of "ripper bills" passed over the governor's veto. Schricker appealed to the courts, and the Supreme Court in a far-reaching decision declared the legislative acts null and void.

During the following administration of Ralph F. Gates a resolution was introduced by the Republicans denouncing the principle of federal aid and urging Indiana congressmen "to vote to fetch our county courthouses and city halls back from Pennsylvania Avenue." One paragraph stood out:

So we propose henceforth to tax ourselves and take care of ourselves. We are fed up with subsidies, doles and paternalism. We are no one's stepchild. We have grown up. We serve notice we will resist Washington, D. C. from adopting us.

The resolution was greeted enthusiastically by the conservative press.

Democrats offered an amendment to the resolution providing that, in the event the resolution was passed, the State Budget Committee was to be instructed to omit all federal financial assistance "and replace the same with State of Indiana funds and increase the budget accordingly." Not surprisingly the amendment was tabled, but the resolution was adopted, its passage in the Senate announced as "thirty-four in favor of Indiana and eleven in favor of Washington" by Lieutenant Governor Richard T. James.

The resolution attracted national attention as it marked the first time a state had gone on record as opposed to the principle of federal aid. For

Indiana's Congressional delegation who had been working to obtain more federal funds for Indiana, the resolution was embarrassing. Even more embarrassing, the legislature within the next three weeks blandly adopted resolutions seeking funds for hospitals, flood control and soil conservation programs. Democrats in the General Assembly gleefully introduced amendments to each of the resolutions calling for "profound apologies to the United States Government" for the passage of the earlier resolution. The amendments were, of course, tabled.

The anti-federal aid position of the Republicans was an issue in the 1948 campaign and undoubtedly played a large part in the smashing victory of Henry F. Schricker, the first man to be elected governor twice under the present constitution. While Thomas E. Dewey carried the state by a mere 13,000 votes, Schricker won by 139,000. The 1949 legislature was divided, but in the 1950 elections Republicans came back into control and in the following legislature created a new crisis—the opening of county welfare records to the public.

The bill, which was passed over the governor's veto, threw into bold relief the problem of state's rights versus federal aid. Under the terms of the Federal Social Security Act, relief rolls were secret, and Indiana was immediately disqualified for 36 million dollars in welfare funds for the next two years. Faced with a financial dilemma, Governor Schricker called a special session of the legislature, which produced a compromise —a bill extending the effective date of the legislation until 1953. The bill became law without the signature of Governor Schricker.

Indiana's action had a reaction in Congress. An amendment by Senator William E. Jenner of Indiana and Everett M. Dirksen of Illinois was eventually passed by Congress permitting opening of the welfare rolls.

Chapter 26

NEW CITY:
INDIANAPOLIS 1970

AS INDIANAPOLIS ENTERED the 1970s, it was undergoing the greatest transformation in its history, an amazing transformation that touched virtually every facet of the city's life. Billions of dollars in new construction that dramatically changed the city's skyline reflected the physical change. But the changes were deeper than new buildings and record-breaking statistics. There were psychological changes in attitudes and positions. The city that had moved so reluctantly from small town to big town, the city once described as a place of "dynamic nostalgia," the city where visitors were advised to turn back their calendars to the nineteenth century, appeared to have cut its umbilical cord to the past.

Indianapolis 1970 was a city awakened, infused with a new enthusiasm for urbanism, a city proud to be a city and determined to be the best of cities. Coiners of phrases called Indianapolis "the boomtown of the Midwest," "City on the Move," "Big League City." The descriptions were accurate, but they failed to capture the basic fact that, above all else, it was a new Indianapolis.

Much of the change was visible. In the downtown area a dozen new skyscrapers, gleaming rectangles of steel, concrete and Indiana limestone, probed the sky—among them the tallest building in the state, the new 37-story Indiana National Bank Tower, the twin towers of the Riley Center apartments, the 28-story City-County Building, the John J. Barton Apartments, the new Hilton Hotel, the Indiana Bell Telephone

Building. Still more buildings were going up: the block-long Federal Building, the Blue Cross-Blue Shield Building, and the 24-million-dollar Indianapolis Convention and Exposition Center, covering two entire city blocks.

New interstates neared completion, seven spokes of wide concrete highways, giving the city more interstates than any other U. S. city. The Thirty-eighth Street Bridge over the White River was opened September 18, 1962. A city of residences became a city of apartments, over 20,000 units of them, a record 7,298 units built in 1969 alone. Twenty-three major shopping centers, two of them enclosed, ringed the city. Three new city high schools, Arlington, Northwest and Marshall, opened and Ritter, Chatard, Latin School, Brebeuf and Roncalli were new names for parochial high schools. School enrollment rose from 85,540 to 108,222. New hospitals were built and multimillion-dollar wings added to others. Weir Cook Airport, completing a $6,500,000 modernization program, immediately embarked on another $3,500,000 program. New airports were created to provide for the growing number of private flyers and their planes. Among the new churches and temples, most of them in the suburbs, were some of the best and boldest examples of contemporary architecture. On the city's west side was an innovative concept in community planning: the 85-million-dollar College Park, the new home of John Burkhart's College Life Insurance Company, to be housed in a group of triangular buildings among a complex of homes, apartments, townhouses and shopping centers.

New citadels of art and culture were created. The magnificent 2,200-seat Clowes Memorial Hall of Butler University, the gift of Mrs. G. H. A. Clowes in memory of her husband, opened in 1963. The home of the famed Indianapolis Symphony Orchestra, conducted by Izler Solomon, it is a center for opera, ballet, concerts, plays, musicals. Northwest of the city is the new Indianapolis Museum of Art, a gift of the heirs of J. K. Lilly to the Indianapolis Art Association. It will eventually cost 25 million dollars and consist of a new museum building, the Lilly Pavilion and a 650-seat outdoor theater.

The city's first zoo, one of the finest small zoos in the Midwest, opened on April 18, 1964. The vast Eagle Creek Flood Control project and reservoir will give the city the largest all-year-round recreational area within the limits of a major U. S. city. Professional sports returned in 1967 with the Indiana Pacers basketball team, which in 1970 won the ABA championship, and the Indianapolis Capitols football team, which captured the 1968 Continental League championship. A domed sports center was on the drawing boards and planned for the 1970s.

A new university complex, its current enrollment 14,000, took form on the near west side as the result of a merger of Indiana University's and Purdue University's regional campuses. Currently operating under the unwieldy title Indiana University-Purdue University at Indianapolis (IUPUI), it is an inventory of superlatives, with the largest medical school in the U. S.; one of the nation's top dental schools; the only nursing school in Indiana offering graduate degrees; the largest law school in Indiana; an art school with an international reputation; the oldest physical education school in America; the state's only school for social workers; and an undergraduate college with schools of business, engineering and the physical sciences.

Expansion and building programs were also underway at the city's private colleges and universities, Butler University, Marian College, and Indiana Central College. In the 1960s Marian College acquired the William B. Stokely estate and the Park School property. The Christian Theological Seminary, once a part of North Western Christian University (Butler), moved into a multimillion-dollar building, a model of contemporary architecture, in 1966.

The dynamics of twentieth-century capitalism was reflected in the city's burgeoning industry. In one four-year span over 23 million square feet of new industrial space was added—more space than that occupied by the city's five largest industries. Another two million square feet was added in 1969. RCA in the 1960s moved its home instrument division to the city, building nine plants in Indianapolis. More new firms came, 60 of them in 1969 alone. The gainfully employed reached a record 467,000 persons and continued to climb. Unemployment that reached a low of two percent in 1967 hovered around 2.3 and 2.4 percent two years later. Over a half-dozen new industrial parks, including Park Fletcher near the airport, were created to provide space for the city's new industries.

It was a decade of major headlines. An industrial arts schoolteacher, Louis Russell, a Negro, received a new heart on August 24, 1968, and in 1970 had lived with a heart transplant longer than any other person. A $3,500,000 fire destroyed the Hygrade Products plant, once the Kingan Brothers pork-packing plant, the largest in the world. The Indianapolis *Times* suspended publication in the fall of 1965, leaving the field open to the conservative *Star* and the *News*. Fire gutted the historic Claypool Hotel on the site of the old Bates House and it fell beneath the wrecker's ball. Indianapolis was headquarters for Robert F. Kennedy in his successful Indiana primary campaign; Kennedy delivered an often-quoted speech here on the night of Martin Luther King's assassination, only weeks before his own death by an assassin's bullet.

As the result of collective community action, a public TV station, WFYI, began regular broadcasts on October 4, 1970.

The city became the capital of auto racing. Besides the famed 500-Mile Race, Indianapolis was the site for the National Drag Races, stock car races, the Hoosier Hundred and other major auto racing events. The first turbine engine appeared at the 500-Mile classic in 1967 and after leading the race for 490 miles was forced out when a six-dollar bearing failed.

Kurt Vonnegut, Jr., a native of Indianapolis and graduate of local schools, became a best-selling author, his irreverent and antiestablishment books providing a sharp contrast to the works of Riley, Tarkington and Nicholson of the Golden Age. Other Indianapolis authors, Jeannette Covert Nolan, Hortense Myers, the late Frank Edwards, Gertrude E. Finney, Gordon Gordon, Joanne Landers Henry, Edah M. Ropkey, and others upheld the city's literary reputation. Former Indianapolis residents John Bartlow Martin, Joseph Hayes and Tristram Coffin turned out major works. Emma Lou Thornbrough added to her reputation as a historian with her *Indiana in the Civil War Era*. Howard Sams, a major publisher of technical electronics manuals, acquired the Bobbs-Merrill publishing company and in the late 1960s both became a part of International Telephone and Telegraph. Beurt SerVaas and his Review Publishing Company acquired new magazine titles, including *Golden Magazine*, to become the nation's largest publisher of children's magazines.

It was a decade in which tragedies were seemingly bigger. Although a Palm Sunday tornado skipped the city in 1965, it struck nearby counties, killing 140 persons and injuring over 1,000. In 1969 a midair collision between an Indianapolis-bound Allegheny Airlines DC9 and a small private plane piloted by a thirty-four-year-old city plumber took 83 lives southeast of Indianapolis. The city's worst tragedy struck on Halloween night, October 31, 1963, in the Coliseum at the Indiana State Fair grounds as an audience of 4,327 persons, many of them families with children, sat watching the finale of a *Holiday on Ice* show. Leaking butane gas that had been collecting under a section of the seats exploded, hurling screaming men, women and children onto the ice. From the jagged crater left by the explosion poured hissing yellow-orange flames.

There was a moment of panic but miraculously the huge crowd gained control of itself and flowed out of the hall. Even as the first of the crowd emerged into the chill October air, police, fire and ambulance sirens punctuated the night. Outside the Coliseum, the grounds resembled a battlefield, with scores of injured to be treated and taken by ambulance and private cars to the city's hospitals (where already Indianapolis citizens were lined up prepared to donate blood, so many, in fact, that hundreds were turned away).

The statistics of the city's worst tragedy were grim: within weeks its death toll reached 74 men, women and children, its list of the injured, nearly 400. Investigation by a Marion County grand jury into the causes of the explosion resulted in seven indictments against state and city fire officials, representatives of the Coliseum and the firm that furnished the bottled gas. None of the cases, however, held up in court. In October 1967, four years later, Federal Judge S. Hugh Dillin announced an out-of-court settlement of all claims growing out of the tragedy; the amount: $3,555,000.

The era brought new political leaders as voters rejected conserva-tive Republicans such as U. S. Senators William E. Jenner and Homer E. Capehart, voted overwhelmingly against Barry Goldwater, but voted twice for the not-so-conservative Nixon. Young liberal Democrats were elected to the U. S. Senate: Birch Bayh, Jr. and R. Vance Hartke, who gave the state a new image and placed it in the political mainstream. Two Democratic governors were elected in a row, the liberal and intel-lectual Matthew E. Welsh and the middle-of-the-road Roger D. Brani-gin. Branigin defeated a modern Republican, Richard O. Ristine, who failed to survive the Goldwater debacle. Indianapolis' Eleventh District sent a young liberal Democratic attorney, Andrew Jacobs, Jr., to Con-gress and continued to reelect him.

In Indianapolis the Democrats elected John J. Barton mayor in 1964. Barton, a former superintendent of the state police, campaigned on the controversial (in Indianapolis) issue of obtaining federal funds for the city. Barton reestablished the Indianapolis Housing Authority, dormant since depression days, and with the aid of federal funds initiated half a dozen low-income housing projects, including Salem Village and a high-rise apartment for elderly citizens. He organized the blue-ribbon Greater Indianapolis Progress Committee, designed to function as an urban coalition.

Barton's bid for reelection in 1967 was a study in contrasts. The sixty-one-year-old white-thatched Barton, running at the head of a strife-torn and divided party, was pitted against a highly articulate thirty-five-year-old businessman and former Rhodes scholar, Richard G. Lugar, with a smoothly functioning Republican machine behind him. Lugar won by 9,000 votes to become the first Republican to win the mayoralty since 1951 and the third Republican chief executive in 40 years.

Lugar has had perhaps the greatest impact on his city of any Indianap-olis mayor. A new breed of Republican, Lugar has proved to be a pro-gressive who blends sufficient amounts of liberalism and conservatism to please both the right and left wings of his party and still earn high marks from the electorate. An intellectual with a brilliant scholastic record and a member of one of the city's older families, Lugar is a U. S.

Navy veteran, a successful businessman and civic leader. As Republican mayor of one of the nation's largest cities he is close to the Nixon administration and in December 1969, ostensibly with administration support, was elected vice-president of the National League of Cities over Mayor John Lindsay of New York. In February 1970 President Nixon brought his Urban Affairs Council to Indianapolis, with Mayor Lugar as host, the first time a President has held such a meeting outside Washington. Lugar, a recognized authority on municipal government, is a member of the President's Advisory Commission on Intergovernmental Relations and member of his Model Cities Advisory Task Force.

The Lugar administration has exploited the city's monumental pride and enlisted top people from business and industry. These men and the other dedicated, hardworking young men around Lugar have often provided a new point of view to old problems. The Employment Task Force, organized in 1968, found jobs for 5,000 unemployed, mostly Negroes. The "Upswing" program designed to use the facilities of Indianapolis' schools during the summer months brought out 25,000 participating young adults. Most of the mayor's projects are locally financed, like "Upswing," which in its first year received $150,000 from the United Fund and $40,000 from Lilly Endowment, Inc.

Although it has brought some protests from the right wing of his party, Lugar has used federal funds to advantage. Shortly after taking office his administration applied for and obtained a Model Cities grant to formulate plans for an extensive urban renewal program. Indianapolis was also selected as one of ten cities for an experimental housing project, "Operation Breakthrough," to be financed with federal funds.

Perhaps the major accomplishment of Lugar's administration was the passage in the 1969 legislature of a bill consolidating the city and county governments, a bold experiment in municipal government popularly known as "Uni-Gov." As a result of the consolidation of the city and Marion County, Indianapolis, formerly ranked twenty-sixth among U. S. cities, became the nation's twelfth largest city on January 1, 1970, ranking just behind Milwaukee and St. Louis. (Tenth in rank according to preliminary 1970 U. S. Census figures.)

The consolidation plan was the work of the Government Reorganization Task Force of the Greater Indianapolis Progress Committee. Co-chairmen of the task force were Beurt R. SerVaas, a publisher and industrialist and president of the county council, and Thomas C. Hasbrook, an executive of Eli Lilly and Company and president of the city council. Some of the city's outstanding legal talent, headed by Lewis Bose, drew up the legislation with lawyers such as Wayne Ponader and Charles Whistler writing key sections.

Basically, Uni-Gov consolidates the City of Indianapolis and all of Marion County—exclusive of Beech Grove, Lawrence and Speedway—

into a single first-class city. The unit is governed by a mayor and a city-county council of 29 members, four elected at large, the others elected from 25 council districts, each district as nearly equal as practical in population. Most important of all, Uni-Gov eliminates the city's and county's hodgepodge of overlapping departments, independent and semi-independent boards. These are reorganized and consolidated into six functional administration departments. Uni-Gov does not, however, provide for a metropolitan police force nor does it affect local school corporations or fire departments.

Perhaps most symbolic of the city's change was its growing concern for the problem of its large black population, estimated at more than 20 percent of the city's population.

Improvement of the black man's lot has been a major thrust of the Lugar administration, which has enlisted community-wide action to solve the problem of black poverty, unemployment, housing and related social problems.

The work of the mayor and dedicated black and white men and women, working independently as individuals or in an organizational framework, has been no easy task in a city once dominated by the Klan and where Negro leadership is diffused. But it is a tribute to the city's improved race relations that among the top 50 American cities Indianapolis has been spared a major riot, its lone outbreak in 1969 confined to a two-block area on Indiana Avenue and sporadic disturbances in other parts of the city. Significantly, the trouble on Indiana Avenue was quickly brought to an end by Negro leaders who moved into the area and worked closely with police and firemen.

Negro employment is at a record high, although unemployment remains a basic black problem. A dozen organizations including the Chamber of Commerce and its Voluntary Advisory Corps, WFBM's Job Line, the Urban League, and the National Alliance of Business are providing job help. Training is provided at the Indianapolis Skill Center, Indiana Vocational Technical College, the Broadway Christian pre-apprentice school and the nearby Camp Atterbury Job Corps.

The federally funded Model Cities planning is concentrated in the city's predominantly black area. Flanner House, a self-help organization, is building a 294-family apartment complex, River House—the first non-profit group in the U. S. to take advantage of new F.H.A. project rules. The Mount Zion Baptist Church operates the city's only total rent subsidy program and is buildng more units. A privately funded organization, I.N.H.I., is building and renovating homes in the inner city, and a church group, H.O.M.E., is funding other renovation projects in black ghettos. Neighborhood associations such as the Butler-Tarkington, Meridian-Kessler and Forest Manor are working for racial balance in their areas.

Dedicated men operate dozens of individual projects for black men and women. A soft-spoken former professional athlete, John Lands, supervises "Our Place" for black youth on Indiana Avenue. The Reverend Andrew Brown of the Southern Christian Leadership Conference runs "Operation Breadbasket" designed to feed the hungry. A white priest, Father Bernard Strange of St. Rita's Church, operates a day-care center and a preschool center, and his parochial school is open to community activities around the clock. An Indiana Avenue supermarket, managed and operated by blacks, represents the collective efforts of individuals, banks, churches, the mayor's office and Allied Grocers.

Increasingly, black men are prominent in the city's life. Dr. Frank Lloyd is director of Medical Research at Methodist Hospital. Willard Ransom sits on the board of the Merchants National Bank—the city's first Negro bank director. Spurgeon Davenport is the assistant chief of police. Henry F. Bundles, president of a large cosmetic firm, Summit Laboratories, heads the mayor's task force on black business opportunities. The dean of Indiana University's downtown campus is Dr. Joseph T. Taylor, the first Negro dean of an Indiana college. Dr. Cleo Blackburn heads Flanner House, and Sam Jones is the executive director of the Urban League. Thomas A. Bolden, Jr. is an assistant vice-president in charge of small business loans at the American Fletcher National Bank. His assistant is Jay Michael Smith, youthful president of the N.A.A.C.P. Clarence Wood is an AFNB branch manager.

The Reverend Landrum E. Shields is president of the Indianapolis Board of School Commissioners, and Robert D. DeFrantz heads up the city's Community Action Against Poverty, C.A.A.P. At the Indiana National Bank, James Shaw is commercial lending officer and Lloyd C. Jones is compensation manager. Juan Solomon, an executive with Eli Lilly and Company, is the city's manpower commissioner. Bill Hardy heads up the city's only black public relations firm, and Snyder-Blackburn Associates, an architectural firm, lists River House Apartments and the city's first integrated country club among its clients.

Much, of course, remains to be accomplished: further desegregation of the city's public schools, more housing, more jobs, more opportunities, improved relations between blacks and police. But Indianapolis blacks and whites are communicating, meeting, organizing and moving forward.

The new City of Indianapolis is the result of many factors, including the city's strategic location in the heart of mid-America and a vigorous economy.

But the lubricant that makes the machinery of the city move forward is civic pride—a pride that extends from the paneled executive suites to modest living rooms deep in the ghetto.

Indianapolis, the city that had to pull itself up by its bootstraps 150 years ago, has a unique roll-up-your-sleeves-and-get-with-it spirit.

Appendix I

MAYORS 1847-1968

Samuel Henderson (Whig) 1847-1849
Horatio C. Newcomb (Whig) 1849-1851 (Resigned November 7, 1851)
Caleb B. Scudder (Whig)1851-1854
James McCready (Whig) 1854-1856
Henry F. West (D) 1856 (Died November 8, 1856)
Charles G. Coulin (D) 1856 (Filled vacancy November 8-22)
William John Wallace (R) 1856-1858 (Resigned May 3, 1858)
Samuel D. Maxwell (R) 1858-1863
John Caven (R) 1863-1867
Daniel McCauley (R) 1867-1873
James L. Mitchell (D) 1873-1875
John Caven (R) 1875-1881
Daniel W. Grubbs (R) 1881-1884
John L. McMaster (R) 1884-1886
Caleb S. Denny (R) 1886-1890
Thomas L. Sullivan (D) 1890-1893
Caleb S. Denny (R) 1893-1895
Thomas Taggart (D) 1895-1901
Charles A. Bookwalter (R) 1901-1903
John W. Holtzman (D) 1903-1906
Charles A. Bookwalter (R) 1906-1910
Samuel Lewis Shank (R) 1910-1913 (Resigned November 28, 1913)
Harry R. Wallace (R) 1913-1914
Joseph E. Bell (D) 1914-1918
Charles W. Jewett (R) 1918-1922
Samuel Lewis Shank (R) 1922-1926
John L. Duvall (R) 1926-1927 (Resigned October 27, 1927)
Claude E. Negley (R) October 27-November 9, 1927 (Acting mayor)

L. Ert Slack (D) November 9, 1927-January 1, 1930 (Appointed by city council)

Reginald H. Sullivan (D) 1930-1935

John W. Kern (D) 1935-1937 (Resigned September 2, 1937)

Walter C. Boetcher (D) 1937-1939

Reginald H. Sullivan (D) 1939-1943

Robert Tyndall (R) 1943-1947 (Died July 9, 1947)

George L. Denny (R) July 9, 1947-1948

Al G. Feeney (D) 1948-1950 (Died November 12, 1950)

Phillip L. Bayt, Jr. (D) November 12, 1950-November 24, 1951 (Resigned)

Christian J. Emhardt (D) 1951-1952

Alex M. Clark (R) 1952-1956

Phillip L. Bayt, Jr. (D) 1956-1959 (Resigned January 1, 1959)

Charles Boswell (D) 1959-1962 (Resigned August 4, 1962)

Albert L. Losche (D) August 6, 1962-1964

John J. Barton (D) 1964-1968

Richard G. Lugar (R) 1968—

Appendix II

POPULATION, CITY
OF INDIANAPOLIS

(U. S. Census Bureau)

1840	2,692	1910	233,650
1850	8,091	1920	314,194
1860	18,611	1930	364,161
1870	48,244	1940	386,972
1880	75,056	1950	427,173
1890	105,436	1960	476,258
1900	169,164	1970	742,613*

* Preliminary estimate, September 1, 1970. The figure represents the combined populations of the City of Indianapolis and Marion County which were consolidated as the result of legislation, popularly known as Uni-Gov, enacted by the 1969 session of the Indiana General Assembly. The new consolidated City of Indianapolis is currently ranked tenth in size among U.S. cities.

Appendix III

TERRITORIAL AND STATE GOVERNORS

TERRITORIAL GOVERNORS

William Henry Harrison (Jeffersonian Republican) 1800-12
John Gibson (Jeffersonian Republican) 1812-13 (Acting governor)
John Posey (Jeffersonian Republican) 1813-16

STATE GOVERNORS

1816-22	Jonathan Jennings (Jeffersonian Republican), Charlestown
1822	Ratliff Boon (Jeffersonian Republican), Boonville
1822-25	William Hendricks (Jeffersonian Republican), Madison
1825-31	James Brown Ray (Democratic Republican), Brookville
1831-37	Noah Noble (National Republican, Whig), Indianapolis
1837-40	David Wallace (Whig), Covington
1840-43	Samuel Bigger (Whig), Rushville
1843-48	James Whitcomb (D), Bloomington
1848-49	Paris C. Dunning (D), Bloomington
1849-57	Joseph A. Wright (D), Rockville
1857-60	Ashbel P. Willard (D), New Albany
1860-61	Abram A. Hammond (D), Indianapolis
1861	Henry S. Lane (R), Crawfordsville
1861-67	Oliver P. Morton (R), Centerville
1867-73	Conrad Baker (R), Evansville
1873-77	Thomas A. Hendricks (D), Shelbyville
1877-80	James D. Williams (D), Knox County
1880-81	Isaac P. Gray (D), Union City

1881-85   Albert G. Porter (R), Indianapolis
1885-89   Isaac P. Gray—*see* 1880-81
1889-91   Alvin P. Hovey (R), Mt. Vernon
1891-93   Ira J. Chase (R), Danville
1893-97   Claude Matthews (D), Vermillion County
1897-1901   James A. Mount (R), Montgomery County
1901-05   Winfield T. Durbin (R), Anderson
1905-09   J. Frank Hanly (R), Warren County
1909-13   Thomas R. Marshall (D), Columbia City
1913-17   Samuel M. Ralston (D), Lebanon
1917-21   James P. Goodrich (R), Winchester
1921-24   Warren T. McCray (R), Kentland
1924-25   Emmet F. Branch (R), Martinsville
1925-29   Ed Jackson (R), Indianapolis
1929-33   Harry G. Leslie (R), Lafayette
1933-37   Paul V. McNutt (D), Bloomington
1937-41   M. Clifford Townsend (D), Grant County
1941-45   Henry F. Schricker (D), Knox
1945-49   Ralph F. Gates (R), Columbia City
1949-53   Henry F. Schricker, *see* 1941-45
1953-57   George Craig (R), Brazil
1957-61   Harold W. Handley (R), LaPorte
1961-65   Matthew E. Welsh (D), Vincennes
1965-68   Roger D. Branigin (D), Lafayette
1968-   Edgar D. Whitcomb (R), Seymour

BIBLIOGRAPHY

Bloemker, Al. *500 Miles to Go*. New York: Coward-McCann, 1966.

Bolton, Nathaniel. *Early History of Indianapolis and Central Indiana*. Indianapolis: The Bowen-Merrill Company, 1834.

Bowers, Claude G. *My Life, The Memoirs of Claude Bowers*. New York: Simon and Schuster, 1962.

———. *Beveridge and the Progressive Era*. Boston: Houghton Mifflin Company, 1932.

———. *The Tragic Era: The Revolution After Lincoln*. Boston: Houghton Mifflin Company, 1920.

Bowman, Heath. *Hoosier*. Indianapolis: The Bobbs-Merrill Company, 1941.

Brown, Ignatius. *City Directory of 1869*.

Burgess, Dale. *Just Us Hoosiers*. Indianapolis: Unified College Press, 1966.

Carmichael, Hoagy, and Longstreet, Stephen. *Sometimes I Wonder*. New York: Farrar, Straus and Giroux, 1965.

Carmody, Donald F., editor. *Indiana, A Self-Appraisal*. Bloomington: Indiana University Press, 1966.

Cathcart, Charlotte. *Indianapolis from Our Old Corner*. Indianapolis: Indiana Historical Society, 1965.

Chronology of Indiana in the Civil War, 1861-65. Indianapolis: Indiana Civil War Centennial Commission, 1965.

Cockrum, William M. *History of the Underground Railroad*. Philadelphia: J. B. Lippincott, 1958.

Cottman, George S. *Indiana, Its History, Constitution and Present Government*. Indianapolis: The Bobbs-Merrill Company, 1925.

———. *Centennial History and Handbook of Indianapolis*. Indianapolis: Max R. Hyman, 1915.

Coughlan, Robert. "Konklave in Kokomo," in *Aspirin Age 1919-1941* edited by Elizabeth Leighton. New York: Simon and Schuster, 1949.

Curtis, John J. "Reminiscences of a Publisher," in *Publishers' Weekly*, May 10, 1930.

Downing, Olive Inez. *Indiana's Poet of the Wildwood*. Marion, Indiana: News Publishing Company, 1941.

Draegert, Eva. "Theater in Indianapolis Before 1880," in *Indiana Magazine of History*, LI (1955).

Dunn, Jacob P. *Greater Indianapolis*, 2 vols. Chicago: Lewis Publishing Company, 1922.

———. *Indiana and Indianians*, 5 vols. Chicago and New York, 1919.

———. *True Indian Stories*. Indianapolis: Sentinel Printing Company, 1908.

Encyclopaedia Britannica, 1961 Edition.

Esarey, Logan. *History of Indiana*, 2 vols. Dayton, Ohio: Dayton Publishing Company, 1922.

Fleming, Charles Francis. *The White Hat. A Political Biography of Henry Frederick Schricker*. Indianapolis, 1966.

Foulke, William Dudley. *Life of Oliver P. Morton*, 2 vols. Indianapolis: The Bobbs-Merrill Company, 1899.

Friedersdorf, Burk, text; George S. Madden, Gene Vaughn and staff of WFBM. *From Crystal to Color, WFBM*. Indianapolis: WFBM Stations, 1964.

Funk, Orville L. *Tales of Our Hoosier Heritage*. Chicago: Adams Press, 1965.

Ginger, Ray. *The Bending Cross: A Biography of Eugene Victor Debs*. New Brunswick, N.J.: Rutgers University Press. (Reprinted as *Eugene V. Debs: A Biography*. New York: Collier Books, 1962.)

Guthrie, J. M. *Sesqui Scrapbook*. Indiana Sesquicentennial Commission, 1966.

Hart, James D., editor. *Robert Louis Stevenson, From Scotland to Silverado*. Cambridge, Mass.: The Belknap Press of Harvard University, 1966.

Hawkins, Hubert H., compiler. *Indiana's Road to Statehood. A Documentary Record*. Indiana Sesquicentennial Commission, 1966.

Hawkins, Hubert H., and McClaren, Robert R. *Indiana Lives*. Hopkinsville, Ky.: Historical Record Association, 1967.

Hill, Herbert R. Selected magazine articles from *Outdoor Indiana*. Indianapolis: Indiana Department of Natural Resources, 1968, 1969.

Historical Commission. *Indianapolis Centennial, 1820-1920*. Indianapolis: Max R. Hyman Company.

Holliday, J. H. *Indianapolis and the Civil War*, Vols. I, IV. Indianapolis Historical Society Publications.

Holloway, W. R. *Indianapolis: A Historical and Statistical Sketch of the*

Railroad City. Indianapolis: Indianapolis Journal Printing Company, 1870.

Holt, Sol. *Dictionary of American History*. New York: McFadden Books, 1963.

Hyman, Max R. *Handbook of Indianapolis*. Indianapolis: Carlon and Hollenbeck, 1897.

————, editor. *Journal Handbook of Indianapolis*. Indianapolis: Journal Publishing Company, 1902, 1907 editions.

Indiana, A Guide to the Hoosier State. Indiana Writers' Project. New York: Oxford University Press, 1941.

Industries of Indianapolis, 1889. Indianapolis: Board of Trade.

Kelly, Fred C. *The Wright Brothers*. New York: Ballantine Books, 1956.

Kull, Irving S. and Nell M. *An Encyclopedia of American History*. New Brunswick, N.J.: Rutgers University Press, 1952.

Leary, Edward A., editor. *Indiana Almanac and Fact Book*, 1967, 1968-69 editions. Indianapolis: Ed Leary & Associates, 1967, 1968.

Leary, Edward A. *The Nineteenth State, Indiana*. Indianapolis: Ed Leary & Associates, 1966-1967 edition.

Leech, Margaret. *In the Days of McKinley*. New York: Harper & Brothers, 1959.

Leibowitz, Irving. *My Indiana*. Englewood Cliffs, N.J.: Prentice-Hall, Inc.

Marlette, Jerry. *Electric Railroads of Indiana*. Indianapolis: Council for Local History, 1959.

Martin, John Bartlow. *Indiana: An Interpretation*. New York: Alfred Knopf, 1947.

Mitchell, John Fowler, Jr. *The Rooster, Its Origin as the Democratic Emblem*. Indianapolis: John F. Mitchell, Jr., 1966.

Newspapers, Indianapolis. Indianapolis *Democrat*
                          Indiana *Freeman*
                          Indianapolis *Gazette*
                          Indianapolis *Journal*
                          Indianapolis *Locomotive*
                          Indianapolis *News*
                          Indianapolis *Sentinel*
                          Indianapolis *Star*
                          Indianapolis *Sun*
                          Indianapolis *Times*
                          Indianapolis *Town Talk*

Nolan, Jeannette Covert. *Hoosier City*. New York: Julian Messner, Inc., 1943.

Nowland, J. H. B. *Early Reminiscences of Indianapolis*. Indianapolis, 1870.

Perry, James E. *Who's Who and What's What in Indiana Politics*. Indianapolis: James E. Perry, 1944.

Phillips, Clifton J. *Indiana in Transition; the Emergence of an Industrial Commonwealth, 1880-1920*. Indianapolis: Indiana Historical Society and Indiana Historical Bureau, 1968.

Pittman, Benn. *The Trials for Treason at Indianapolis*. Cincinnati: Moore, Wilstach and Baldwin, 1865.

Rabb, Kate Milner, and Herschell, William. *An Account of Indianapolis and Marion County*. Dayton, Ohio: Dayton Historical Publishing Company, 1924.

Roll, Charles. *Indiana: One Hundred and Fifty Years of American Development*. 5 vols. Chicago, Ill., 1931.

Rose, Ernestine Bradford. *The Circle: Center of Our Universe*. Indianapolis: Indiana Historical Society, 1957.

Shaw, Wilbur. *Gentlemen, Start Your Engines*. New York: Coward-McCann, 1955.

Shumaker, Arthur W. *A History of Indiana Literature*. Indianapolis: Indiana Historical Society, 1962.

Simmons, Virgil, editorial chairman. *Indiana Review*. Indianapolis: State of Indiana, 1938.

Smith, William Henry. *The History of the State of Indiana from the Earliest Explorations of the French to the Present Time*. 2 vols. Indianapolis, 1903.

Statistical Abstract of the U. S., 1967, 1968, 1969. Washington, D. C.: Department of Commerce.

Stickney, Ida Stearns. *Pioneer Indianapolis*. Indianapolis: The Bobbs-Merrill Company, 1907.

Stone, Irving. *Adversary in the House*. Garden City, N.Y.: Doubleday, 1947.

Sulgrove, B. R. *History of Indianapolis and Marion County*. Philadelphia: L. H. Everts and Company, 1884.

———. *The City and the Bank*. Privately printed. Indianapolis: Merchants National Bank and Trust Company of Indianapolis, 1965.

———. *The Hoosier House*. Indianapolis: The Bobbs-Merrill Company, 1923.

Thompson, Dave O., Sr. and Madigan, William L. *One Hundred and Fifty Years of Indiana Agriculture*. Indianapolis: Indiana Sesquicentennial Commission, 1966.

Thornbrough, Emma Lou. *Indiana in the Civil War Era.*, Vol. III of a projected 5-vol. history of Indiana. Indianapolis: Indiana Historical Bureau and Indiana Historical Society, 1965.

Thornbrough, Gayle and Riker, Dorothy, editors. *Readings in Indiana History*. Indianapolis: Indiana Historical Bureau, 1956.

Thornton, J. F. and Reade, Anna R. *Indiana, The Story of a Progressive Commonwealth*. Chicago, Ill.: Mentzer, Bush & Company, 1926.

Wilson, William E. *Indiana, A History*. Bloomington: Indiana University Press, 1966.

———. *The Angel and the Serpent: The Story of New Harmony*. Bloomington: Indiana University Press, 1964.

World Book Encyclopedia, 1962 Edition.

Index

Abe Martin, 163-164, 183
Academy of Music, 120, 189
Accidents, auto, 168, 195
Adams, J. Ottis, 120
Ade, George, 157-158, 165
A.F.L.-C.I.O., 186-187, 216
Airplanes, 195, 225
Airports, 119, 225
Alabama Street, 79, 197, 216
Alhambra Theater, 183
Allegheny Airlines, 227
Allied Grocers, 231
Allison, James A., 175, 176, 177, 180, 181-182, 208
Allison Division, General Motors, 189-190, 215
American Automobile Association, 178, 220
American Bicycle Company, 177
American Fletcher National Bank, 219, 231
American Legion, 190-191, 195, 204, 211, 222
American Motor Car Co., 169, 170
American Order of Workingmen, 140
American Railway Union, 152, 186
American Society of Professional Automobile Racing (ASPAR), 219
Americans for Conservative Action, 221
Anderson (Indian chief), 6-7, 15
Anthony, Susan B., 121
Anti-Saloon League, 191
Antlers Hotel, 217
Apartments, 159, 208, 225, 228, 230, 231
Apperson, Elmer and Edgar, 145
Armistice, World War II, 190
Armstrong, Nell, 183
Art, 56-57, 120, 139, 182, 225
Art Association of Indianapolis, 140, 182, 225

Arthur, Joseph, 139
Athenaeum, 189, 194
Athenaeum Theater, 81, 100
Atkins, Elias C., 69
Attucks, Crispus, High School, 182, 204
Authors, 157-166
Automobile racing, 168, 175-179, 208, 219, 227
Automobiles, 145, 167-172, 174; list of autos made in Indianapolis, 170-171
Avery, P. C. (inventor), 176
Axtell, Mary J. and Harriett, 43
Ayres, A. C., 137
Ayes, L. S., & Co., department store, 123, 136, 197
Ayres, Lyman S., 123, 181
Ayr-Way Discount Department Stores, 123

Bacon, Hiram, 88
Bagwell, Billy, 26
Baker, (Gov.) Conrad, 127
Baker, E. G. (Cannonball), 178
Baker, J. Worth, 220
Baldwin & Miller, 136
Balloons, 175, 176, 177-178
Bank robberies, 124-125
Banks, 42-43, 83-86, 117, 129, 207, 218-219, 231
Banks, Henry, 220
Baptists, 23, 230
Barbers, early, 13, 47
Barbers union, 216
Barnard, (Dr.) Harry E., 189
Barnes, (Rev.) Benjamin, 22
Barton, (Mayor) John J., 228
Barton, John J., Apartments, 224, 228
Baseball, 142, 195
Basketball, 182, 195, 198, 225
Bates, Hervey, 19, 43, 70
Bates House, 70, 95, 126, 135, 226

Batts, Robert L., 198-199
Bauman, Frederick, 155
"Baxter Law," 122
Bayh, (U. S. Sen.) Birch E., Jr., 228
Bayt, (Mayor) Phillip L., Jr., 218
Beatty Farm, 134
Beech Grove, 180, 229
Beecher, (Rev.) Henry Ward, 44-45, 46, 54, 58, 66, 80
Beecher, (Mrs.) Henry Ward (*nee* Eunice Ballard), 44-45
Beehive Store, 181
"Beer riots," 76
Beiderbecke, Bix, 193
Belt line railroad, 133-134, 143, 209
Ben Hur: A Tale of the Christ, 158-159
Benham's Musical Review, 124
Berry's Trace, 17
Beveridge, Albert J., 163, 184-185
Bicycles, 141, 167, 175, 177
"Big Field, The," 14
Bigger, (Gov.) Samuel, 54
Binford, Thomas, 220
Bingham, J. J. (editor), 111, 112
Birch, John, Society, 221
Black, Charles H., 145, 167
Blackburn, (Dr.) Cleo, 231
Blackford, (Judge) Isaac, 28, 33, 62
Blackford's building, 100
Blackledge, Elden (magician), 194
Blake, James, 23, 25, 46, 62, 115
Blind, Asylum for the, 72
Block, William H., 198
Block, William H., Company, 181, 217
Bloemker, Al, 219
"Blue Laws," 72
Blythe, Benjamin, 11, 35
Bobbs, (Dr.) John S., 119-120
Bobbs, William C., 136, 160, 162
Bobbs-Merrill Company, 35, 160, 161-163, 227; *see also* Bowen, Stewart & Co.; Bowen-Merrill Co.
Boetcher, (Mayor) Wallace A., 217
Bolton, Nathaniel, 19-20, 35, 72, 82
Bolton, Sarah, 35, 72, 82
"Bone-dry" law, 75
Book, William Henry, 220, 221-222
Booker, Samuel P., 10
Boosters Club, 182
Bose, Lewis, 229
Boswell, (Mayor) Charles, 218
Bounty system, 101-102
Bowen, Silas T., 64
Bowen, Stewart & Company, 64, 136
Bowen-Merrill Company, 136, 142, 160, 161-163
Bowers, Claude C., 135, 153

Bowles, (Dr.) William A., 112
Boxing, 195
Branigin, (Gov.) Roger D., 228
Bread riot, 134
Bridgeport Brass, 216
Bright, Jesse D., 91-92
Bright, Richard J. (publisher), 124
Broad Ripple, 50, 66, 192
Broadway Christian pre-apprentice school, 230
Brotherhood of Locomotive Engineers, 122
Brown, (Rev.) Andrew, 231
Bruce, (U. S. Rep.) Donald C., 221
Brush, John T., 136, 142
Bryant and Stratton, 140
Buchanan, James (publisher), 130-131
Buchanan, Thomas, 130-133
Bucktown, 117
"Buffalo Boy," 47-48
Bumbaugh, (Capt.) G. L., 176, 177, 178
Bundles, Henry F., 231
Burbank, Lucinda M., 104
Burckhardt, (Dr.) Louis, 140
Burkhart (Buckhart), Dave ("Old Dave"), 38
Burkhart, John (insurance company president), 225
Bush, Donnie, 195
Business, *see* Indianapolis; Industry; Manufacturing
Butler, Ovid, 71, 88, 90, 91
Butler-Tarkington Neighborhood Association, 230
Butler University, 71, 88, 117, 121, 140, 141, 182, 194, 195, 225, 226
Butsch, Valentine, 81, 120

Cadets of Temperance, 57
Cadle Tabernacle, 197, 203
Camp Atterbury Job Corps, 230
Camp Dellwood (Girl Scouts), 183
Camps, Civil War, 97-98; Camp Morton, 100, 111, 113, 139
Canals, 48-52, 53, 65, 67
Capehart (U. S. Sen.) Homer E., 228
Capital, state, *see* Indiana
Capitol, state, *see* Statehouse *under* Indiana
Capitol Avenue, 36, 72
Carlton and Hollenbeck, 181
Carmichael, Hoagy, 192, 193-194
Carnahan, James A. (G.A.R.), 154
Carr, John (state agent), 10, 17
Carter, Tommy (auctioneer), 18
Carter's Tavern, *see* Rosebush Tavern
Casino Gardens, 193, 194

Catherwood, Mary Hartwell, 157, 163
Caven, John, 119, 122-123, 133-134, 143
Center Township, 22
Central Avenue, 119, 177
Central Canal, 49-52, 53, 65, 67
Central College of Physicians and Surgeons, 140
Central Electric Railway Association, 173
Central Labor Council, 152
Central Union Telephone Company, 143
"Chain Gang," 38
Chain stores, 194
Chanticleer, The, 90
Chapman, George A., 54
Chapman, Jacob Page, 54, 80, 90
Chapman, John, 55
Chase, William Merritt (artist), 120
Chenoweth family, 177
Chevrolet, Art, 169, 178
Chevrolet, Louis, 169, 176
Chevrolet Brothers, 169, 170
Chislett, F. W., 120
Cholera epidemic, 45-46
Choral Union, 120
Christ Church, 42, 156
Christian Theological Seminary, 226
Chrysler Corporation, 216
Churches, 14, 22-23, 42-44, 72-73, 136, 182, 198, 225, 231
Churchman Avenue, 209
Cigarette laws, 183
Circle, the, 12-13, 14, 33, 37, 39, 42, 44, 45, 55, 58-59, 70, 71, 115, 118, 135-136, 138, 144, 149, 154-155, 184, 187, 189, 190, 196, 198, 212, 216
"Circle Park," 154-155
Circle Theater, 183, 198
Circuses, 65, 81, 183
Citizens Committee for Research, 221
Citizens' Executive Committee, 156
Citizens' Industrial Association of America, 186
Citizens Railway Company, 119
"City of Indianapolis" (airplane), 196
Civil War, 95-96, 97-103, 104-112, 113-114, 139, 148, 190
Clark, (Mayor) Alex M., 218, 220
Classical School for Girls, 121
Claypool, Henry, 70
Claypool Hotel, 186, 226
Clemens, W. F. (Jap), 168
Cleveland, (Pres.) Grover, 146, 149-152
Clothing, see Fashion
Cloutier, Joe (speedway executive), 219
Clowes, (Mrs.) G. H. A., 225
Clowes Memorial Hall, 225

Clubs, 121, 135, 137, 140, 149, 152
Cochrane, Homer (broker), 219
Coe, (Dr.) Isaac, 16, 23, 25, 50, 62
Coffin, Tristram, 227
Cold Spring Road, 181
Cold Springs, 124
Cole, E. P., 63-64
Coliseum, 198, 227-228
College Life Insurance Company, 225
College Park, 225
Colleges, see Universities
Colored Methodist Church, 44
"Colored Town," 50
Columbia Club, 149, 184, 196-197
Columbia Conserve, 209-210
Commercial Club, 135, 137, 152, 185
Congress of Industrial Organizations, 210, 216
Conner, John, 5, 6
Conner, William, 5-6, 9, 15, 27
Conscription Acts, 102
Conservatives, 221
Constitutional convention, 1951, 82-83
Construction, see buildings under Indianapolis
Contemporary Club, 140
Cook, John (state librarian), 57
"Copperheads," 108-111
Corbaley, Jeremiah, 8, 13
Cornelius, George, 181
Corydon, 4, 9, 10, 11, 19, 23, 25, 30, 36
Costigan, Francis, 70
Counties, 180
County Seminary, 43, 58, 63
Court Street, 120
Courthouse Square, 120
Cox, (Mrs.) A. G., 120
Cox, Jacob, 56-57, 120
Cravens, (Rev.) William, 14, 23
Crime, 57, 74-75, 99, 146, 192, 198-199
Crossroads of America, 87
Crowe, Ray (basketball coach), 182
Crown Hill Cemetery, 120, 154, 161, 192
Culley, David V., 70
Currency depreciation, 130-131
Curtis, John J., 136, 162
Cyclorama, 139

D-A Lubricant, 220
Daily Commercial, 124
Daily Mirror, 124
Daily Sentinel, 102
Daily Telegraph, 124
Dan Patch, 139
Dancing, 18-19; dancing era, 194
Daniels, Samuel P. (librarian), 57

Daughters of the American Revolution, 151
Daughters of Temperance, 57
Davenport, Spurgeon, 231
Davis, Charlie (bandleader), 196
Davis, Joseph W., 77-78
Dawson, Joe (race driver), 179
Debs, Eugene Victor, 152, 161, 185, 186-187
Decatur, Illinois, 126
Decatur Township, 22
Defrees, John, 91, 92, 95
Delaware Indians, 3, 6-7, 15, 27
Delaware Street, 18, 64, 120, 136, 148
Delaware Township, 22
Democrat, 34, 54, 80, 88
Democrats, 54-55, 90-96, 107-112, 126-128, 131-133, 146, 151, 211-212, 213-214, 218-219, 220-223, 228-229
Denison Hotel, 161
Denny, (Mayor) Caleb S., 146, 218
Denny, (Mayor) George L., 218
DePalma, Ralph, 178-179
Department stores, 127, 136, 181
Depressions, 168, 174, 207, 209, 216
DePuy, Henry (publisher), 88
Desegregation, 230-231
Detroit, Michigan, 168
Deutsche Haus, Das, 135, 189
Dewey, Thomas E., 223
Diamond Chain Division, 177
Dice, (Mrs.) Marguerite, 221
Dillin, (Judge) S. Hugh, 228
Dillinger, John, 213
Dillon, Jack (boxer), 195
Dillon, John Brown, 57
Disasters, 114, 121, 142, 173, 184, 227-228
Disciples of Christ, 71, 222
Dodd, Harrison H., 111-112
Downie, George B. (bandleader), 81
Draft, Civil War, 102-103
Drag races, 227
Drake, Aaron, 20
Drama, *see* Theater
Dramatic Club, Inc., 140
Dreiser, Theodore, 157, 158
Duesenberg, Augie, 169, 172
Duesenberg, Fred, 169, 172
Duesenberg auto, 169, 170, 172, 179
Dumont, Ebenezer, 96, 98
Duncan House, 70
Dunlap, (Dr.) Livingston, 16, 56
Dunn, Jacob Piatt (historian), 40
Duvall, (Mayor) John, 203, 206

Eagle Clothing Store, 69, 181

Eagle Creek, 56
Eagle Creek Flood Control project, 225
Eagle Machine Works, 69, 80
Eagle Tavern, 13, 20
Eaton, Joseph O., 56-57
Edison, Thomas A., 144, 183
Edison Telephone, 143
Education, *see* Schools; Universities and colleges
Edwards, Frank, 227
Eggleston, Edward, 157
Eggleston, George, 157
Eight-Hour Leagues, 122
Eighteenth Amendment, 191
Elections, *see* politics *under* Indiana; Indianapolis
Electric lights, 143-144, 149
Emhardt, (Major) Christian J., 218
Emmerich, (Prof.) Charles E., 139-140
Empire Automobile Company, 169, 170
Employee-operated company, 209-210
Employment, 117, 129, 136, 215, 226, 230
Employment Task Force, 229
Enabling Act, 5
English, William E., 138, 154
English, William E., Foundation, 216
English, William H., 130, 138, 154, 155
English Hotel, 138, 216
English Opera House, 138, 156, 196, 216
Enlistments, Civil War, 101-102
Ensaw, Ephraim, 13
Entertainment, *see* Circus; Music; Opera; Theater; Vaudeville
Epidemics, 15-16, 24, 45-46, 56
Episcopal Church, 42, 156
Equal Suffrage Society, 121
Equitable Life Assurance Society, 216
Ernestinoff, Alexander (conductor), 208
Erwin, Daniel P., 182
Estates, 181-182
Evangelical United Brethren Church, 182
Evans, Charles (city librarian), 118
Evans, (Dr.) Hiram Wesley, 201, 203-205
Explosions, fairgrounds, 121, 227-228

FM radio, 217
Fairbanks, (Vice-Pres.) Charles Warren, 185, 188
Fairview Park, 145, 182
Fall Creek, 6, 8-9, 15, 28, 56, 99, 119, 184
Fall Creek Settlements, 5, 7
Farmers, 88, 130, 151, 164, 188
Farmers' Alliance, 151-152

Farmers' Mutual Benefit Association, 151-152
Fashions, 47, 140-141, 196
Fayette County, 6
Federal aid, 221, 222-223, 228-229
Federal Building, 224
Feeney, (Mayor) Albert G., 218
Fehrenbatch, John, 122
Fenian Brotherhood, 123
Ferries, 22, 72
Fertig, Fred, 156
Fidelity Trust Company, 219
Fifteenth Amendment, 126-128
Fifteenth Street, 99
Fifth Street, 71, 118
Finley, John, 40-41, 82
Finney, David D., 221
Finney, Gertrude E., 227
Fire fighting, 31, 58-59, 76-78
Fires, 142-143, 226
First English Lutheran church, 43
First Indiana Cavalry, 127
First National Bank, 117, 130
First Presbyterian Church, 115
Fisher, Carl G., 175-179, 180, 181-182, 192
Fitch, Graham, 92
"500 Festival," 220
500-Mile Race, see Indianapolis Motor Speedway
Flanner House, 222, 230, 231
Flat Tire Club, 181
Fletcher, Calvin, 13, 24, 25, 28, 42-43, 46, 47, 62-63, 71, 91, 147
Fletcher, (Mrs.) Calvin, Jr., 114
Fletcher, Louisa, 166
Fletcher, Stoughton A., 43, 166, 177
Fletcher and Churchman Bank, 43
Fletcher's Bank, 43
Fletcher's Swamp, 15
Floods, 21, 56, 184
Flower Mission Fair, 138
Foley, Michael, 189
Football, 225
Foote, Obed, 13, 23, 47
For America Committee, 221
Forbes, Gilbert, 198
Fordham, Elias, 11, 13
Forest Manor Neighborhood Association, 230
Forsyth, William, 120
Fort Benjamin Harrison, 189
Fortnightly Club, 140
Fortune, William, 137
Forty and Eight, 191
Forty-second Rainbow Division, 189
Foster, (Gen.) John W., 156

Foster, (Gen.) Robert S., (G.A.R.), 126
Foster's Jewelry Store, 42
Fourteenth Amendment, 125
Fox, Bill, 219
Foyt, A. J., 179, 220
Franklin Institute, 43
Free Democrats, 91
Free Soil Democrats, The, 88
Free Soil Democratic Association, 90
Free Soil party, 90-91
Freeman, John, 88-89
Freeman, Samuel J., 220
Freie Presse, 88, 124
French Lick Springs Hotel, 146
Frenzel, John P., 140, 145, 153
From Dawn to Daylight, 45
Fugitive Slave Law, 87-89

Gangsters, 192, 198, 213
Garfield Park, 154
Gas, see Natural gas
Gates, A. B., 137
Gates, (Gov.) Ralph F., 222
Gatling, (Dr.) Richard (inventor), 100
General Motors, 169
Gennett Records, 193
Gentleman from Indiana, The, 165-166
Gentry, Earl, 205
Georgia Street, 20, 44, 71, 72, 142
German Singing Societies, 81
Germans, 43, 50, 74-76, 81, 87, 93, 101, 118, 122, 124, 137, 189
Ghettos, 230-231
Gibson Girls, 140
Giesendorff's mill, 105
Girl Scouts, 182-183
"Golden Age of Literature," 157-166, 227
Golden Hills, 182
Goldkette, Jean, 193
Goldsmith, Gardner, 91
Golf, 141, 195
Goodrich, (Gov.) James P., 188, 189
Goodwin, (Rev.) T. A., 88
Gordon, Gordon, 227
Gould and Jackson, 67
Government Reorganization Task Force, 229
"Governor's house," 33-34, 37-38, 42, 45, 70
Grand Army of the Republic, 126, 154, 156, 190, 217
Grand Opera House, 138-139, 159
Grand Theater, 183
Grange, 130, 151
Grayson, (Mrs.) Jane, 114
Great National Turnpike Road, see National Road

Greater Indianapolis, 133
Greater Indianapolis Progress Committee, 228, 229
Green, William, 186
Greenback Clubs, 132
Greenback-Labor Party, 151-152
Greenback Party, 131-133, 151
Greenbackers, 130, 151-152
Greenfield, 54-55, 159, 161, 172
Greenlee, Pleas E., 213-214
Greenough, (Mrs.) Walter S., 196
Greenwood and Franklin Electric Railway, 167
Gregg, Harvey, 20
Gregg school, 43
Gregory, (Sen.) James, 25, 30
Gresham, Otto, 149
Gresham, Walter G., 152
Grubbs, (Mayor) Daniel W., 146
Guminsky brothers (Von Tilzers), 144
Gurley, Bob (editor), 204
Gurley, (Rev.) Phineas, 115

H.O.M.E., 230
Haag drugstores, 194
Hadley, William, 118
Haggerty, (Capt.) James, 123
Haggerty, Judson, 218
Hamilton, Francis (radio pioneer), 197
Hammond, (Rev.) Rezin, 14
Hampton, Slide, 194
Hanley, (Gov.) J. Frank, 183
Hanna, (General) Robert, 35-36
Hannaman, William, 106
Hannegan, Steve, 208
Hapgood, Powers, 210
Hapgood, William, 209-210
Harding, Eliakim, 22
Harding, Mordecai, 13
Harmonic Society, 120
Harrington, (Judge) Henry W., 132-133
Harrison, Abraham W., 63
Harrison, (Pres.) Benjamin, 133, 146, 148-151, 155, 156, 163, 184-185
Harrison, (Mrs.) Benjamin (Caroline Scott), 148, 151
Harrison, (Mrs.) Benjamin (Mary Dimmick), 151
Harrison, Christopher, 10, 11-12, 17
Harrison, Elizabeth, 151
Harrison, (Pres.) William Henry, 7, 53-55, 155
Harrison Marching Society (Columbia Club), 149, 150
Harroun, Ray, 175, 179
Hartke, (U.S. Sen.) R. Vance, 218, 228
Hasbrook, Thomas C., 229

Hascall, (Gen.) Milo S., 109
Hastings, Don, 198
Hatfield Electric Company, 197
Havens, (Rev.) James, 38
Hawkins, John, 23
Hawkins' tavern, 13, 20
Hay and Willits Company, 177
Hayes, B. S., 120
Hayes, Joseph, 227
Haynes, Elwood, 145, 167
Haynes-Apperson Car, 145
Hays, Will H., 188-189
Haywood, Bill, 186-187
Heffren, Horace, 112
Heischler, Theodore (publisher), 88
Henderson, Samuel, 20, 38, 62, 65, 68
Henderson's Grove, 79, 101
Hendricks, (Gov.) Thomas A., 30, 92, 108, 110, 115, 127
Henneman & Duzen, 69
Henry, Charles L., 172
Henry, Joanne Landers, 227
Herff-Brooks Company, 169, 170
Herron, John, 182
Herron, John, Art Institute, 182
Herschell, William, 194
Hibernians, Ancient Order of, 140
Highways, 168, 195, 225
Hilgenberg, Mr. and Mrs. Noble, 197
Hilton Hotel, 224
Hinkle, Paul D. (Tony), 195
Hitt, George C., 159
Hodgkins, John, 56
Holiday on Ice, 227
Holland, Bill, 219, 220
Hollenbeck, John C., 99
Holliday, John H., 117, 124, 152
Holloway, William R., 81, 86
Home for Friendless Women, 118
Home guards, 113
Homes, 21, 141, 215, 230
Honeybee (Indianapolis, New Castle and Eastern), 173-174
Hook, August F. (Bud), 181
Hook, John, 181
Hooker's Female School, Miss, 43
Hook's Economy Drug Store, 181, 194
"Hoosier," origin of word, 40-41, 92
Hoosier Art Colony, Munich, 120
Hoosier Democratic Club, 214
Hoosier dialect, 194
Hoosier Farmer, 212
Hoosier Hundred, 227
Hoosier Motor Club, 181
Hoosier Schoolmaster, The, 157
"Hoosier's Nest, The," 40-41, 82
Horse cars, 119

Horse Thief Association, 203
Horse track, 139
"Horseless carriages," 145, 167
Horsey, Stephen, 112
Hospitals, 100, 119, 140, 182, 225, 231
Hotels, 10, 70, 135, 138, 224
House of Refuge for Boys, 118
House of a Thousand Candles, The, 162
Housing, experimental, 229
Hovey, (Gov.) Alvin P., 64, 111, 112, 155
Howard, Roy, 190, 196
Hubbard, Kin (Frank McKinney), 157, 163-164
Hubbard, (Mrs.) Frank McKinney, 164
Hubbard block, 67, 181
Huffman, Wallace S., 170
Hulman, Anton (Tony), Jr., 219-220
Hulman & Company, 219
Humphrey, Andrew, 112
Hygrade Products plant, 226
Hyman, Max, 36

I.N.H.I., 230
"Ice King" (Volney Malott), 117
Illinois Street, 10, 18, 37, 42, 54, 69, 95, 119, 120, 142, 145, 181, 193, 195
Independent Party, 131-132
Independent Relief Company, 58
Indiana
  capital: at Corydon, 4; move argued, 5; new site approved, 9; move delayed, 24-25; move to Indianapolis, 30-31; new capitol, 137-138
  Civil War statistics, 114
  constitutional convention, 1851, 82-83
  Deaf and Dumb School, 71-72
  first auto license plates, 168
  first gasoline tax, 168
  first highway department, 168
  first senior U.S. senator, 28
  first state librarian, 57, 82
  first statehouse in Indianapolis, 36-37
  first Thanksgiving Day, 52
  free public school system established, 83
  funds misappropriated, 183
  General Assembly, 10, 19, 20, 25, 30-31, 42, 51, 62, 83, 108, 152, 154, 168, 184, 190, 191, 212, 222, 223; see also House of Representatives, Senate under Indiana
  governor's house, 33-34, 37-38, 42, 45, 70

Indiana—Continued
  Historical Building, 208
  Hospital for the Insane, 72
  House of Representatives, 3, 37, 82, 90, 133, 211
  Internal Improvements Bonds, 49
  labor laws, 183
  "New Purchase" treaty, 3
  politics, 53-55, 89-96, 125-128, 131-133, 149-154, 184-186, 210-212, 213-214, 220-223, 228
  population, 4, 180, 216
  prohibition law passed, 74-75
  Public Utilities Commission, 214
  Senate, 37, 82, 90, 133, 211
  State Board of Agriculture, 79, 139
  State Board of Health, 168
  State Budget Committee, 222
  State Bureau of Labor, 183
  State Council of Defense, 189
  State Fair, 79, 121, 139, 143, 208, 217
  State Fair grounds, 119, 139, 168, 181, 198, 227
  state funds, 222
  State Library, 57, 208
  State Office Building, 216
  State parks, 195
  State Police, 218
  State Sanitary Commission, 102, 106, 107
  Statehouse, 36-37, 131, 133, 134, 216; new building, 137-138
  Superintendent of Public Instruction, 204
  Supreme Court, 28, 37, 64, 75-76, 149, 222
  territory capital, 4
  voting rights, 83
"Indiana, Miss" (statue), 156
Indiana American, 88
Indiana Avenue, 10, 118, 119, 230, 231
Indiana (balloon), 177
Indiana Bell Telephone Building, 224
Indiana Brigade, 98
Indiana Central College, 182, 226
Indiana Central Medical Society, 25
Indiana in the Civil War Era, 227
Indiana Dental College, 140
Indiana Farm Bureau, 212
Indiana Federation of Business and Professional Women, 183
Indiana Federation of Labor, 186, 216
Indiana Federation of Trade and Labor Unions, 152
Indiana Freeman, The, 88
Indiana Grange, 130, 151
Indiana Greenback Party, 132, 151

Indiana High School Athletic Association, 182
Indiana Historical Society, 40
Indiana Home Owners Loan Corporation, 214
Indiana and Illinois Central Railroad, 100
Indiana Journalism Hall of Fame, 217
Indiana Law School, 140
Indiana League, 196
Indiana Legion, 105
Indiana Medical College, 119-120
Indiana National Bank, 117, 153, 219; Tower, 224
Indiana Pacers, 225
Indiana Peace Society, 188
"Indiana Plan," 131
Indiana Railroad, 174
Indiana Roof, 194
Indiana Sentinel, 11, 16-17, 67, 131
Indiana Soldier in the War of the Union, The, 121
Indiana State Sentinel, 54-55
Indiana Theater, 193
Indiana II (balloon), 178
Indiana University, 182, 193, 211, 225-226, 231
Indiana University Law School, 211
Indiana University Medical Center, 208
Indiana University-Purdue University at Indianapolis, 226
Indiana Vocational Technical College, 230
Indiana Volunteers, 148, 154
Indianapolis
  "ager" epidemic, 15-16
  Board of Councilmen, 74
  board of health organized, 45
  Board of Park Commissioners, 154
  Board of School Commissioners, 140, 196, 203
  buildings, new, 135-136, 180, 196, 224-225
  business conditions, 55-56, 69-71, 117, 123, 136-137, 181, 196-197, 207-208, 215-216
  camp meetings, 22, 38
  canals and railroads, 48-52, 53, 65, 67
  capital: site selection, 5-9; named, 10-11; move delayed, 24-25; move from Corydon, 30-31; Civil War capital, 95-96, 97-103; new capitol, 137-138
  charter adopted, 61, 62; new charter, 74, 137
  cholera epidemic, 45-46

Indianapolis—*Continued*
  City Council, 63, 73, 98, 102, 133, 143-144, 176, 189, 192
  City-County Building, 180, 216, 224
  City Hall, 216
  City Hospital, 119
  City Market, 138
  Civil War boom explodes, 129-134
  Civil War Gov. Morton and, 104-112
  coins in use, 42
  country town, metropolis, 136
  crime and vice, 57, 74-75, 99, 146, 192, 198-199
  election of officials, 61-63, 74
  fashions, 47, 140-141, 196
  ferry fees, 22
  Fire Department, 58-59, 76-78, 142-143, 190
  first amateur acting group, 57
  first apartment house, 159
  first auto-industry capital, 167
  first banker, 13
  first black man, 13
  first board of trustees president, 62
  first brewery, 34
  first brick house, 21
  first budget, 73
  first burial, 16
  first Catholic church, 44
  first Catholic school, 71
  first cheese-dairy farm, 88
  first child born, 13
  first churches, 23
  first circuit court session, 24
  first Civil War casualty, 99
  first Civil War unit, 98
  first college, 182
  first college without restrictions, 71
  first constable and bailiff, 13
  first council meeting, 63, 73
  first dancing party, 18-19
  first doctor, 13
  first electricity station, 144
  first electricity usage, 144
  first Episcopal church, 42
  first fire fighting group, 31
  first floods, 21
  first Fourth of July, 23
  first free library, 118
  first full-time newspaper cartoonist, 163
  first Germans in, 43
  first golf links, 141
  first G.A.R. encampment, 126
  first hangings in city, 124
  first high school, 63

Indianapolis—*Continued*
  first house with incandescent lights,
    149
  first ice cream parlor, 56
  first insurance company, 35
  first interurban, 172
  first Irish in, 35
  first justice of the peace, 13
  first labor organization, 70
  first lot sold, 18
  first Lutheran church, 43
  first mayor, 62, 68, 73
  first mayor born in, 146
  first Methodist church, 23
  first military execution, 101
  first municipal scandal, 73
  first murder, 47
  first musical comedy, 139
  first musical skit, 26
  first Negro to arrive and leave, 13, 47
  first Negro voting, 146
  first newspaper, 19
  first officials elected, 61-64
  first permanent radio station, 197
  first postal service, 20
  first postmaster, 62
  first Presbyterian church, 23
  first public building, 36-37
  first public execution, 28
  first public school system, 61-62
  first radio station, 197
  first railroad trains, 64, 66
  first resident preacher, 14
  first school, 18, 22
  first smithy, 8
  first stagecoach lines, 31, 32
  first store, 13
  first street numbering, 73-74
  first summer, 15
  first superintendent of schools, 64
  first telegraph lines, 66-67
  first telephone exchange, 143
  first theater, 81
  first theatrical production, 26
  first theatrical season, 46
  first town government, 38-39
  first town sheriff, 43
  first turbine engine at 500-Mile Clas-
    sic, 227
  first two-story house, 21
  first wedding ceremony, 13
  first white settlement, 5
  first wholesale dry goods house, 46
  first winter, 18
  first woman to die, 16
  floods, 21, 56, 184

Indianapolis—*Continued*
  general charter adopted, 74
  "golden years," 135; of literature, 157-
    166, 227
  high schools, 63, 118, 139, 165, 182, 192,
    204, 205, 225
  Housing Authority, 228
  log jail, 31
  lot auctions, 17-18, 37
  mail services, 20, 32, 34, 47-48, 54, 71,
    120, 134, 180, 195
  mayors, 62, 68, 73, 146
  Mayor's Commission on Human
    Rights, 222
  mile square, 12-13, 18, 21, 79
  militia organized, 23
  naming of, 10-11
  Negroes in, *see* Negroes
  new market house, 47
  newspapers, 19-20, 34, 40, 79-80, 88
  Northern town, Southern style, 39-40
  one-hundredth birthday, 191
  park system, 147
  police force problems, 74-76, 99
  Police Department, 192, 198, 203
  politics, 62-63, 146, 218, 220-223, 228-
    230
  population, 21, 24, 33, 69, 87, 137, 180,
    216, 229
  public buildings, 36-37, 71-72
  Public Library opened, 118-119
  railroads in, 48-49, 64-67, 68
  roads: planned, 19; conditions, 32;
    state highway system, 34; plank-
    ing of, 70-71
  salaries of officials, 64, 74
  schools: started, 18, 22, 25; female
    seminaries, 43; Old Seminary, 58;
    public system try fails, 61-62, es-
    tablished, 63-64; growth of, 139-
    140
  smallpox scare, 56
  squirrel epidemics, 24, 56
  street improvements, 73-74, 137
  taxes, 61-62, 63, 74, 117, 118
  temperance crusades, 46, 57, 75-76,
    90, 121
  town government abolishment at-
    tempt, 53
  volunteer fire fighters, 58-59, 76-78
Indianapolis, Peru and Chicago Rail-
    road, 117
Indianapolis Athletic Club, 189, 197, 198,
    204, 219
Indianapolis Automobile Racing Asso-
    ciation, 168

Indianapolis Band, 81
Indianapolis Benevolent Society, 71, 118
Indianapolis Board of Trade, 143, 185
Indianapolis Business College, 140
Indianapolis Business University, 140
Indianapolis Capitols, 225
Indianapolis Chamber of Commerce, 137, 173, 188, 215, 220, 221, 230
Indianapolis and the Civil War, 117
Indianapolis Concert Band, 197
Indianapolis Convention and Exposition Center, 225
Indianapolis Council of Women, 140
Indianapolis Country Club, 141
Indianapolis Daily Live Stock Journal, 137
Indianapolis Democrat, 20
Indianapolis Evening News, 124
Indianapolis Female Institute, 43
Indianapolis Freight Terminal, 173
Indianapolis Gas & Coke Company, 70
Indianapolis Gazette, 19-20, 21, 34, 80
Indianapolis Home for Colored Children, 118
Indianapolis Hotel, 35
Indianapolis Indians, 142
Indianapolis Journal, 20, 40-41, 44, 54, 66, 69, 79-80, 82, 86, 95, 102, 111, 114, 124, 126, 130, 132, 133, 154, 159, 181
Indianapolis Literary Club, 140
Indianapolis Lying-In Hospital, 140
Indianapolis Manufacturing Company, 137
Indianapolis Motor Speedway, 175-179, 189, 192, 195, 198, 208, 217, 219, 220, 227
Indianapolis Museum of Art, 225
Indianapolis News, 124, 135, 162, 163-164, 183, 185, 194, 197, 198, 217, 219, 221, 226
Indianapolis Orchestra, 208
Indianapolis Power & Light Company, 143, 197
Indianapolis Practical Business Military and Lecture College, 118
Indianapolis Sentinel, 20, 55, 79-80, 95, 98, 109, 111, 112, 114, 124, 150, 181; building, 119, 124
Indianapolis and Seymour Line, 174
Indianapolis Skill Center, 230
Indianapolis Stamping Company, 177
Indianapolis Star, 181, 197, 217, 226
Indianapolis Stockyards, 133
Indianapolis Street Railway Company, 145
Indianapolis Suffrage Society, 121
Indianapolis Sun, 130, 131-132, 196

Indianapolis Symphony Orchestra, 208, 222, 225
Indianapolis Thespian Corps, 57
Indianapolis Times, 137, 196, 197, 198, 204, 205, 218, 226
Indianapolis Traction Terminal, 173
Indianapolis Typographical Union, 122
Indianapolis Union Depot, 69, 100, 106, 110, 115, 116, 119, 134, 144, 145, 173, 196; new depot, 138
Indianapolis Water Company, 67, 140
Indianapolis Woman's Club, 121, 140
Indianapolis Young Ladies Institute, 71
Indianola (Stringtown), 56
Indians, 3-4, 6, 15, 23, 26-28, 32
Industrial Terminal, 173
Industry, 69-70, 116, 136-137, 194-195, 209, 215-216, 226
Ingals, Mitchell, 13
Internal Improvements program, 49-51
International Telephone and Telegraph, 227
International Workers of the World, 186-187
Interstates, 225
Interurbans, 172-174
Irish, 35, 43, 50, 75, 87, 101, 122-123, 137, 146
Irvington, 117, 201

Jackson, (Gov.) Ed, 198, 201, 204, 205
Jacobs, (U.S. Rep.) Andrew, Jr., 228
James, (Lt. Gov.) Richard T., 222
Jameson, (Mrs.) Ovid Butler, 165
Jameson, (Dr.) P. H., 119
Jazz, 192-194
Jenner, (Sen.) William E., 223, 228
Jennings, (Gov.) Jonathan, 4-5, 8-9, 10-11, 13
Job Corps, 230
Johnson, (Pres.) Andrew, 125-126
Johnson, J. J., 194
Johnson, Jerry, 13
Johnson, (Vice-Pres.) Richard M., 54
Jones, Sam, 231
Jordan, Arthur, 182
Jordan Hall, 182
Journal of Commerce, 124

Kahn Tailoring, 136
Kansas Aid Society, 91
Kansas-Nebraska Act, 90-91, 105
Keith's B. F., theater, 197
Kennedy, (Sen.) Robert F., 114, 226
Kentucky Avenue, 12, 18, 42, 72, 116
Kern, (Mayor) John W., 217
Ketcham, (Mrs.) J. L., 114

Keys, Harry S., 153
Kiddie Klan, 203
Kiefer, August, 123
Kiley, Bill, 198
King Oliver's Creole Jazz Band, 193
Kingan, Thomas D., 131
Kingan Brothers, 226
Kingan & Company, Ltd., 116, 226
Kirby, Durward, 198
Kitchen, (Dr.) John M., 119
Knefler, Fred, 155
Knights of the Golden Circle, 108
Knights of the Ku Klux Klan, see Ku Klux Klan
Knights of Labor, 122, 140
Knights of Pythias, 140
Know Nothings, 91
Kresge building, 201
Krout, Caroline Virginia, 157
Ku Klux Klan, 191, 198, 199, 200-206, 230
Kuntz, (Rev.) Theodore J. E., 44

Labor unions, 70, 122, 130, 134, 140, 152, 180, 186, 216
Ladies' Home, 106
Ladies' White Ribbon Clubs, 121
Lafayette, 49, 50
Lake County Jail, 213
Lander, (Lt.) Edward, 55
Landers, Franklin, 132
Lands, John, 231
Lane, (Gov.) Harry S., 92-94
Langsdale, George J., 154-155
Lawrence, (Mr. and Mrs.) Rice B., 22, 25
Lawton, Henry W., 154
Lazarre, 163
League of American Wheelmen, 177
League of Women Voters, 196
Lecture programs, 56, 80
Legislature, see General Assembly; House of Representatives; Senate under Indiana
Leibowitz, Irving, 218
Lemcke, Julius, 155
Levee, 145-146, 184
Lewis, E. I., 196
Lewis, Jim, 15
Lewis, John L., 186, 210
Libby Prison, 107
"Liberty Guards," 189
Liberty Loan drives, 189
Liberty party, 88
Libraries, 57, 82, 118-119
Lieber, H., Company, The, 69
Lieber, Herman, 155
Lieber, Richard, 188, 195

Lilly, Eli, 123, 137, 152, 156
Lilly, Eli, Base Hospital 32, 189, 190
Lilly, Eli, and Company, 123, 229, 231
Lilly, Josiah K., 123, 225
Lilly Endowment, Inc., 229
Lilly Pavilion, 225
Lincoln, (Pres.) Abraham, 92-96, 97, 107-108, 110-112, 125; assassination, 114; funeral train, 115
Lincoln, (Mrs.) Abraham, 115
Lindbergh, Charles A., 195-196
Lindsay, John, 46
Liquor Control Act, 212
"Literary club," 121
Literature, Golden Age of, 157-166, 227
Little, Joseph, 77
Little & Company, 69
"Little Orphant Annie," 160-161
Little Sower, The, 124
Lively, Chaney, 47
Lloyd, (Dr.) Frank, 231
Lockefield Gardens, 208
Lockerbie Street, 161
Locomotive, 79-80
Lodges, 140
Losche, (Mayor) Albert J., 218
Love, John W., 120
Love-Gookins art school, 120
Lugar, (Mayor) Richard G., 228-230
Lumber, 56
Lutherans, 43-44
Lynch bill, 183
Lyric Theater Ballroom, 194

MacArthur, (Gen.) Douglas, 189
McCartney, William, 22
McCarty Street, 123
McCauley, (Gen.) Dan, 123
McClung, (Rev.) John, 14, 23
McClure, (Dr.) John E., 45-46
McClure's Publishing Company, 165
McCollum, D. C., 155
McCormick, James, 8
McCormick, John, 7-8, 9, 22
McCormick, Samuel, 8
McCoy, Kid (boxer), 195
McCray, (Gov.) Warren, 192
McCready, James, 57, 75
McCulloch, George F., 181
McCulloch, Hugh, 84
McCutcheon, George Barr, 157
McCutcheon, John T., 163, 165, 166
McDonald, Joseph E., 111
McGuire, Douglass, 20, 35, 46
McHale, Frank, 204, 213
McIllvaine, James, 13, 21-22
McKay, (Capt.) Horace, 121

McKay, (Mrs.) Horace, 121
McKay, Jesse, 18
McKay, (Mrs.) Martha Nicholson, 121
McKinley, (Pres.) William, 153-154, 184,
    185, 186
McKinney, E. Kirk, 214
McKinney, Frank E., 218-219
McKinney, (Mrs.) Frank E., 220
McKinney's Cotton Pickers, 193
McMasters, (Mayor) John B., 146
McNamara, John and James, 187
McNeely, J. A. (editor), 80
McNutt, (Gov.) Paul Vories, 166, 211-
    214, 218, 221
Machinists' and Blacksmiths' Union, 122
Macy, David, 70, 117
Macy House, 70
Madden, Thomas J., & Company, 137
Madison and Indianapolis Railroad, 49-
    50, 53, 64-67, 68
Madison and Indianapolis Stage, 32
Maennerchor, 81, 189
Magnificent Ambersons, The, 165, 166
Magruder, Tom, 45
Mahoney, John J., 155
Main Chance, The, 162
Major, Charles, 157, 162
Mallory, David, 13
Mallory, P. R., Company, 194-195, 217
Malott, Volney T., 84, 117
"Mammoth Improvement Bill, The," 49-
    50
Mansions, 136, 181-182
Mansur, Isaiah, 66, 98
Mansur, Jeremy, 66
Manual High School, 192
Manufacturers' Natural Gas Company,
    143
Manufacturing, 117, 129
Marathons, dance, 194
Marian College, 208, 226
Marion, (Gen.) Francis, 19
Marion County, 19, 21-22, 25, 46, 47, 55,
    88, 114, 146, 150, 180, 214, 218, 229
    Courthouse, 19, 25, 31, 36, 135-136,
        216
    first agricultural exhibit, 46
    first county officers, 21-22
    first poorhouse, 46
    Grand Jury, 205-206
    library, 57
    Poor Farm, 118
    Seminary, 43, 58, 63
    Superior Court, 210
Marion County Democratic Committee,
    218
Marion County Medical Association, 119

Marion Firehouse, 77
Marion Fire, Hose and Protective As-
    sociation, 39, 58, 63
Market Street, 21, 23, 36, 37, 44, 51, 57,
    71, 118, 138, 139, 143, 146, 148, 173,
    181
Marmon, 169, 171, 172, 175
Marott, George J., 197; Hotel, 197; Shoe
    Store, 136
Mars Airport, 196
Marshall, Leonard, 219
Marshall, (Vice-Pres.) Thomas R., 147,
    164, 185
Martin, Abe, *see* Abe Martin
Martin, Gaylord, 211
Martin, John Bartlow, 168, 227
Martindale, Charles, 149
Martson, Gilman, 43
Marvin, David, 143
Maryland Street, 19, 22, 34, 81
Masonic Hall, 70, 72, 80, 82-83, 89, 94,
    96, 130
Masons, 72, 140, 220
Massachusetts Avenue, 59, 77
Matinee Musicale, the, 120, 140
Maxwell, (Mayor) Samuel D., 94
May, Edwin, 137-138
May Festival, 138
Mayer, Charles, store, 119, 136, 141
Meaning of the Times, The, 163
Mechanics Mutual Protections, 70
Medical College of Indiana, 140
Memorial Hall, 191
Merchants Bank Building, 180, 186
Merchants Heat & Light Company, 197
Merchants National Bank, 117, 231
Meridian-Kessler Neighborhood As-
    sociation, 230
Meridian Street, 10, 12-13, 58, 77, 81,
    120, 123, 136, 137, 180, 190, 196, 197,
    209
Meridian Street Methodist Church, 184
Merrick pumper, 39
Merrill, Catharine, 30, 33, 114, 121
Merrill, Charles W., 162
Merrill, Meigs and Company, 136
Merrill, Priscilla, 30-31
Merrill, Samuel, 10, 30-31, 35, 37, 38, 42-
    43, 62, 65, 69, 121, 136
Merrill, (Mrs.) Samuel, 30-31
Merrill, Samuel, Jr., 69, 151
Merz, Charley, 168, 178
Meskinges, 6-7, 15
Methodist Hospital, 182, 231
Methodists, 14, 22, 23, 38, 44, 89, 182, 191
Metropolitan Theater, 81, 96, 99, 120,
    139

Metzner, August (artist), 120
Mexican War, 55, 97, 99, 155
Meyer-Kiser Bank, 218
Miami Indians, 3, 15, 27
Michigan Road, 32, 48, 70-71
Michigan Street, 8, 118, 195
Midland United Company, 174
Mile square, 12-13, 18, 21, 79
Military Park, 55, 79
Miller block, 120
"Millerites," 59-60
Milligan, Carrie F., 121
Milligan, Lambdin P., 111-112
Milliken, Mary, Fund, 182
Minton, Sherman, 214
Mississippi Street, 57
Missouri Compromise, 90
Missouri Street, 17, 18, 19, 20, 99
Mitchell, (Dr.) Samuel G., 13, 16, 25
Mitchell, (Mayor) Thomas, 123
Model Cities, 229-230
Model Cities Advisory Task Force, 229
Moffett, Dorothy Dell, 183
Monsieur Beaucaire, 165, 166
Montgomery, Wes, 194
Monument Circle, 187, 196
"Monument Place," 155
"Monument for the Soldiers," 155
Moody, William Vaughn, 157, 158
Morgan, John Hunt, 113-114
Morgan's Art Exhibition, Matt, 139
Morris, Betheul F., 43
Morris, Morris, 21, 37
Morris, Seaton W., 42-43
Morris, Thomas Armstrong, 53, 65, 69, 98-99
Morris Street, 184
Morrison, Alexander F., 80
Morrison, (Dr.) Frank, 189
Morrison, James, 39
Morrison, Robert, 42
Morrison, William (residence of), 149
Morton, (Gov.) Oliver P., 38, 91, 92-94, 96, 97-98, 113, 114-115, 125-127, 128, 135, 155, 221; war governor, 104-112
Morton Place, 119
Motherhead's Drugstore, 58
Motor Car Manufacturing Company, 169, 170
Motorcars, see Automobiles
Motorcycle racing, 177-178
Mount, (Gov.) James A., 153
Mt. Jackson, 35, 72
Mount Zion Baptist Church, 230
Moving pictures, 183, 196
Munsell, (Dr.) Luke, 57
Murders, 47, 124, 202; Indian, 26-27

Murray, A. M., 72
Music, 26, 56, 80-82, 120, 138-139, 192-194, 228
Myers, Hortense, 227
Myers, T. E. "Pop," 195, 219

Naismith, James, 182
National Alliance of Business, 230
National Association of Manufacturers, 185-186
National Balloon Races, 178
National Currency Act, 117
National Drag Races, 227
National Grange of the Patrons of Husbandry, 130
National Guard, Indiana, 153, 189
National Independent Greenback Party, 131-132
National League of Cities, 229
National Motor Vehicle Company, 169, 171, 177
National Republicans, 53
National Road, 9, 17, 31-32, 34, 35, 38-39, 47, 48, 56, 70-71, 118, 159
National Road Bridge, 34, 35
National Woman Suffrage Committee, 121
Natural gas, 143
Naval Reserve Armory, 208
Negro Methodist Church, 44
Negroes, 8, 13, 23, 38, 44, 45, 47, 50, 72, 83, 87-89, 101, 108, 118, 121, 125, 126-127, 137, 146, 150, 154, 181, 193, 204, 208, 229, 230-231
Neighborhood associations, 230
New, Harry, 149
New Deal, 166, 211, 212, 220, 221
New Harmony, 57
"New Light," denomination, 14
"New Purchase," 3, 5, 7, 8, 11, 15
New York Central Railroad, 180
New York Stock Exchange, 207
New York Store, 69
New York Street, 59, 180
Newby, Arthur C., 175, 177
Newby Bicycle Racing Oval, 177
Newcomb, Horatio, 71
Newspapers, 19-20, 34, 40, 79-80, 88, 123-124, 137, 181, 202, 217, 226
Nicholson, Meredith, 157, 162, 227
Nickelodeons, 183
Nicknames, 40
Nineteenth Amendment, 196
Nineteenth Street, 79, 119
Nixon, (Pres.) Richard M., 228, 229
Noble, (U. S. Sen.) James, 28
Noble, (Gov.) Noah, 36, 37, 45, 49

Noblesville, 5, 19, 21, 143, 205
Noel, (State Rep.) S. V. B., 62
Nolan, Jeannette Covert, 227
Noland, Elizabeth, 35
Nordyke & Marmon Company, 171, 172
North Street, 10
North Western Christian University (Butler), 71, 88, 117, 121, 226
North Western Farmer, 130
Northwest Confederacy, 112
Northwest Territory, 4
Nowland, Matthias, 8, 17, 18
Nurses, Civil War, 114

Oberholtzer, Madge, 204-205
Occidental hotel, 70
Odd Fellows Building, 72
Ohio River, 4, 17, 19, 32, 48, 50, 88, 99, 107, 109, 113
Ohio Street, 10, 43, 47, 119, 145, 180
Old Capitol Hotel, 10
Old Ferry, 72
"Old Graveyard," 16
"Old Pike, The," 32
Old Swimmin' Hole, The, 159, 161
Oldfield, Barney, 176
Oliver, (Dr.) John, 189
Oliver Avenue, 169
Ollaman's wagon shop, 46
Olleman, Ezra O., 130-133
"Open-shop town," 180
Opera, 80, 138, 139, 225
"Operation Breadbasket," 231
"Operation Breakthrough," 229
Order of Chosen Friends, 140
O'Reilly, Henry, 66
"O'Reilly's Line," 66-67
Oriental hotel, 70
Orphan's Home, 71, 118
Orpheum Theater, 183
Orr, Benjamin, 56
Orth, Godlove S., 133
Osborne, John T., 22
Osbourne, (Mrs.) Fanny, 142
Osbourne, Samuel, 142
Outing Bicycle Team, 177
"Outlots," 13, 18
Over the Tea Cup (women's club), 140
Overall, John, 38
Owen, Robert Dale, 57, 83

"Paddle Your Own Canoe," 82
Paige, Robert, 194
Painters union, 216
Palmer, Nathan B., 46
Palmer House, 70
Panic of 1837, 43, 50, 53, 86

Panic of 1857, 84-86
Panic of 1873, 129, 131, 135
Panic of 1893, 152-153
Panic of 1907, 180
Parish, Mitchell, 193
Park Fletcher, 226
Park School, 226
Park Theater, 81, 139
Parker, (Rev.) Theodore, 80
Parochial schools, 71, 118, 225, 231
Parry, David Maclean, 137, 169, 181-182, 185-186
Parry Manufacturing Company (carts and carriages), 137, 169
Parry Motor Car Company, 169, 171, 185
Patrons of Husbandry, 130
Paxton, (Rep.) James, 23, 25, 30
"Peace Democrats," 108-111
Pearl Harbor, 215
Pearl Street, 137
Pembroke Arcade, 181
Pendleton, 21, 27-28
Penney, J. C., 216
Pennsylvania Street, 12-13, 23, 34, 71, 72, 119, 120, 136, 140, 141, 144, 176, 180, 182, 191, 217
Penrod, 165, 166
People's party, 75, 90-91, 105, 151-152
Peoples State Bank, 218
Perkins, (Judge) Samuel E., 64, 75-76
Perry, Oran S., 149
Peters, Earl, 214
Pfaff, (Dr.) O. G., 189
Phonographs, 144
Pierce, Franklin, 105
Pierson, H. J. (Joe), 221
Pierson's, 181
"Pioneer Poet Laureate," 82
Pitts, George W., 76
Plainfield, 118
Pocahontas, 57
Pogue, George, 7-8, 15
Pogue's Run, 8, 12, 15, 31, 110; Valley, 55
Politics, *see* Indiana; Indianapolis
Ponader, Wayne, 229
Pope, Dr. Abner, 56-57
Populist Party, 131, 152, 153, 186
Porter, (Gov.) Albert G., 140, 151
Porter, Gene Stratton, 157
Post Office, 20, 62, 71, 180
Potawatomi Indians, 3, 32
Powell, Dick, 194
Presbyterians, 23, 44, 72, 89, 115
President's Advisory Commission on Intergovernmental Relations, 229
Pressley Farm, 177

Presto-Lite Company, 168, 176, 189, 198
Prince of India, The, 159
Printers, 181
Prisoners, Civil War, 100, 107
Proctor, (Rev.) C., 23
Prohibition, 75, 122, 191-192
Propylaeum, 135, 140
Protestant Evangelicalism, 202
Public Depository Law, 183
Public schools, *see* Schools
Public Utility Act, 174
Publishing center, 88
Pulitzer Prize, 165, 185, 204
Pulliam, Eugene Collins, 217
Pullman Company, 152
Purdue University, 165, 198, 226

Quakers, 89
Queen Mab's, 146
Quinn, Joseph L., Jr., 219-220
Quinn, (Bishop) Paul, 44

Radical Reconstructionists, 125
Radical Republicans, 125-126
Radio, 197-199, 217
Radio Corporation of America (RCA), 195, 216, 226
Railroad Managers' Association, 152
Railroads, 48-49, 50, 53, 64-67, 68, 133-134, 137, 138, 172
Ralston, Alexander, 11-13, 14, 22, 36, 43
Ralston, (U. S. Sen.) Samuel, 147
Ransdell, Daniel M., 155
Ransom, Willard, 231
Rapp, Frederick, 5
Ravenswood, 192
Ray, (Gov.) James Brown, 28, 33, 48
Ray, James M., 18, 21, 23, 43, 120
Reagan, Jane, 13
Reconstruction issue, 125-128
Recordings, 144, 193
Recreational area, 225
Recruiting, Civil War, 101-102
Red Cross, 222
Red Men (Lodge), 140
Redman, Don, 193
Reed, Joseph C., 18, 21-22, 25
Reform tickets, 146
Reformatory School for Females, 118
Relief Company, 63, 77
Relief programs, 130, 152
"Remember the *Maine*," 153
Reno Gang, 124-125
Republicans, 53, 75, 90-96, 107-112, 125-128, 133, 146, 149, 151, 153, 185, 188, 206, 211, 214, 218, 220-223, 228-229
Review Publishing Company, 227

Richards, Samuel, 120
Richmond, Charles, 78
Rickenbacker, (Capt.) Eddie V., 195, 208-209, 219
Riley, James Whitcomb, 155, 156, 157, 159-161, 164, 165, 182, 194, 227
Riley Center Apartments, 224
Riots, 76, 134, 146
Ristine, Richard O., 228
River House Apartments, 230, 231
"Riverboat Shuffle," 193
Riverside Park, 181, 194
Roads, 19, 32, 34, 70-71, 168, 195; *see also* National Road
Robberies, 124-125, 174
Robert Hanna (steamboat), 35-36, 65
Roberts, James E., Fund, 182
Robinson, Susanah, 166
Robinson, W. F. "Yankee," 81
Robson, George, 220
Roman Catholics, 44, 71, 118
Romeo and Juliet, 81
Rooker, Samuel S. (councilman), 63
Roosevelt, (Pres.) Franklin D., 166, 210-211, 213-214
Roosevelt, (Pres.) Theodore, 185
Rooster, crowing, symbol, 54
Ropkey, Edah M., 227
Rose, Mauri, 208, 219
Rosebush Tavern, 14, 25, 26, 31, 35
Ross, (Dr.) David, 189
Royal Arcanum, 140
Rugby, 141
Runnel, (Dr.) O. S., 140
Russell, Alexander, 13, 23
Russell, (Col.) Charles, 101
Russell, Louis, 226

Saengerbunds, 81
Saengerfest, 81
St. John's school, 71
St. Joseph Street, 119
St. Mary's, Ohio, 3, 7
St. Paul's German Lutheran Church, 44
St. Rita's Church, 231
Salem, 4, 88
Salem Village, 228
Sams, Howard, 227
Sanders, Jemima, 100
Sanders, (Dr.) John H., 37
Sand's Nathan & Company American Circus, 81
Sanitary Fairs, 106
"Sanitoriums," 140
Saturday Mirror, 159
Schmitz, Bruno, 155
Schnull, Henry, 182

Schnull & Company, 69
Schools, 18, 22, 25, 43, 61-64, 71, 83, 118, 139-140, 225, 226, 229, 231; high schools, 63, 118, 139, 165, 182, 204, 205, 225
Schricker, (Gov.) Henry F., 222-223
Schurz, Carl, 93
Scott, (Rev.) James, 22
Scott, Thomas R., 42-43
Scrip, 51, 55, 129
Scripps-Howard, 190-196
Scudder, Caleb, 23, 39
Scudder, Jacob, 35, 106
Sebastian, William, 54
Second Adventists, 59-60
Second Presbyterian Church, 44, 118
Second State Bank of Indiana, 42-43, 51, 53, 84-85
Segregation, 23, 50, 83, 87-88, 204
Seibert, Mr. (teamster), 30-31
Senate Avenue, 36
Seneca Indians, 15, 27
SerVaas, Beurt R., 227, 229
Seventh Street, 101
Sevitsky, Fabien, 208
Sewall, May Wright, 121, 140
Seward, William H., 92, 96, 105
Shaefer, Ferdinand, 208
Shaffer, Daniel, 13, 16
Shank, Bob, 195
Shank, (Mayor) Samuel Lewis, 197
Shaw, Wilbur, 219
Shawnee Indians, 6, 15, 27
Shopping centers, 225
Short Flights, 162
Shortridge, (Prof.) A. C., 118
Shortridge High School, 118, 139, 165
Shoup, (Capt.) Frank, 97
Shumaker, Arthur W., 161
Shumaker, (Rev.) Seitz, 191
Sidener, Merle, 181, 198
Sigma Delta Chi, 217
Silent Waverly Electric, 169
Silver Bell (boat), 52
Simmons, Franklin, 135
Simmons, ("Colonel") William Henry, 201-202
Sissle, Noble, 194
Sisters of Providence, 71
Sisters of St. Francis, 208
Sixteenth Street, 182, 193
Skinner, Otis, 163
Slavery question, 88-89, 90-91
Sloan's Drug Store, 136
Slums, 118
Smallpox, 56
Smith, Caleb B., 92, 95

Smith, George, 13, 19-20, 34
Smith, Gerald D., 217
Smith, Jay Michael, 231
Smith, R. N., & Company, 123
Smith and Yandes, 122
Smiths, the (theatrical performers), 26
"Smoky Row," 50
Snyder-Blackburn Associates, 231
Social-Democratic Party, 186
Socialist Party of America, 186, 201, 210
Socialists, 185-187, 209
Society of Friends, 89
"Soldier, The," 156
Soldiers' Home, 106
Soldiers' and Sailors' Monument, 154-156
Solomon, Izler, 225
Solomon, Juan, 231
Song writing, 144
Sonntag, Marcus, 190
Sons of Liberty, 109-112
Sons of Temperance, 57
South Street, 10, 55, 64, 77, 169
Southeastern Avenue, 32
Southern Christian Leadership Conference, 231
Southern Club, 222
Spanish-American War, 153-154, 184, 217-218
Sparks, (Judge) Will H., 205
Speakeasies, 192
Speedway, see Indianapolis Motor Speedway
Speedway City, 176, 180, 229
Sports, 141-142, 182, 195, 225
Springsteen, Jefferson, 75, 76
Squirrel invasions, 24, 56
Standard Grocery, 194
Stanton, Elizabeth Cady, 121
Stapp, Milton, 50
"Stardust," 193
Stark, George, 209
Stark, Wetzel & Company, 209
Starr Piano Company, 193
State Bank of Indiana, 42, 85
State Temperance Society, 35, 57
Steele, T. C., 120
Stegemeier's, 181
Stein, Evaleen, 157
Stempfel, Theodore, 155
Stephenson, David Curtis, 191, 200-206, 221
Stevenson, Marion E., 217
Stevenson, Robert Louis, 142
Stewart and Bowen, 69
Stockman, George, 116
Stokely, William B., 209, 226
Stokely-Van Camp, 209

Stone, Asahel, 106
Stone, George B., 64
Stone, Lucy, 80-81
Stonecutters union, 216
Stores, 13, 25, 46, 55, 69, 117, 136, 194, 207
Stowe, Harriet Beecher, 44-45, 89, 121
Strange, (Father) Bernard, 231
Strange, John, 33
Strauss, L., & Company, 181
Street Railway Company, 119
Streetcars, 144-145
Streets, 73-74, 117, 136, 137, 181; see also names of
Streight, Abel D., 107
Strikes, 129, 133-134, 219
Studebaker, 172
Stutz, Harry C., 169, 172
Stutz Bearcat, 169, 170, 198
Suburbs, 117, 225
Suffrage, Negro, 121, 125, 126-127, 146, 150
Suffrage, women, see Women's rights
Sulgrove, B. R., 77
Sullivan, (Judge) Jeremiah, 10-11, 207
Sullivan, (Mayor) Reginald H., 207, 214, 217
Sullivan, (Mayor) Thomas L., 146, 207
Summit Laboratories, 231
Superstitions, 40
Surgical Institute, 142-143
Sweetser, (Mrs.) James V., 182
"Symbol of Indiana," 155

TAT-Maddux Transcontinental Airline, 196
Taggart, Thomas, 146-147, 188-189, 221
Talbot, George, 138
Talbot Street, 182
Talbott, Washington Houston, 100
Tarkington, Hauté, 165
Tarkington, Laurel, 166
Tarkington, Newton Booth, 140, 157, 158, 164-166, 182, 188, 227
Tarzian, Sarkes, 217
Tatewiler, Henry, 63
Taxes, 61-62, 63, 74, 117, 118, 168, 194, 208
Taylor, (Dr.) Joseph T., 231
Tecumseh, Chief, 54
Telephones, 143
Television, commercial, 194, 217; public, 226
Temperance Hall, 35
Temperance movements, 35, 57, 75-76, 90, 121
"Ten O'Clock Line," 4

Tennessee Street, 20, 47, 71, 72, 81, 118
"Tenth of June Convention," 131
Terre Haute, Indianapolis and Eastern (interurban), 174
Terrell, Adjutant General, 121
Thanksgiving Day, 52
Theater, 26, 46, 56, 57, 81-82, 120, 138-139, 183, 196
Third Christian Church, 198
Third State Bank of Indiana, 83-84
Thirtieth Street, 177, 217
Thirty-Eighth Street, 139, 196, 225
Thompson, Maurice, 157, 162-163
Thornbrough, Emma Lou, 227
Tinker Street, 101
Tipton, John, 5, 8-9
Tomlinson, Stephen D., 138
Tomlinson's Hall, 138, 149, 153, 156, 184, 188, 195, 210
"Toolmaker of the Nation," 215
Tornadoes, 91, 227
Town Talk, 124
Townsend, (Gov.) Clifford M., 214
Traction terminal, 173
Transportation, 192; see also names of types
Traveler's Hall, 35
Tremont House, 70
Trotter, Lem, 176-177
Trusty, (Rev.) Clay, Sr., 204
Turner, Augustus, 44
Turner, (Mrs.) J. J., 153
Turnverein, 189
Turpie, David, 108
Twenties, Roaring, 69, 191-199
Twenty-eighth Street, 176
Twenty-second Street, 193
"Two Percent Club," 214
Tyler, Edward S., 57
Tyndall, (Mayor) Robert H., 189, 217-218

Uncle Tom's Cabin, 44-45, 81, 89, 159
"Underground Railroad," 88
Unemployment, 130, 152, 208, 226, 229, 230
Uni-Gov, 229-230
Union Carbide and Carbon Corporation, 176
Union Clubs, 109
Union Depot, see Indianapolis Union Depot
Union Firehouse, 77
Union Labor Party, 151
Union Leagues, 109
Union Railway Company, 69
"Union Sunday School," 23

Union for Working Girls, 152
Unions, *see* Labor unions
United Fund, Indianapolis, 216, 222, 229
United Methodist Church, 182
United Mine Workers, 186, 210
United Press, 190
United Spanish War Veterans, 154
U.S. Arsenal, 120
United States Auto Club, 220
United States Census, 229
U.S. Sanitary Commission, 106-107
U.S. Supreme Court, 112
Universities and colleges, 71, 88, 117, 118,
    119-120, 121, 137, 140, 141, 165, 182,
    193, 194, 195, 198, 208, 211, 225-226,
    230, 231
University of Indianapolis, 137
University Park, 191
University Square, 113, 149, 163, 191, 208
"Upswing" program, 229
Urban Affairs Council, 229
Urban League, 230, 231

Van Blaricum, 8, 25
Van Blaricum, Jesse, 76
Van Blaricum, Michael, 47
Van Buren, (Pres.) Martin, 46, 54
Van Camp Packing Company, 209
Van Nuys, (Sen.) Frederick, 214
Vandalia Railroad, 106, 137
Vandalia Road, 133
Vandegrift, Frances Matilda, 142
Vaudeville, 183, 194, 196
Veterans, 150, 154, 190; *see also* American Legion
Veterans of Foreign Wars, 190
Vice, 74-75, 99, 146
"Victory" (statue), 156
Victory Gardens, 189
Vigilante groups, 183-184
Virginia Avenue, 10, 91, 181
Volksblatt, 79, 88, 93
Voluntary Advisory Corps, 230
Volunteer Firemen's Association, 77
Von Tilzer, Harry and Albert, 144
Vonnegut, Clement, 69
Vonnegut, Kurt, Jr., 227
Vorhees, Daniel, 110
Vorhees, J. & P., Company, 34
Voss farm, 139
Voting rights, 83
Voyles, Samuel B., 155
Vukovich, Bill, 220

WBBZ radio, 198
WFBM radio, 197-198
WFBM-FM, 217

WFBM-TV, 217, 230
WFMS-FM, 217
WFYI-TV, 226
WIRE radio, 198, 217
WISH-TV, 217
WKBF radio, 198
WKNF radio, 198
WLW-I-TV, 217
WMDZ radio, 198
WOH radio, 197
WTTV-TV, 217
Wabash and Erie Canal, 48-49, 51
Wade and Company, 67
Walcott, Benjamin, 149
Walcott, Mary N., 121
Walker, (Mrs.) C. J., 181
Walker, C. J., Manufacturing Company,
    181
Wallace, Aaron, 13, 47
Wallace, (Gov.) David, 37, 52
Wallace, (Mrs.) David (Zerelda), 121
Wallace, Lew, 55, 97-99, 105, 107, 113,
    121, 155-156, 157, 158-159
Wallace, William, 57
Walpole, Hugh, 22
Walton, Samuel, 34
Wapehani, 3
Wapeminshink, 6
War Memorial Plaza, 190-191
War Prohibition Act, 191
War Savings Bonds, 215
Ward, Rodger, 220
Warner, C. G., 76, 159
Washington Hall hotel, 70
Washington Hall Tavern, 20, 58
Washington Hotel, 201
Washington Park, 142, 195
Washington Street, 8, 12-14, 17-18, 20, 22,
    23, 31-32, 34, 36, 38, 43, 47, 54, 55,
    56, 58, 66, 69, 70, 72, 75, 77, 81, 88,
    95, 99, 101, 115, 119, 120, 123, 135, 136,
    142, 143, 145-146, 163, 181, 183, 184,
    195, 198, 204; *see also* National Road
Wasson, H. P., 136, 181
Water-Works Company of Indianapolis,
    67, 140
Watkins, John A., 142
Watson, Carl, 198
Watson, Noble, 198
Watts, Jane, 182
Waverly, 5, 7
Waverly Company, 169, 171
Wayne Township, 22, 46
Wea Indians, 3
Weaver, James B., 152
Webb, Clifton, 194
Weekday Religious Education, 222

Weir Cook Airport, 225
Welsh, (Gov.) Matthew E., 228
Werneg, William, 34
West, Henry F., 63
West Street, 10, 18, 19, 75, 79, 106, 123
Western Censor and Immigrant's Guide, The, 20, 25
Western Presage, The, 88
Western Electric Company, 216
Western Union, 67, 144
Westinghouse Lamp Works, 195
Wetzel, Erwin, 209
Wheeler, Frank H., 175, 177
Wheeler, Joe, 154
Wheeler Rescue Mission, 198
Wheeler Schebler Caburetor Company, 177
Wheeler Schebler Race, 178
Wheeling League, The, 141
When Department Store, 136, 142
When Knighthood Was in Flower, 162
Whetzel, Cyrus, 6
Whetzel, Jacob, 5, 7, 9
Whetzel Trace, 8, 17
Whigs, 53-54, 90-92
Whistler, Charles, 229
Whitcomb, (Gov.) James, 37, 62, 65, 155
White, (Sen.) Albert S., 120
White River, 3-9, 15, 21, 22, 24, 25, 34, 35-36, 46, 47, 56, 70, 72, 124, 133, 147, 176, 184, 193, 225
"Whitecaps," 183
Whiteman, Paul, 193
Whitewater Bridge, 114
Whitewater River, 6, 7, 16, 18
Whitewater settlements, 8, 21
Whitridge, T. W., 56
Wick, (Judge) William W., 19, 23, 24, 28
Widows and Orphans Society, 82
Wilcox, Howard (Howdy), 178, 208
Wilcox, Howard S., 220
Wilkins, John, 38
Willard, Ashbel B., 91
Willard's Musical Visitor, 124
Williams, John D. ("Blue Jeans"), 132-133, 134
Williams, Martin, 120
Willich, August, 101
Willis, J. M., 72
Willkie, Wendell, 211, 214
Willys-Overland Co., 169, 171
Wilmot, Robert, 13, 15
Wilson, Captain, 22
Wilson, Isaac, 8

Wilson Sewing Machines, 69
Winchester, Walter, 176
Wingate, Henry, 63
Winsell (Winchell), Andrew, 28
Wishart, Spencer, 178
Wolcott, Anson, 132-133
Women's activities, 121
Women's Christian Temperance Association, 121-122
Women's Franchise League, 196
Women's Peace Party, 188
Women's rights, 57, 83, 121
Women's Rights Association, 121
Women's School League, 196
Wood, James, 63
Wood, John, 34, 43
Woodburn "Sarvin Wheel" Company, 116
Woodruff, James D., 117-118
Woodruff Place, 117-118
Woodstock Country Club, 141
Woollen, Evans, 137, 189
Woollen, (Dr.) G. V., 119
Woolworth's, 194
Workingman's Convention, 122
World, end of the, 59-60
World Peace Foundation, 188
World War I, 172, 174, 179, 187, 188-191, 192, 194, 195, 202, 221
World War II, 198, 215, 217
Wright, James, 149
Wright, (Gov.) Joseph A., 38, 84-85
Wright, Joseph H., 58
Wright, Wilbur and Orville, 178
Wright Building, 148
Wyandotte, John, 15
Wyant, John, 18
Wygart, William D., 43

Yandes, Daniel, 22
Yandes, Simon, 71
Young, (Mr. and Mrs.) Jacob, 124
Young, John L., 34
Young Men's Christian Association, 80, 121, 135, 188
Young Men's Literary Society, 80
Young Women's Christian Association, 121
Youth programs, 229

Zig-Zag Cycling Club, 141, 177
Zion's Church, 43-44
Zoo, 139, 225
Zouave Regiments, 97-99, 105